Conquering the American Wilderness

CONQUERING THE AMERICAN WILDERNESS

The Triumph of European Warfare in the Colonial Northeast

GUY CHET

University of Massachusetts Press / Amherst and Boston

LC 2002151285
ISBN 1-55849-366-2 (library cloth); 382-4 (paper)

Designed by Mary Mendell
Set in Quadraat by Graphic Composition, Inc.
Printed and bound by The Maple-Vail Book Manufacturing Group

Library of Congress Cataloging-in-Publication Data

Chet, Guy, 1968–
    Conquering the American wilderness : the triumph of European warfare in the
colonial northeast / Guy Chet.
        p. cm.
Includes bibliographical references and index.
ISBN 1-55849-366-2 (lib. bdg. : alk. paper) — ISBN 1-55849-382-4 (pbk. : alk. paper)
1. New England—History—Colonial period, ca. 1600–1775.
2. New England—History, Military—17th century.
3. New England—History, Military—18th century.
4. Military art and science—New England—History—17th century.
5. Military art and science—New England—History—18th century.
6. Military art and science—Europe—History.
7. Indians of North America—Wars—1600–1750.
8. Indians of North America—New England—History.
9. British Americans—New England—History.
10. Frontier and pioneer life—New England.   I. Title.

F8 .C49 2003
974'.02—dc21

                                2002151285

British Library Cataloguing in Publication data are available.

To Mom and Dad. Thank you for putting this
good fortune in my path to stumble upon.

And Wee doe by these present for vs Our Heires and Successors Grant Establish and Ordaine that the Governor of our said Province or Territory for the time being shall have full Power . . . to traine instruct Exercise and Governe the Militia there and for the speciall Defence and Safety of Our said Province or Territory to assemble in Martiall Array and put in Warlike posture the Inhabitants of Our said Province or Territory and to lead and Conduct them and with them to Expulse Repell Resist and pursue by force of Armes aswell by Sea as by Land within or without the limitts of Our said Province or Territory and alsoe to kill slay destroy and Conquer by all fitting wayes Enterprises and meanes whatsoever all and every such Person and Persons as shall at any time hereafter Attempt or Enterprize the destruccon Invasion Detriment or Annoyance of Our said Province or Territory.

—Charter of the Province of Massachusetts Bay

CONTENTS /

ILLUSTRATIONS /

WHEN I BEGAN THIS PROJECT, my intent was to trace the process by which the settlers of New England were transformed from a collection of farmers into an "Americanized" military society. I saw it as a military and psychological transformation—competition with the Indians over territory and resources taught the colonists to free themselves from the rigid constraints of "civilized" warfare and acquaint themselves with the pragmatic and rational means by which to contend with the unique tactics of New England's native population. I was excited about the prospect of charting the gradual progress of colonial armed forces—how, through imitation and innovation they enhanced their potency and effectiveness against Indian forces.

This thesis, however, did not withstand the evidence. Like other scholars of early American history, I was struck by the trends of cultural continuity rather than the glimpses of an Atlantic cultural divide. The settlers—especially those of the New England colonies—are often presented as prophets of a new era and a uniquely American culture. Some military historians share this view, arguing that the colonial era saw the development of an "American way of war," setting the stage for the stunning victory of American forces over the British during the American War of Independence. By the nature of their profession, historians tend both to discern patterns and to impose them on the past. It is important, however, to keep in mind that not all pre-Revolutionary developments were precursors to the Revolution. An examination of the miitary accomplishments of colonial armed forces in the Northeast clearly demonstrates this point.

Analyses of military affairs revolve around strategy, logistics, and tactics. The term *strategy* refers to the planning of a diplomatic, political, and military course of action, the formulation of a tactical doctrine, and the deployment of forces in accordance with that doctrine. Logistics involve the mobilization and movement of men and matériel (military equipment). Whereas strategy and logistics involve preparations for battles, the term *tactics* refers to actual combat—the method by which a military force attempts to accomplish its mission on the field, during a battle. The distinction between an army's tactical role and a society's political role in relation to its neighbors is crucial. Tactics relate strictly to battlefield conduct. Thus, in any military contest, the aggressor—the side that promoted antagonism, sought armed conflict, or even launched the first strike—can assume either offensive or defensive tactics. The other side, as well, is not compelled by its defensive role in the political arena to adopt a defensive role on the battlefield.

Another clarification of terms is required to identify the three types of English armed forces in North America: regular forces were composed of professional soldiers; provincial forces consisted of colonists who volunteered or were drafted for service for a single expedition or campaigning season, in return for financial compensation; militia units were used for local assignments of communal defense. Service in the militia was compulsory for all men of fighting age.

The military adventures of the New England settlers make for an interesting and instructive tale. It is a tale that involves horrifying incidents, which I have deliberately chosen not to focus on (after reading one of my chapters, Bernard Bailyn commented that it was remarkably "clean"; he had expected to find the pages awash with blood). New England's military history is indeed filled with gory battles, torture scenes, atrocities, near-atrocities, and counteratrocities committed by both Indian and English troops. These are a matter of common knowledge and of human nature. Such incidents are not unique to America and can be found in most societies and in any era of human history. Attempts to locate the chronological and geographical origin of "total war" —a concept that has been hollowed by excessive application—are bound to be as fruitless as attempts to pinpoint the birthplace of warfare.

Descriptions of English violence and cruelty are more prominent here than tales of the Indians' painful treatment of the settlers. I saw no need to present a balanced account of the reciprocal violence and cruelty, since my objectives lie elsewhere. I hope that this work will prompt a debate about "Americanization," "American tactics," and American exceptionalism, rather than re-ignite the debate over the assignment of blame or guilt for cruelty and belligerence. Although I have dealt with material that is relevant to these issues, my purpose was to investigate other matters.

This leads me to another imbalance in this work that I wish to address. The military history of colonial New England is the history of the English settlers, the region's Indian tribes, and the French settlers of Canada. I deal almost exclusively with the English component of the story. This book is not meant to be a comprehensive narrative of the military encounters between Indians and Europeans in this region. Rather, it is a study of the transportation of English culture—military culture—to the frontier of European civilization. Thus, I discuss Indian and French culture and history only insofar as it illuminates the topic as I have defined it.

Similarly, as scholars of European history will undoubtedly recognize, my first chapter is not offered as a comprehensive treatment of the development of European armies and tactics in the early modern era. Instead, it is an introduction to the weaponry and basic tactical maxims of European warfare, offering the necessary background for understanding the dynamics of warfare in the colonies.

Throughout, I use modernized dates rather than the old-style dates of the Julian calendar used in the seventeenth century. In quotations from contemporary sources, I retain the original spelling and punctuation, except when using a secondary source in which the original text has already been modernized.

ACKNOWLEDGMENTS /

I AM INDEBTED TO John Demos for much valuable early advice and patient guidance through the years. His support for my work, as well as his genuine kindness and good humor, has been a great asset to me on both a personal and a professional level. Jon Butler's helpful tips on writing and other tricks of the trade have made this massive undertaking more enjoyable and productive than it might have been. To Mary Habeck, I owe a special debt for her help. I am also grateful to Patrick Malone for his friendship and encouragement. Although we disagree on points of historical interpretation, he has graciously offered helpful comments as well as generous portions of his time and advice. I would also like to thank Linda Colley, Paul Rahe, Ingrid Walsoe Engel, and Ayala Dvoretzky for all they have done to help me along.

My research was supported by grants from Yale University, Brown University, and the University of North Texas. Preparing my book for publication has been an interesting experience. I am indebted to my editors at the University of Massachusetts Press, Clark Dougan and Carol Betsch, and to my copy editor, Deborah Smith, for their support and helpful advice throughout this process. For assisting me with the production of the maps and illustrations, I thank Chad Maloney, at the Center for Media Production of the University of North Texas, and Margit Kaye, at Yale University's Sterling Memorial Library Map Collection, as well as Kevin McBride, Bob Halloran, and Jon Ault, at the Mashantucket Pequot Museum and Research Center, Archives and Special Collections.

It has been said that if you steal from one author, it's plagiarism; if you steal from two, it's research. What I have written here is very much a product of the findings and perspectives provided by other historians, such as Ian K. Steele, Daniel Beattie, John Shy, and Patrick Malone, to whom I am, for this reason, very grateful. I would also like to thank Fred Anderson for his encouragement, as well as Karen Kupperman, Bernard Bailyn, and Peter Harrington, the editor of the John Hay Library Military Collection at Brown University.

To Carrie I intend to show my gratitude and my affection for years and years to come. A special thanks goes out to my friends at the Rochdale (most notably John, Bryan, Eric, Gwyn, Christopher, and Dave), who have done their very best to distract me from my research and impede my academic career. The Art History touch-football crew—Kerr Houston in particular—has made my years in New Haven (or Sundays at the very least) so much brighter and happier. I just wish we had photos, in case memory fails me in years to come.

Conquering the American Wilderness

IN 1754, GEORGE WASHINGTON led a Virginia regiment to defeat at Fort Necessity, ending the battle that inaugurated the Seven Years' War in North America. Convinced that any English commander would have suffered the same fate, Washington emphasized the tactical importance of Indian allies: "Indians are the only match for Indians, and without these, we shall ever fight on unequal terms."[1] Indeed, there is a popular image in American schools and American scholarship of British soldiers in America fighting in an outdated fashion ill-suited for American conditions. Americans, on the other hand, relying on Indian military conventions and common sense, preferred a more practical, *offensive*, and effective form of warfare—mobile soldiers advancing independently, using concealed and accurate fire. In such assessments, Benjamin Church, the hero of King Philip's War, is usually given credit for initiating the tactical transformation of military forces in colonial New England by adopting characteristics of Indian warfare.[2]

The military adventures of the English settlers in New England illuminated the tensions between American conditions and European training and conventions. European tactics were ill-suited to the uneven and wooded terrain of New England. The great mobility and loose formation of Indian forces, as well as their hit-and-run tactics, further undermined the effectiveness of defenders' firepower. Successful Indian attacks on colonial forces during King Philip's War, combined with the celebrated exploits of Benjamin Church, have led some contemporary and modern observers to conclude that the combination of firearms and Indian tactics was too potent for English forces relying on conventional European tactics. Consequently, it has been argued, exposure to Indian tactics (during King Philip's War, King William's War, and Queen Anne's War) improved the efficiency of English military forces. Battlefield experience forced colonial commanders to "unlearn" what their European military manuals had taught them. Thus, only by employing the Indians' tactical methods against them were colonial commanders able to reverse the tide of Indian victories, achieve tactical success against Indian forces, and consequently win the war.

This assumption is not supported by the evidence. King Philip's War and the later colonial wars were won not through a succession of tactical victories but through a campaign of attrition. Furthermore, the colonies' military and political leadership never rejected European military conventions. Benjamin Church's accomplishments, as well as his legacy, have been overstated by Church himself and by generations of admirers. European tactics were not outdated or ineffective in the American wilderness, as the Seven Years' War in North America clearly demonstrated. Reliance on European defensive tactics—in both offensive and defensive operations[3]—often enabled the English to overcome and overwhelm their opponents. A comparison between the first generation of New England's military commanders (conventional-minded European veterans) and the supposedly "Americanized" commanders of the later colonial wars reflects poorly on the latter. Colonial commanders, as a group, were not "Americanized"; they were simply remarkably inexperienced and unprofessional. Thus, colonial forces were often tricked into abandoning the tactical defense, with disastrous results. Some authors (such as Stephen Saunders Webb and John Ferling) assert that colonial New England was a militarist society. A close examination of colonial armed forces (after the 1650s), however, indicates that this was a society of military novices, plagued by astonishing carelessness and neglect in military matters and undermined by its own ad hoc approach to military affairs.

The debate on the formulation and adoption of "American tactics" is inevitably linked to the question of the effectiveness of Indian tactics. Proponents of the Americanization thesis concede that the English enjoyed a strategic and logistical advantage over their Indian adversaries.[4] They assume, however, that the settlers could not match the Indians' tactical skills. Thus, they argue that the settlers' success against Indian troops resulted from their reliance on Indian allies; only these could match the enemy's speed and tactical skills. None of these authors, however, provides evidence to sustain their assumption. Indeed, little evidence exists to demonstrate that on a tactical level, Indians were more effective than Englishmen against Indian troops. In fact, the data suggest that Indian alliances were a political and strategic asset, rather than a tactical one.

The colonists' military ordeals in New England during the late seventeenth and early eighteenth centuries did not lead to a reevaluation and transformation of their military doctrine. Rather than revitalizing the settlers' military establishments, these episodes highlighted the ongoing degeneration of colonial armed forces. In fact, it was the poor performance of colonial forces in King Philip's War and King William's War that led eighteenth-century colonial magistrates to address the shortcomings of their military forces through a greater reliance on British forces and imperial administrators.

The military history of the northeast illustrates that when sufficient men and resources were invested, European warfare could be imposed on the American wilderness. The misconception regarding the colonists' successful adjustment to wilderness warfare prior to the American Revolution was promoted by eighteenth- and nineteenth-century popular historians and biographers.[5] It has been sustained by some cultural and military historians. Such works exhibit three inaccuracies that need to be addressed. First, one can see more continuity than innovation in colonial military tactics. Second, the tactical innovations initiated at times by colonial forces did not represent an ideological departure from European military doctrine; the settlers were not won over by a new philosophy of war. Finally, European tactics were not ineffective in North America.

WINSTON CHURCHILL claimed that war is the story of the human race. Indeed, war is often the means by which communities form, progress, or disintegrate. The conquest of the North American wilderness and its native population by the English settlers shaped American society, culture, and ideology, and still illuminates central aspects of contemporary American culture. Thus, because a civilization's military doctrine, institutions, and reputation are a unique and emotionally charged cultural tag, the debate on "American tactics" is a corollary of the ever-widening controversy over American cultural exceptionalism and the colonies' relation to the British Empire.

Most accounts of the colonies' military history focus on the cultural interaction between Europeans and Indians. Writers such as Robert A. Williams

(The American Indian in Western Legal Thought), Nicholas P. Canny (The Elizabethan Conquest of Ireland), Anthony Pagden (The Fall of Natural Man) and Harry Culverwell Porter (The Inconstant Savage) focus on the durability of the European "just war" tradition in America. They demonstrate how justifications for subjugation, as well as the criteria for defining and gauging "savagery," were transported to the New World and applied to Indians. These justifications relied on preconceived and self-realizing expectations regarding the Indians, informed by European experience.

Like the aforementioned authors, Charles Segal and David Stineback (Puritans, Indians, and Manifest Destiny), Neal Salisbury (Manitou and Providence), and John Ferling (A Wilderness of Miseries) focus on the cultural aspects of military conflicts. However, they draw a different conclusion from the colonies' military history. Stressing the local roots of the settlers' Indian policies, Segal and Stineback argue that anti-Indian militancy served to rally and unite Englishmen behind their political and religious institutions, thus reversing the waning commitment to Puritanism.[6] Ferling claims that the colonists brought with them to America a brutal and pragmatic European attitude regarding warfare (an attitude that was shaped by the Wars of Religion and the Thirty Years' War). He argues that cultural conflict with the Indians fed the colonists' racism and militarism, sustaining their total-war tradition, whereas in Europe these were on the decline during the late-seventeenth and early-eighteenth centuries.[7]

Alden T. Vaughan (New England Frontier) and Roy Harvey Pearce (Savagism and Civilization) deny that the colonists' enmity toward the Indians was racist. They acknowledge the prejudices and brutality of seventeenth-century Europeans but discern a genuine belief among settlers that Indian culture rather than Indian nature led them to evil. Both Vaughan and Pearce reject assumptions regarding the colonists' genocidal aims and their introduction of total war to New England. Indeed, the cruelty and brutality of warfare in America was not novel or unique and should not, therefore, be viewed as a symptom of exceptional racial or cultural animosity. The use of fire against enemy forts was not an American invention; neither was the primitive biological warfare employed at times by the English (the use of blankets infested with small pox). Similar measures (catapulting plague-infected limbs into besieged fortresses, for example) had been used successfully in Europe and the Near East since antiquity. Richard Johnson ("The Search for a Usable Indian") and James D. Drake (King Philip's War) further challenge the assertions of Ferling,

Salisbury, and Segal and Stineback by stressing that important military and cultural alliances existed between Englishmen and Indians. Thus, lines of battle were not drawn neatly along ethnic lines.

Studies that examine interactions between Europeans and Indians from a strictly military perspective are characterized by a similar division between those who stress the continuity of European experience and influence, and others, who focus on the transforming effect of American conditions on English settlers. Patrick Malone (*The Skulking Way of War*) describes how New England Indians appropriated European military technology and how this appropriation transformed their way of waging war, as well as their way of life. He also discusses the "Indianization" of the colonists' tactics, technology, and logistics.[8] Explaining that King Philip's War exposed the incompatibility of English military maxims and the unique realities of warfare in America, Malone argues that the colonists were forced to adjust their tactics to their surroundings and to the tactics of their enemies. This view is shared by other historians, such as John Ferling ("The New England Soldier"), Steven Charles Eames ("Rustic Warriors"), John M. Dederer (*War in America to 1775*), and Armstrong Starkey (*European and Native American Warfare*).[9]

Ferling and Eames go on to assert that provincial troops' bad reputation was unjustified in view of the special security needs of frontier communities. They argue that the political organization of colonial society and the exceptional nature of frontier warfare created a soldiery whose success depended not on discipline and large-scale cooperation, but on individual action and expertise. These modifications reflected not only the settlers' need for a smaller, nimbler, and more offensive-minded military, but also their commitment to republican and democratic values (that is, their fondness for military institutions with flat hierarchical structures).

In opposition to such assessments, Stanley McCrory Pargellis (*Lord Loudoun in North America* and "Braddock's Defeat"), Ian Kenneth Steele (*Guerrillas and Grenadiers*), and Daniel J. Beattie ("The Adaptation of the British Army to Wilderness Warfare") offer refreshingly original and nuanced accounts of the conduct of British forces in North America, primarily during the Seven Years' War.[10] Disregarding established stereotypes, they offer readers a glimpse into the *conventional* means (creation of supply centers and secure lines of communications, mass deployment, fort construction, and defensive tactics) by which the army countered the challenges posed by North America's terrain and by its rivals' irregular tactics.

Although these works are not recent, supporters of the Americanization thesis have yet to address the challenge presented by Pargellis, Steele, and Beattie. The fact that most "Americanizationists" have focused primarily on colonial forces has enabled them to sidestep the arguments and evidence provided by Pargellis, Steele, and Beattie, whose works focus primarily on British forces. Thus, these scholarly camps have coexisted in relative peace by arguing past one another and turning a blind eye to the activities of the other. This strange dialogue echoes the heated dispute over the military and civic merits of a militia, as opposed to a standing army. More significant, however, it highlights the dangers of viewing colonial history and culture as presaging the American Revolution.

The transmission of European military culture to the periphery of the empire was a characteristic of a transatlantic English civilization. When examined within the context of imperial history, the story of warfare, politics, and culture in colonial North America reads as a process by which the colonies gravitated toward England's cultural and administrative sphere of influence, rather than attempting to liberate themselves from it.

CHAPTER ONE /
The Beginnings of a Colonial Military Tradition

ANALYZING MILITARY TACTICS is a fairly simple task. It is a military axiom that, on a tactical level, the offensive is predicated on mobility, whereas the effectiveness of the defense is predicated on firepower. A defending force is dedicated to preserving the gap between it and the opposing army. Firepower—projectile weapons used en masse—is the most effective means of achieving this goal. By sending sheets of lead across the battlefield at a consistent rate, defenders inhibit the enemy's ability or willingness to charge.

Whereas defenders attempt to keep attackers at bay, the offensive's goal is to eliminate this gap between the two armies. To achieve success, an offensive force must either advance, under fire, and engage the defenders at close quarters or flank the defensive line and attack its rear (swiftness being essential for both a frontal assault and a flanking maneuver). For this reason, European warfare in the seventeenth and eighteenth centuries often frustrated its practitioners. Throughout this period, technological and tactical innovations dramatically increased the firepower of European armies but not their mobility. Thus, commanders were dissuaded by heavy defensive fire from attacking, and battles often devolved into expensive tactical stalemates.

Linear formations maximized the effectiveness of firearms, making it much easier for defenders to maintain the gap between themselves and the enemy. Offensive forces, however, could target the main weakness of these defensive formations—their lack of depth. The key to overcoming the superior position of the defense was attacking its flanks or rear. Exposing the defenders' weak side was seen as essential to an offensive's success. This vulnerability of the defensive line resulted from its delicate psychological dynamics.

> The tactical line provides a means by which each man (or each unit in the line), save those on the extreme flanks, may protect the sides of his neighbor and be protected by the enlightened self-interest of that neighbor. Once this line is severed, broken into, or smashed, safety is gone. . . . Every member wishes to separate himself from the band when it is in danger. Indeed, the wish to decamp is always strongest at just that point, the tactically critical point, where the group is in the greatest danger. The prime object of discipline and training is to prevent this.[1]

To prevent offensive flanking, European commanders "anchored" their formations, positioning the line between barriers, such as a river or a fort, or even a concentration of infantry companies, that would prevent or inhibit the advance of the enemy. It is for this reason also that the overwhelming majority of large-scale European battles were fought on flat terrain. Uneven terrain disrupted the continuity of the line and threatened its integrity; in effect, it created flanks in the middle of the line.[2]

Toward the end of the seventeenth century, three technological innovations dealt a seemingly fatal blow to the offensive. The replacement of the matchlock musket with the flintlock and the introduction of prepacked cartridges for muskets (a ball and a charge of powder wrapped in paper, ready for loading and firing) simplified and shortened the loading procedure, increasing both the volume and range of fire. The prepacked cartridge created a greater breech pressure behind the ball, increasing its velocity. Armed with a flintlock and provided with cartridges, a well-trained soldier could fire two rounds per minute. Set in three ranks, a defensive line could, therefore, produce a massive volley once every ten seconds. From the late 1680s, with the wholesale adoption of the flintlock and prepacked cartridges, an attacking force had to cover 150 yards under defensive fire, compared with 60 yards during the matchlock era.[3] Even more devastating in this respect was the advent of bayonets. Despite its being a shock (close combat) weapon, the bayonet dramatically increased firepower and reduced the probability of close-quarters combat. Before its introduction to the battlefield, infantry forces consisted of musketeers (roughly 66 percent) and pikemen (33 percent), whose role it was to defend the musketeers with their long pikes when a cavalry or infantry charge reached the line (the musketeers being utterly useless at close combat).[4] The bayonet provided musketeers with the means of defending themselves. Thus, the role of the offensively unproductive pikemen was abolished and the number of musketeers on the line increased by 150 percent. Not only were the musketeers more numerous with the elimination of the pike; they were also positioned more densely, thus producing a more devastating volley.

The rapidly growing importance of musketry in European warfare was coupled with a marked decline in the utility of skilled marksmanship. Contemporary tactics required musketeers to load and fire their firearms uniformly, on command, in volleys, and by ranks. Since both sides were similarly organized in close formations, European armies became increasingly vulnerable to massed fire. The growing number of musketeers on the line made volume and constancy of fire much more important than individual accuracy. Furthermore, although the flintlock smoothbore musket was effective against infantry formations at 150 yards, it took a skilled marksman to hit an individual target at a range of 40 to 50 yards.[5] In other words, at a range of 150 yards, all that could be expected of a soldier was to hit the broad side of a barn, or of a mile-long enemy line. It is estimated that 15 to 20 percent of shots fired by well-trained infantry formations hit their targets. More often than not, this was sufficient to inhibit offensive mobility. Thus, military men felt that numbers adequately compensated for lack of marksmanship.

The dramatic increase in firepower enabled more innovative European armies (such as the Dutch, Prussian, and British armies) to reduce the number of ranks on the line from five to three, thus creating longer formations. The firepower produced by these formations kept offensive forces at bay, while the increased frontage further inhibited mobility on the field. Orchestrating offensive advances on such a massive scale was a demanding task. Furthermore, flanking such immense defensive lines was a slow and difficult project that allowed the defense the time required to adjust its position.

These developments significantly diminished the effectiveness of shock troops. Nevertheless, tactical innovators such as Gustavus Adolphus, the Duke of Marlborough, and Frederick the Great refused to forsake the offensive. They attempted to break the tactical stalemate by emphasizing the importance of breaking through the defensive line rather than flanking it and quickly engaging the enemy at close quarters.

The Nine Years' War (1689–98) and the War of Spanish Succession (1701–

13) provided John Churchill, later Duke of Marlborough, with the opportunity to experiment with innovative offensive tactics. The key to his offensive success was the fact that he did not attempt to push back the entire defensive line. Marlborough's objective was to weaken a certain point along the line, break through it, and then attack from the rear. Repeated assaults on the enemy flanks forced his opponents to stretch their defense, thus weakening the center. After hours of successive assaults on the flanks, Marlborough made the final assault on a predetermined section at the center of the defensive line, relying heavily on his artillery and on his most mobile shock troops, the cavalry, to initiate this assault.[6]

Marlborough emphasized the importance of firing volleys by ranks while advancing toward the enemy line. The objective of this practice was to pressure the defenders with projectile volleys and increase this pressure with the threat of a bayonet charge. Sometimes three to four minutes of this type of pressure were sufficient to bring about the disintegration of a defensive line; when Marlborough's forces managed to reach bayonet range, the enemy was often already in flight.

Like Marlborough, Frederick the Great believed that one could overcome the superior position and firepower of the defense with a combination of maneuver and numbers. His oblique order formation was designed to achieve this. The Prussian system also targeted only a certain portion of the line, attempting to break through and then attack the rear. The Prussians challenged their enemies' defensive doctrine by positioning their troops in an oblique formation and heavily reinforcing the wing closest to the defensive line. Thus, this wing could absorb defensive fire and still launch an effective charge toward the enemy. Moreover, the increased firepower of this reinforced wing enabled it (with artillery support) to weaken the defensive units facing it. Whereas numerical superiority and increased firepower compensated for the positional weakness of the offensive wing, distance compensated for the numerical inferiority of the weaker Prussian wing.

These offensive tactics required elaborate and exact coordination that took years of training to perfect and were very costly in terms of casualty rates. In Marlborough's most impressive victory, at Blenheim, he lost 25 percent of his men. In an era when the soldier was the most expensive piece of military equipment on the field, these successful offensives sometimes turned out to be Pyrrhic victories. The battles of Napoleon, who is viewed as a successor to Marlborough and Frederick, were also characterized by horrifying casualty rates. Unlike his predecessors, however, Napoleon enjoyed a virtually unlimited supply of men (who were also poorly trained and, therefore, more expendable). Despite these statistics, these innovators demonstrated that a combination of mobility and superior offensive firepower (that is, numerical superiority at the point of engagement) could, if only for a limited time, overcome defensive firepower. The unorthodox approach of these commanders challenged the maxims of European military doctrine. Indian warfare posed a similar challenge for English settlers in New England. The uneven and wooded terrain of New England was less than perfect for the employment of European tactics. The great mobility and loose formation of Indian forces, as well as their hit and run tactics, further undermined the effectiveness of defenders' firepower.

THE COLONISTS LIVING in New England during the first half of the century were, generally speaking, military novices. Most of them were totally inexperienced in military affairs, combat, and firearms and unaware of the great improvements in the practice of European warfare.[7] The governing bodies of the New England colonies tried to compel their constituents to acquire military skills. Colonists who failed to report to their units on training days or failed to furnish themselves with firearms were severely fined.[8] Nevertheless, the authorities' designs were often frustrated. Moreover, training days seemed more like a country fair than a military gathering, with eating and drinking the paramount activity, rather than drilling.[9]

Although colonial military leaders such as Miles Standish and John Endicott advised the colonists to arm themselves with flintlocks, most settlers at this time preferred the less expensive matchlock (see Fig. 1).[10] The matchlock was a heavy and unwieldy weapon. Its weight and size compelled the musketeer to use a forked rest to support and stabilize it. The lock, by which fire was admitted, consisted of a pan containing powder. The burning serpentine (that is, the "slow match") was held on a cock. When the pan was opened and the trigger was pulled, a simple mechanism pressed the serpentine to the pan. Sparks from the ignited powder shot into the barrel through a little opening, igniting the powder charge that propelled the bullet or shot. The procedure of preparing, loading, charging, aiming, and firing a matchlock musket was slow, clumsy, and laborious.[11] For this reason, and many others,[12] the matchlock proved unsatisfactory in New England. Throughout the 1640s, 1650s, and 1660s, colonial authorities purchased flintlocks for their

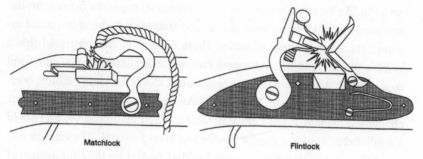

1. Matchlock and flintlock mechanisms.

military establishments. Matchlocks were still in private and public use in New England in 1675–76, during King Philip's War, though colonial authorities outlawed their use as public arms later in the decade.[13] A similar shift from matchlocks to flintlocks took place in most European armies during the 1680s and 1690s.

In Europe, the advent of the flintlock and the bayonet brought about the elimination of the pike. In colonial New England the pike was discarded as well, though much earlier, and for different reasons. In keeping with European conventions, the settlers brought with them from Europe both pikes and muskets. By the same conventions, one-third of colonial infantrymen were pikemen.[14] The pikes proved, however, to be ineffective in America. They were best suited for Europe's massive armies and for the terrain of the low countries. In the New England wilderness and against an enemy that shunned pitched battles, they were relatively useless. For this reason, the Court of Assistants in Boston decreed as early as 1634, "that every trayned soldier, as well pykemen as others, shalbe furnished with musketts, bandoleroes,[15] & rests, powder and shott according to the order for musketeers."[16]

CHAPTER TWO /
Muskets and Bows

ALTHOUGH ENGLISH SETTLERS in New England were willing to modify their military equipment to their new surroundings, they did not reevaluate the military maxims with which they were familiar. They were not forced to do so. In fact, their adherence to European conventions was a key factor in their remarkable military accomplishments during the first generation after settlement. Despite the glaring differences between the plains of the low countries and the terrain of the New England wilderness, and between the massive professional armies of Europe and Indian war bands, the European martial education of New England's military leaders served them well in the New World.

The first English emigrants who landed on New England's shores were not military men; very few of them had had any military experience in Europe. Nevertheless, they expected military confrontations with the "savage and brutish" natives of America and came equipped for such encounters. The pilgrim "saints" brought along with them a company of "strangers," led by Captain Miles Standish, to whom the security of the community was to be entrusted. They also brought with them muskets, pikes, armor and artillery pieces, and a supply of powder and ammunition.[1] Public records from this early stage of settlement demonstrate the settlers' preoccupation with military affairs. The knowledge that civilization and Christendom in New England extended only to the range of European guns facilitated this preoccupation.[2]

Most of the military leaders employed by the settlers in the 1620s were English soldiers of fortune who had served in the armies of the Protestant princes during the Dutch wars of independence. First and foremost among these commanders was Miles Standish of Plymouth. Born in Duxbury, Lancashire, in 1584, he received a soldier's education and was commissioned as a lieutenant in England's military establishment in the Netherlands. The books found in Miles Standish's private library indicate that he read contemporary military theorists (William Barriffe was the most prominent of these), as well as the classics.[3] Very little is known about his career in Holland. After leaving the service, Standish settled in Leyden, where he became acquainted with John Robinson's flock of Brownist separatists. He lived with them, though not as a member of the church.[4] When the community decided to emigrate to America, Standish was commissioned by William Bradford, Edward Winslow, and Isaac Allerton as the military commander of their party.[5]

Like Miles Standish, John Mason, John Underhill, Daniel Patrick, Richard Morris, and Lion Gardiner served in the English military establishment in the Netherlands. All of them served under the command of Sir Thomas Fairfax at some point in their military career in Europe.[6] They emigrated to Massachusetts in the early 1630s. John Mason—"energetic, of a stern, but not headlong disposition; moral yet not religious"—served in Boston and, as a captain, in Dorchester in the early 1630s.[7]

Lion Gardiner, "engineer and master of works of fortification" in the service of the Prince of Orange, was approached in 1635 by the Puritan community in Rotterdam on behalf of the New England Company. He accepted their offer of a four-year commission and set sail for Massachusetts with his wife. In Boston, he was entrusted with the task of completing the fortifications on Fort Hill.[8] From the very beginning, Lion Gardiner displayed meticulous attention to details that other, more adventurous commanders tended to neglect or overlook. He was methodical and conservative in preparing for war, always careful to conserve his resources. In 1636, for example, he was requested to evaluate the fortification works required in Salem. Upon his return, he reported that the people there were more in danger of starvation than of any potent enemy. He recommended to defer any fortification plans. In spring 1636 Connecticut's governor, John Winthrop Jr., commissioned Gardiner to construct and command a fort at Saybrook, on an elevation on the west bank of the Connecticut River, flanked by the river, the Long Island Sound, and by salt marshes.[9] The only overland access route was defended with a palisade. Gardiner commanded the fort for four years, until 1640.[10]

Although early fortification projects (such as the fortification of Castle Island) indicate that the settlers felt threatened by European naval powers, the settlers were very much aware also of their vulnerability with regard to the Indians. Ever since the discovery of America, Europeans had been informed by travelers' horrific accounts of Indian violence and license, as well as by their own cultural and religious prejudices, about what they could expect of the natives in America. Colorful and gruesome tales of Indian social, religious, and martial ethics had been circulating in Europe for over a century before the pilgrims set sail for America. Thus, when the pilgrims left Europe, they expected to encounter a savage, cruel, and treacherous people, who "delight to tormente men in the most bloody manner that may be; [skinning] some alive with the shells of fishes, cutting of the members, and joyntes of others by peesemeale & broiling on the coles, eate . . . their flesh in their sight while they live with cruelties horrible to be related."[11]

William Bradford's description of the New England landscape indicates that after their arrival and settlement, the settlers of Plymouth found nothing that would dispel their fears and insecurities: "a hideous and desolate wilderness, full of wild beasts and wild men—and what multitudes there might be of them they knew not."[12] Weakened by a two-month voyage and by near-starvation,[13] with no allies in sight, the settlers were acutely aware of their isolation and vulnerability. Before they met any Indians, they saw the smoke from their camps, and at night they could hear their cries.[14] A quick glance at a map illustrates the cause of the colonists' intense sense of isolation and insecurity (see Fig. 2). Although ravaged by disease, the New England Indians vastly outnumbered the colonists. By 1621, Plymouth Plantation numbered one hundred men, women, and children. Only fifty men were of military age. The Wampanoags alone, despite being decimated by successive epidemics, could field five hundred warriors at this time.[15] So intensely fearful were the Europeans—and so aware of the Indian presence around them—that during the first winter they buried their dead at night and leveled the graves to hide the fact that their numbers were rapidly decreasing.[16]

By spring 1621, the colonists had learned from Samoset (an Indian interpreter, guide, and teacher) of the amazing effectiveness of European diseases in decimating and weakening their Indian neighbors. Samoset explained that although the coastal Indian tribes were hostile toward the settlers, they feared the white man's god. Thus, their hostile actions against the settlers were limited to magic and witchcraft.[17]

The first military confrontation between the settlers and Indians took place

2. New England, 1637.

in December 1620. An armed company of nine men, led by Miles Standish, set out December 6 to explore the Cape Cod area. Their mission was to locate a site for settlement, with a good harbor. In two previous expeditions the settlers came across some abandoned Indian dwellings and saw some Indians at a distance. Every night the explorers built a man-high barricade around their campsite. They lit a fire at the center of camp and set sentinels around it. They also took care to wrap their matchlocks in blankets or coats for the night to protect them from the morning dew. On December 7, while fortifying their campsite, the explorers accompanying Captain Standish heard "a hideous and great cry." Assuming that it came from wolves, they discharged two muskets and the howling ceased. Early the next morning they heard the same cry once again. Immediately, one of the sentinels ran in shouting, "Men, Indians! Indians." A barrage of arrows followed him, and then Indians charged the camp.[18]

The men ran for their firearms. But only four men, including Captain Standish, had their muskets nearby; the rest of the muskets were already loaded on the boat. Standish fired his flintlock at the attackers, and one of his men followed suit, giving the armed men behind the barricade time to charge and load their weapons.[19] "In the mean time, of those that were ther ready, tow muskets were discharged at them, and 2. more stood ready in the enterance of ther randevoue, but were comanded [by Standish] not to shoote till they could take full aime at them; and the other 2. charged [and loaded] againe with all speed, for ther were only 4. had armes ther, and defended the baricado which was first assalted."[20]

Captain Standish ordered the four armed men to stay with him to defend the barricade and the remaining five men to charge for the boat, a few meters behind the barricade. It was essential that they recover their muskets and defend the vessel to protect the company's rear (and their only route of escape). The Indians tried to prevent this charge but were too late. They "soone got their armes, and let flye amongs them, and quickly stopped their violence.[21] . . . They left some to keep the shalop [boat], and followed them aboute a quarter of a mille, and shouted once or twise, and shot of 2. or 3. peces, and so returned. This they did, that they might conceive that they were not affrade of them."[22]

Before leaving the battlefield, Captain Standish and his men christened it "First Encounter." The battle of First Encounter is instructive. Captain Standish's conduct demonstrated a European approach to warfare adapted to non-European conditions. His company fortified its camp and sent out sentinels every night. When hostilities began, he kept his men on the defensive, relying on the firepower of his musketeers. In protecting his rear, he displayed the disciplined and methodical care of a veteran—while his company pursued the fleeing Indians, six men were left behind to guard the boat, "for we were carefull of our businesse."[23]

Captain Standish ordered his very few men not to fire at will. In keeping with European defensive tactics, the defenders at the barricade were commanded to maintain a steady rotation of fire, in effect, firing by "ranks."

Shortage of men on the defensive "line," however, required a tactical adjustment: accurate fire became essential in the absence of volume. William Bradford describes an Indian warrior who was firing at the colonists from behind a tree; he was fired upon but did not flee, "till one taking full aime at him, and made the barke or splinters of the tree fly about his ears, after which he gave an extraordinary shrike, and away they wente all of them."[24]

Fortunately for the colonists, the battle of First Encounter did not escalate into war with the New England Indians. Thanks to the efforts of Squanto and Samoset, the Plymouth colonists and the Wampanoag sachem, Massasoit, agreed on a peace settlement. In September 1621 three other Indian chiefs—Corbitant (Massasoit's brother) and two chiefs of the Massachusetts tribe—came to Plymouth and added their names to the treaty.[25] By this treaty the Indian signatories declared themselves—probably unwittingly—loyal subjects of King James and his heirs, "and gave unto them all the Lands adjacent, to them and to their Heirs forever."[26] The treaty was resigned in 1639 by Massasoit and his son and heir-apparent, Wamsutta (referred to by the English as Alexander), and ratified by the colonial government. It remained in effect until the end of Massasoit's reign and his succession by his son Metacom (King Philip).

The colonists realized that Massasoit had agreed to a peace settlement with them because of a perhaps misplaced belief in their capabilities—Squanto had diligently spread the rumor among the Indians that the English had buried the plague under the floorboards of their storehouse (where, in fact, they had buried barrels of gun powder).[27] Squanto and Samoset informed the settlers that Massasoit was eager to find allies, "because he hath a potent adversary, the Narragansetts, that are at war with him, against whom he thinks we may be some strength to him, for our pieces are terrible unto them."[28]

ON MARCH 23, 1623, Miles Standish was ordered by the authorities to lead a group of men to Weymouth (Wessagusett), twenty-five miles to the north of Plymouth, to assist the sixty English colonists who had settled there in 1622. The new settlement was not a success. With the arrival of winter, the settlers there sold their possessions to their Indian neighbors, the Massachusetts, in exchange for food. Some were forced to find employment with the Indians, as workers and servants. Others, however, "fell to stealing both night and day from the Indians, of which they [the Massachusetts] grievously complained."[29]

Plymouth's decision to assist the Weymouth settlers was more a matter of expediency than a testament to English solidarity. The Plymouth settlers felt that the Indians' anger toward Weymouth was justified, and they were careful to explain to their Indian neighbors that they were distinct from the Weymouth settlement.[30] They felt compelled to come to Weymouth's aid, however, once they had learned from Massasoit that the Massachusetts planned to attack the new settlement,[31] because they feared the Massachusetts—whose enmity toward Massasoit was well known—would not discriminate between the two English groups. Furthermore, fear of Indian violence was running high at the time because the news had recently arrived from Virginia that an Indian raid on Jamestown had left three hundred colonists dead.

On his arrival (April 5, 1623), Captain Standish established command over the Europeans at Weymouth, rationing to each a pint of corn a day from the supplies brought for his men and ordering them, on pain of death, not to stray from the settlement. (The settlers were accustomed to gathering berries and working the fields surrounding the village.)[32] Captain Standish avoided a battle with the Massachusetts by undertaking a series of assassinations that became known as the Weymouth massacre. On Massasoit's recommendation, minor Massachusett sachems were lured to a hut, where they were murdered one after the other.[33] The following morning Hobomac, Massasoit's war captain, defeated and drove off the remaining Massachusetts warriors. On his return to Plymouth, Captain Standish presented the impaled head of Wituwamet, the chief conspirator against the English, at the entrance to Plymouth's modest fortress (a blockhouse that served also as a meeting house and house of worship).[34]

Throughout this period, regional politics intensified the settlers' sense of insecurity. At the end of 1621 the one hundred settlers living in Plymouth faced a new threat. Through their alliance with Massasoit and the Wampanoags they had acquired the Narragansetts (thirty thousand strong) as their enemies.[35] Cannonicus, the Narragansett sachem, declared war on Plymouth Plantation soon after the peace settlement with Massasoit.[36] Consequently, the settlers decided to erect defensive fortifications around the town: "Knowing our own weakness, notwithstanding our high words and lofty looks towards them, and still lying open to all casualty, having as yet (under God) no other defence than our arms, we thought it most needful to impale our town."[37] Miles Standish supervised the construction of a palisade ten to twelve feet high that encircled the town, as well as part of the adjacent Burial

Hill. Four companies of sentinels guarded the palisade's three gates day and night.[38] Each company had a specific assignment in case of attack.[39]

The fortifications were completed by March 1622. Before summer's end, however, these were deemed insufficient. In the aftermath of the Jamestown massacre, the settlers at Plymouth felt that their Indian neighbors were growing bolder and more impertinent; the Massachusetts and Narragansetts in particular, but "now also [Massasoit] seemed to frown on us, and neither came or sent to us as foremerly."[40] Thus, in June, the settlers began construction of a fort.[41]

> The fort is a large, square house, with a flat roof, made of thick, sawn planks, stayed with oak beams, upon the top of which they have six cannon, which shoot iron balls of four or five pounds, and command the surrounding country. The lower part they use for their church, where they preach on Sundays, and the usual holidays. They assemble by beat of drum, each with his musket or firelock, in front of the captain's door. . . . Thus, they are on their guard, night and day.[42]

The fort was built on Burial Hill, within the limits of the town's palisades. The guns on its roof commanded the town and the harbor. Although the colonists' ordnance in the early seventeenth century was directed primarily at European navies,[43] it was effective also against Indian attacks overland. Artillery played a very minor role, however, in New England's Indian wars; it was most effective psychologically, as a deterrent: "[The] redoubling echo rattling in the rocks caused the Indians to betake themselves to flight (being a terrible unwonted sound to them)."[44]

In time, a communication system was established between the various settlements. The colonial government instituted a system of communal defense.

> It is agreed . . . That when an Alarum is made and continued in Plymouth Duxborrow or Marshfeild There shalbe twenty men sent from Plymouth and as many from Duxborrow and tenn from Marshfeild to releeve the place where the Alarum is so continued. And when any of these places stand in neede of help upon the continuance of the Alarum Then a Beacon to be fyred or els a great fyer to be made from Plymouth upon the Galhouse hill, on the Captain Hill for Duxborrow And on a hill by Mr. Thomas his house for Marshfeild.[45]

Until the late 1620s, Plymouth was the largest and most prominent of New England's "Puritan colonies." In 1630, however, the arrival of one thousand settlers to the Massachusetts Bay area immediately transformed the Bay Colony into the region's largest and strongest colony. Between 1629 and 1632 the population of the Massachusetts Bay Colony grew from roughly 450 to over 2,000. By 1634 the population was 4,000, and by 1637 over 8,000.[46] The expansion and ascendance of the Massachusetts Bay Colony coincided with a new wave of epidemics among the Indians, the worst since 1617. Indian communities as far as the Connecticut Valley and the Piscataqua River in Maine were severely affected by the plague; these Indian societies were crumbling politically because of internal tensions related to the epidemics and to Indian-European interactions. Consequently, by 1632, several Massachusett and Narragansett sachems traveled to Boston to sign peace treaties with the Bay Colony.[47]

Massachusetts Bay was much better equipped and prepared for war than was Plymouth.[48] During the early 1630s, the Court of Assistants in Boston enacted and enforced legislation designed to provide the various settlements with mutual support and capable defenders: frontier communities (such as Dorchester and Watertown) were required to established nightly watches;[49] weekly drills were made mandatory for all militia units;[50] stiff penalties were imposed on absentees from training and watch duty; all citizens were instructed to equip themselves with a musket, one pound of powder, twenty bullets, and two fathoms of match (serpentine); towns were authorized to impress men into service for purposes of security; and travelers on the frontier were forbidden to travel alone or unarmed.[51] To complement these defensive preparations, a beacon was constructed in Boston in 1635 to be fired in case of attack by land or sea—hence the name Beacon Hill.[52] The court involved itself heavily in matters of security. No other issue received as much attention.[53] In 1634, every town was instructed to appoint an overseer of powder and shot. The sale of arms and ammunition to Indians was strictly forbidden and had been since the Massachusetts Bay Company received its royal charter in 1629. Captain John Endicott, the resident agent of the New England Company, was instructed by the Massachusetts Bay Company to arrest offenders and send them to London for trial.[54] Similarly, the first Connecticut General Court convened in Hartford, April 26, 1636, forbade the sale of firearms and ammunition to Indians.[55]

In 1637, war broke out between the New England colonies (Connecticut,

Massachusetts Bay, and Plymouth) and the Pequot Indians, who inhabited the lower Connecticut Valley. The declaration of war was the culmination of an acrimonious investigation into the murder of Captain John Stone (a Virginia merchant), Captain Walter Norton, and their ship's crew in spring 1634. In July 1636 another merchant, Captain John Oldham, was murdered and his ship captured by a tributary tribe of the Narragansetts on Block Island. Although Cannonicus, the Narragansett sachem, was persuaded by the Bay Colony's outrage to return the property and captives, he claimed that he could not extradite the murderers. They had allegedly found shelter with the Pequots.[56]

After a peace and cooperation treaty was signed between the Bay Colony and the Narragansetts, ninety volunteers were sent to Block Island, under the command of John Endicott and John Underhill. Captain Endicott's orders were to take possession of the island and put to death all the men there. Then he was to proceed to Pequot territory and demand the murderers of Stone and Oldham, as well as reparations and hostages.[57]

When the troops came ashore on Block Island they were met by a force of roughly sixty Indian warriors armed only with bows and arrows, who shot arrows at them from the shelter of a low dune. The Englishmen retreated into the water; when they were out of effective range, they fired one volley toward the Indians, who immediately fled.[58] Endicott and Underhill occupied the village and prepared themselves defensively for an Indian counterattack, but no attack came. The Indians retreated to the swamp, where they were protected from English fire.[59] Unchallenged, the colonists began burning and pillaging. They confiscated the Indians' corn, killed their dogs, burned their huts, and destroyed property.[60]

After two days they set sail for Saybrook, from which they were to continue toward Pequot territory to begin peace negotiations. Lion Gardiner, the commander of the fort at Saybrook, was not pleased to see them: "You come hither to raise these wasps about my ears, and then you will take wing and flee away." Expecting the worst and knowing that when hostilities broke out, enemy cornfields were often the first target, Lieutenant Gardiner immediately ordered his men to harvest Saybrook's cornfields.[61] Indeed, the negotiations were not successful. The Pequots refused to comply with Endicott's demands, and so the English decided to

> beat up the drum and bid them battle. Marching into a champaign field we displayed our colors; but none would come near us, but

standing remotely off did laugh at us for our patience. We suddenly set upon our march, and gave fire to as many we could come near, firing thir wigwams, spoiling their corn, and many other necessaries that they had buried in the ground we raked up, which the soldiers had for booty.[62]

After a day spent "burning and spoiling the country," Endicott returned to Boston and the Pequots began raiding settler communities along the Connecticut River. The first victims were the soldiers Gardiner had sent to the settlement's cornfields. Two were captured and tortured. Five days later, the Pequots raided Saybrook itself. On February 22, 1637, Lieutenant Gardiner himself was ambushed. He and nine of his men left Fort Saybrook to clear the woods that handicapped the fort's command of the adjacent territory. The company stumbled upon three Indians, whom they pursued until they realized that they were tricked. Suddenly they were surrounded and charged by hundreds of Indians.[63] Three Englishmen were slain. The rest "made their way through the salvages with their swords, and so got under the command of the cannon of the fort. . . . The Indians thus fleshed and encouraged, besieged the fort as near as they durst approach."[64]

Lieutenant Gardiner sent a messenger to Boston, asking for relief. By then the number of English fatalities exceeded thirty. Consequently, the Massachusetts General Court convened on April 18 and approved the enlistment of 160 soldiers, to be levied proportionally from the towns. Two weeks later, the Connecticut General Court followed suit. Meanwhile, on April 23, the Pequots raided Wethersfield, killing nine people and capturing two young women. On the way back they taunted Gardiner's troops, waving the English clothes of their victims as they passed by Saybrook in their canoes.[65]

John Mason of Windsor received command over Connecticut's forces and Robert Seely was appointed as his lieutenant.[66] Hartford, Windsor, and Wethersfield were instructed to levy the men required for Mason's proposed campaign. Massachusetts, preparing its forces for war, quickly dispatched a company of twenty men, under Captain Underhill, and another company of forty men, under Captain Patrick to join and assist Major Mason.[67] Plymouth raised a company of fifty men under Lieutenant William Holmes, but it did not take part in the war.

John Mason arrived at Fort Saybrook with eighty English soldiers and eighty Mohegans, under the command of Uncas.[68] Lieutenant Gardiner was shocked that Mason had allied himself with Uncas: "Then I asked them how they durst trust the Mohegin Indians, who had but that year come from the Pequits. They said they would trust them, for they could not well go without them for want of guides. Yea, said I, but I will try them before a man of ours shall go with you or them."[69] Gardiner summoned Uncas and informed him that to join the campaign he would have to prove his sincerity and allegiance by killing or capturing a group of six Pequots that had been spotted the day before at Bass River.[70] Uncas agreed. He took twenty of his men and soon returned with four bodies and one captive.[71]

The Connecticut Court instructed Major Mason to attack the Pequots' main fort, at the mouth of the Pequot (Thames) River. Mason felt, however, that a frontal assault from the beach would be a mistake. Approaching from the sea, the English would have been visible from the fort. Furthermore, "their numbers far exceeded ours, . . . [and they] were on land, and being swift on Foot, might much impede our Landing, and possibly dishearten our Men." By approaching from the east, overland through Narragansett territory, Mason points out, "we should come upon their Backs, and possibly might surprise them unawares, at worst we should be on firm Land as well as they."[72]

Some of Mason's officers objected to his plan and urged him to follow the court's letter of instruction. He decided to consult the company's chaplain, Stone. He asked Stone "that he would commend our Condition to the Lord, that night, to direct how and in what manner we should demean ourselves in that Respect."[73] Fortunately, as Mr. Stone notified the officers in the morning, the Lord was in full agreement with the major, and so with His endorsement, Mason's proposal was approved. The next morning (May 19, 1637) they set sail eastward, past Pequot Harbor, to Narragansett Bay.

Mason urged the Narragansett sachems Miantonomo and Cannonicus to side with the English against Sassacus, the Pequot sachem. They agreed and supplied the English with soldiers and guides.[74] While Mason and his troops were at Cannonicus's fort, an Indian messenger arrived from Roger Williams, informing Mason that Captain Patrick and his men had just arrived in Providence and that Patrick wanted the attack delayed until he could join Mason's force. Mason, however, decided to move quickly. He set out toward Mystic on Wednesday, May 24, 1637, with plans to attack the smaller of the two Pequot forts on the Mystic River (see Fig. 3).[75] That night, his force camped in the territory of the Niantics, whose sachem, Ninigret, was related to Sassacus and loosely allied with him. Fearing that Ninigret would notify Sassacus of their approach, the English encircled Ninigret's fort for the night. The next night,

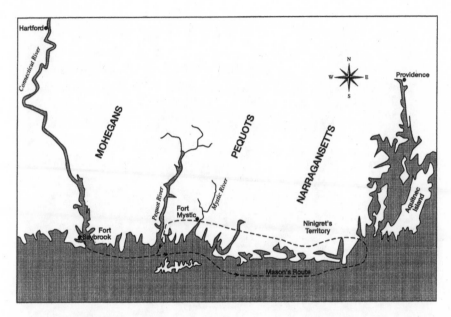

3. Mason's expedition, 1637.

they camped two miles away from Fort Mystic, at Porter's Rock (a space at the edge of a swamp, enclosed from three directions by granite rocks) and prepared to attack at dawn (May 26).[76]

At daybreak, Mason arrived within view of the fort, on the western side of the hill. He sent Underhill's contingent to the southern slope and, after allowing them enough time to get in position, he started his approach toward the palisade. Despite their silent advance, the English were detected by the Pequots' dogs. The English fired through the palisade and then charged both entrances to the fort simultaneously, "having our swords in our right hand, our carbines or muskets in our left hand." When the Indians started firing from within their huts, Mason ordered a retreat. He and Underhill blocked the entrances to the fort and then set it on fire, stoking the fire with gun powder. The English and their Indian allies formed two rings around the burning fort; those who escaped the fire were "received by the soldiers and entertained with the point of the sword."[77] Mason's force suffered two fatalities and twenty casualties. Of Mystic's six hundred inhabitants, only seven survived (see Fig. 4).

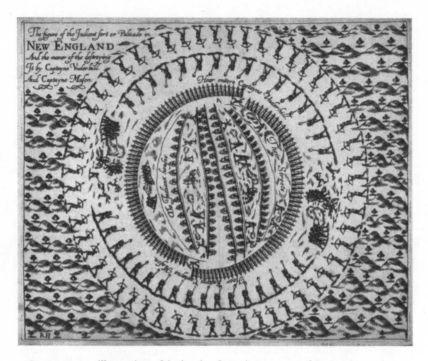

4. Contemporary illustration of the battle of Mystic (courtesy of the Mashantucket Pequot Museum and Research Center).

Despite this seemingly decisive victory, Mason's force was still in a danger-ous position—deep in enemy territory (seven miles away from the rendez-vous point with their boats) and burdened with twenty casualties.[78] Soon af-ter Mystic was razed, roughly five hundred Pequot warriors, led by Sassacus, arrived from the larger and stronger Pequot fortress on the Pequot River. They rushed toward Mason's retreating troops. Two files at the rear (each eight strong), under Underhill's command, fired volleys at the charging Pequots to inhibit or delay their pursuit, while Mason—leading the column—pressed forward to the boats. After this first volley, the Pequots kept their distance. They kept harassing the English and impeding their retreat by firing from be-hind rocks and trees, but they did not charge them: "the Peqeats came upon us with their prime men, and let fly at us . . . but they finding our bullets to outreach their arrows, forced themselves after to retreat."[79] According to John

Mason, the English even had time enough to stop at the river's bank to refresh themselves, "having by that time taught [the Pequots] a little more Manners than to disturb us."[80] Mason's advancing force cleared the thickets ahead of these snipers with musket fire. By the time Mason got to within two miles of Pequot Harbor, the Pequots had abandoned the battlefield.

At one point during this retreat, the Mohegans and Narragansetts charged the Pequots. Observing their mode of combat, John Underhill remarked that "they might fight seven years, and not kill seven men." He felt that the settlers' Indian allies were surprised and impressed by the Europeans' method of combat. They were unaccustomed to such wholesale slaughter as took place at Mystic and were in awe of the ferocity and deadliness of the Englishmen.[81]

John Underhill had another opportunity to demonstrate the efficacy of European tactics against Indian forces six years later, as a Dutch commander. On November 15, 1637, the Massachusetts General Court disarmed Underhill and dismissed him from all offices and services as punishment for publicly supporting Anne Hutchinson.[82] Later banished from the colony with other Hutchinsonians, he moved to the territory of New Hampshire before returning to Massachusetts in 1640.[83] There, following a ceremony of public humiliation, he was forgiven but was never again welcome in the colony. Ever on the move, he spent a year in the service of the fledgling town of Stamford, Connecticut. A restless and adventurous man, Underhill was dissatisfied and bored with defensive assignments. Thus, in 1643 he sought and received a commission in New Netherland.[84]

The imprudent Indian policy of William Kieft, the Director-General of New Netherland, resulted in an outbreak of hostilities that year. Seven Indian nations, fielding fifteen hundred warriors, united for campaigns against New Netherland's outlying settlements. The European survivors of the fighting gravitated toward New Amsterdam, pressuring Kieft into action.[85] By mid-September, Underhill had given up his office in Stamford. Always on the lookout for greater and grander tasks, he capitalized on the opportunity offered by New Netherland's predicament. On September 29, 1643, he and a company of Englishmen that he had recruited independently took an oath of allegiance to New Netherland, and by October, Underhill was appointed to Kieft's war council. With Isaac Allerton he went to New Haven, on Kieft's behalf, to request military assistance (one hundred men) in exchange for Dutch subsidies. The New Haven colony declined the offer.[86]

General Johannes de la Montagne, a doctor with no previous military experience, led the Dutch forces.[87] This "army"—130 men in all—included forty burgher guards (professional Dutch soldiers), thirty-five Englishmen (under Lieutenant George Baxter), and Sergeant-Major Underhill's company.[88] New Netherland's first campaign, against a small Indian force on Staten Island, was not a success. By the time the Dutch arrived, the Indians had already left. All that remained for the soldiers to do was harvest as much corn as they could and return to New Amsterdam. The army's next campaign, at Greenwich, was equally uneventful.

Since 1642 the English settlers of Greenwich had been under Dutch jurisdiction. Their military leader, Captain Daniel Patrick, fearing an Indian attack because of an altercation between settlers and Indians that resulted in the death of an Indian sachem and three colonists, demanded protection and assistance from William Kieft. He threatened to dissolve the settlement's ties with New Netherland if help did not come.[89] Consequently, the Dutch army boarded three boats and set sail for Greenwich with the mission to locate and attack the threatening Indian band. By the time they landed, however, the Indians were long gone. Tension and frustration resulted in a violent confrontation between Underhill and Patrick. Underhill charged Patrick with treachery, for "causing 120 men to come to him upon his promise to direct them toward the Indians, . . . but deluded them. Whereupon the captain [Patrick] gave him ill language and spit in his face, and turning to go out, the Dutchman [Underhill] shot him behind in the head, so he fell down dead and never spake."[90]

Meanwhile, William Kieft was informed of altercations with the Canarsee Indians of Long Island. Their sachem, Chief Pennewitz, had led a number of raids on outlying farms on the island. After Robert Fordham of Hempstead (an English settlement on Long Island) had caught and arrested seven Indians for killing three pigs, he requested Kieft's assistance.[91] Kieft responded quickly, dispatching John Underhill, with fifteen men, to Hempstead. Three of the prisoners were killed immediately on his arrival. Two more were tortured to death.[92] The remaining two were taken to Fort Amsterdam.[93] Kieft had sent his remaining eighty men (under Captain Peter Cook) to attack Matsepe, the Canarsee's largest village. Captain Cook's force was successful in carrying out its orders, killing over one hundred Indians there in a nocturnal surprise attack (while suffering only four casualties).[94]

The last battle of the war took place near Stamford in February 1644. This time, John Underhill commanded the entire Dutch army. His conduct there is reminiscent of his actions in the battle at Fort Mystic. After landing near Greenwich, the small Dutch force (130 men) followed Underhill's Indian guide across two rivers and over snow-covered hills to a large Weequaesgeek fort, at Pound Ridge, northwest of Greenwich.[95] They arrived there late in the evening, suffering severely from the near-freezing temperature. Since they could not risk lighting fires, Underhill decided not to encamp but to attack immediately, despite the full moon and the fact that the Indians were still awake and on their guard. The Dutch divided into small groups and silently proceeded to encircle the village. Indians who attempted to charge the surrounding line of musketeers were shot. When the Indians then fired their bows at the Dutch from within their huts, Underhill ordered his men to torch the village. The villagers "tried every means to escape, not succeeding in which, they returned back to the flames preferring to perish by the fire than to die by our hands. What was most wonderful is, that among this vast collection of men, Women, and Children not one was heard to cry or scream."[96] The number of Indian fatalities is estimated at between three hundred and seven hundred. Only eight survived. The Dutch encamped for the night and tended to their wounded. The next morning they started the march toward Stamford.[97]

Like the battle of Mystic, John Underhill's complete victory over the Weequaesgeek at Pound Ridge (also known as the battle of Strickland Plains) horrified neighboring Indian tribes and resulted in the signing of several bilateral peace treaties. Even before Underhill returned to New Amsterdam, he was approached in Stamford by a group of sachems (from today's Westchester and Dutchess Counties in New York) who asked him to apply for peace on their behalf to the governor of New Netherland.[98] It is doubtful that John Mason and John Underhill had planned their campaigns with this strategic purpose in mind. Nevertheless, the battles of Mystic and Pound Ridge demonstrated that despite their overwhelming numerical inferiority, the Europeans could intimidate their Indian neighbors into submission by employing extreme violence. The near annihilation of the Pequots and the Weequaesgeek allowed the English and the Dutch thereafter to rely on deterrence (that is, on their reputation for ferocity) as a first line of defense. The willingness of Indian tribes to join or support the settlers' enemies was undermined by the reputation established by men such as Mason and Underhill.

The critical tactical objective in Indian warfare was surprise and encirclement. Indian wars, therefore, did not involve pitched battles.[99] If surprise was impossible, Indian armies usually tried to lure the enemy into a trap by such means as feigning a retreat—as the Pequots had tricked Gardiner outside the walls of Fort Saybrook.[100] Indian military doctrine was offensive—relying on mobility and the targeting of enemy troops rather than on holding strategically strong positions. Indian forces repeatedly abandoned the battlefield, preferring to use their mobility by drawing the enemy in pursuit and then encircling it.

European military doctrine, in contrast, was defensive, relying on strength in numbers and firepower. European armies were trained to fight en masse; they were best suited for high-intensity warfare and close combat against concentrated and fortified forces. By targeting and holding positional targets, such as forts or other strategically strong locations, they forced the enemy to attempt hazardous and costly offensives against fortified positions.

These doctrinal and tactical differences reflect the cultural characteristics of these societies. The unprofessional character of Indian armies in colonial New England, as well as their offensive doctrine, reflected the flexibility that seasonal migration offered Indian societies in the Northeast.[101] Unencumbered by the imperatives of sedentary communities, Indian armies were not compelled to maintain their position on the battlefield (that is, to defend their territory). English military establishments in New England shared some of these characteristics: modest size, lack of professionalism, and poor training. Thus, the settlers quickly became aware of the incompatibility of their armed forces and their security needs as sedentary communities. William Bradford expressed the settlers' appreciation of their tactical and strategic vulnerabilities with regard to the Indians before the Pequot War.

> In the mean time, the Pequents . . . sought to make peace with the Narigansets, and used very pernicious arguments to move them therunto: as that the English were strangers and and begane to overspred their countrie, and would deprive them therof in time, if they were suffered to grow and increse; . . . and if they should harken to them [the Pequots], they should not neede to fear the strength of the English; for they would not come to open battle with them, but fire their houses, kill their katle, and lye in ambush for them as they went abroad upon their occasions; and all this they might easily doe without any or litle danger to them selves. The which course being held, . . . the English could not long subsiste, but they would either be starved with hunger, or be forced to forsake the countrie.[102]

John Winthrop recorded a similar concern in his diary when rumors of a Narragansett conspiracy reached Boston in September 1642: "We found ourselves in very ill case for war, and if we should begin, we must then be forced to stand continually upon our guard, and to desert our farms. . . . Further, it was considered that our beginning with them could not secure us against them: we might destroy some part of their corn and wigwams, and force them to fly into the woods, etc., but the men would be still remaining to do us mischief, for they will never fight us in the open field."[103] Winthrop found New Netherland in the early 1640s equally vulnerable. "The Indians did so annoy them by sudden assaults out of the swamps, etc., that [William Kieft] was forced to keep a running army to be ready to oppose them upon all occasions."[104] To compensate for this strategic weakness—to eliminate the element of surprise—the New England settlements established an alarm system to warn neighboring communities of impending attacks.[105]

Although trained on the battlefields of Europe, where the rigid, cumbersome formations of immense armies made it almost impossible to approach the enemy quickly or undetected, New England's professional military leaders relied heavily on their ability to surprise the enemy. Their military doctrine was not un-European in this respect. The objective of seventeenth- and eighteenth-century commanders—both European and Indian—was to threaten or attack the enemy's weak side, thus causing confusion and panic. European armies, with their lengthy defensive formations, improved firepower, and impregnable fortresses, were able to effectively protect their rear. Indian war bands, in contrast, were unable to do so not only because of their technological and organizational limitations (that is, their limited firepower) but also because of their numerical limitations. Naturally, the effectiveness of a defensive formation is predicated on its ability to provide individual soldiers with a sense of security. When the battlefield is too vast or the number of defenders too few, the individual soldier cannot rely on his fellow soldiers for security; very likely, he will not maintain his position.

Indian and colonial military forces were therefore not as effective defensively as European armies. They could not field enough soldiers to repel an attack and secure their rear.[106] The successful ambush of Lieutenant Gardiner outside Fort Saybrook in February 1637 may serve as a demonstration: they were "surrounded by hundreds of them, who let fly their arrows furiously, and came desperately upon the muzzles of their muskets, though the English discharged upon them with all the speed they could."[107] Gardiner's men could not produce enough firepower to keep the attackers at bay. Lack of discipline and professional training—for both Indian and European soldiers in America—certainly contributed to the success of the offensive, but professionalism could not have compensated for this numerical weakness. The modest size of armies in America not only made them more susceptible to surprise attacks; it also enabled offensive forces to approach the defenders more quickly and undetected, especially in New England, where the wooded and hilly terrain provided effective cover for approaching troops. Realizing the need for surprise, Major John Mason had decided to ignore his orders and approach the Pequots overland, from the east. Thus, "we should come upon their Backs, and possibly might surprise them unawares."[108]

The successful surprise attacks by Miles Standish at Weymouth and John Mason and John Underhill at Mystic and Pound Ridge should not suggest that these men had Americanized their tactics or that they had rejected the tenets of European military doctrine. Their imperatives and objectives remained as they were in Europe. In both battles, the colonists took a defensive stance.[109] By encircling the Indian forts—taking the *strategic offensive*—they limited the size of the battlefield and threatened their opponents, forcing the enemy into launching frontal assaults. Thus, a small number of men, relying on the *tactical defense*, were able to maintain their position. What was novel in New England was the fact that for the first time in their careers, Standish, Mason, and Underhill faced an enemy that was vulnerable to flanking approaches. Whereas European commanders were forced by strong and alert defensive formations to attempt frontal assaults (with increased firepower, rigorous discipline, and high casualty rates), these colonial commanders were able to achieve success—threatening the enemy's weak side—with stealth.[110]

The European education and training of these men was evident also in their defensive orientation. For example, in Miles Standish's explorations on Cape Cod, he fortified his camp nightly and sent out sentinels in the European fashion. Similarly, the settlers at Plymouth and later in the Bay Colony erected European fortifications around their towns as soon as they suspected hostilities with the Indians. By defending strategically strong positions rather than targeting enemy troops, they displayed a defensive, positional doctrine like that of the large, professional armies of Europe. The palisades that the settlers erected around their towns were similar to the defenses surrounding Indian forts.[111] It would be a mistake, however, to assume that the Europeans adopted this Indian technique. During Miles Standish's first exploration expedition at Cape Cod in November 1620, the company saw its first Indian fort. The construction seemed so familiar to these European immigrants that they assumed the fort "had beene made by some Christians."[112]

Indeed, in the early seventeenth century, New England towns and fortifications followed a traditional English pattern of a nuclear settlement.[113] The home lots were grouped closely together, surrounded by a system of individual plots that extended from that nucleus to the bounds of the town grant. This pattern was used almost uniformly by English settlers beyond England's borders (on the Continent, in Wales, and in Ireland), though in England itself types of settlements varied from county to county.[114] The nuclear settlement was a conventional organizational technique utilized by Englishmen in frontier settlements, when surrounded by a numerically superior native population. Anthony Garvan argues, therefore, that the glaring similarities between the defenses of towns in Ulster and in New England (such as Saybrook, Guildford, and New London) were not incidental.[115]

The forts or garrison houses, despite the strategic locations of these settlements (sometimes surrounded by natural barriers from three directions, allowing overland access from one route only), were not designed or positioned to defend the town itself. Instead, like medieval fortresses in Europe, they provided a defensible sanctuary for the townspeople in case of native attacks but not defenses. Descriptions and illustrations of the fortifications at Plymouth, Saybrook, New Amsterdam, and other colonial towns indicate that forts and blockhouses were relatively isolated from the home lots.[116] As John Underhill testified, these forts did provide effective security against Indian attacks.[117] However, controlling these forts did not necessarily translate into control of the countryside.[118] Thus, before the Pequot War broke out, Lion Gardiner and his men "were little better than besieged" in Fort Saybrook. As the Pequot raid on Wethersfield in April 1637 demonstrated, Gardiner was unable to prevent the Indians from traveling up and down the river at will.

Nevertheless, the Pequots never attacked the fort itself. They "came to the fort jeering of them, and calling, Come and fetch your Englishmen's clothes again; come out and fight, if you dare; you dare not fight; you are all one like women."[119] Gardiner, however, remained behind his defenses, choosing not to waste lives and resources on an unproductive assault on the Indians. He was a conservative and methodical commander. Throughout his career in New England, he displayed a strategist's view of warfare: "War is like a three-footed stool, want one foot and down comes all; and these three feet are men, victuals, and ammunition."[120] As the commander of Fort Saybrook, he devoted his efforts to keeping his store rooms well supplied with corn and powder at all times; he was rarely reckless with his men's lives.

Gardiner displayed his conservative (defensive) doctrine on the battlefield as well. In an incident in which two of his men were threatened in the field by a group of Indians, he rushed to their aid with six others. They reached the two men, "keeping all abreast, in sight, close together."[121] Although fighting did not break out—cannon fire from the fort killed some Indians and dispersed the rest—this incident illustrates that Gardiner planned to engage the Indians in a European fashion. By ordering his men in a close defensive formation, he prepared his troops to *repel* an Indian assault. Only once did he act in an offensive manner, targeting enemy soldiers rather than relying on the strategic advantage of a strong position. His impulsive pursuit of the three Pequots outside Fort Saybrook (February 22, 1637) led his men to a dangerous and costly ambush. He never repeated the mistake.

John Underhill's experiences taught him different lessons. Successful on the offensive and bored on defense, Underhill was more inclined to seek out enemy troops than to build fortifications, store supplies, and wait patiently for the enemy to charge.[122] Lion Gardiner personified Machiavelli's fourth and sixteenth Rules of War: "It is better to conquer the enemy with famine than with yron: in the victory of which, fortune may doe much more than valour". . . . "He that prepareth not necessary victuals to live upon, is overcome without yron."[123] The offensive-minded Underhill, in contrast, personified the twenty-sixth: "Men, yron, money and bread be the strength of the Warre; but of these four, the first two bee most necessary: because men & yron find money and bread."[124] Yet, despite Underhill's aggressive demeanor, he still relied on the collective firepower of the musketeers, rather than resorting to raiding tactics. He had quickly realized that his men's buff coats provided them with adequate protection against Indian arrows. They were further protected from Indian fire because the range of their muskets exceeded the range of Indian arrows, allowing them to be effective while remaining invulnerable to defensive fire.[125] The use of fire against Indian villages at Mystic and Pound Ridge carried this objective—inflicting casualties on the enemy from a distance, with little risk to one's own soldiers—to its logical extreme. After the destruction of Mystic and the skirmishes that took place during the English retreat, Underhill lost respect for the Indians' soldiery.[126] He felt confident in his ability to inflict heavy casualties on Indian forces with concentrated musket fire.

Overall, the first generation of military commanders in New England was not particularly innovative. Nearly all of New England's military leaders at this period were professional soldiers, educated on the battlefields of Europe. Their attitudes and practices reflected their military training. John Underhill was anomalous in this respect. Yet although his adventurous and undisciplined nature compelled him to adopt a more offensive stance than that of most of his colleagues, he too relied on coordinated and massed fire.

One significant innovation to European military maxims—the emphasis on individual marksmanship—was seemingly evident in two of the conflicts mentioned above. During the battle of First Encounter, Miles Standish faced attackers in loose formation (in contrast to the large, dense target of an advancing European army) with few defenders, cumbersome firearms, and a very limited supply of ammunition. Standish, therefore, ordered his men to restrain themselves—not to fire at will but to take careful aim and make each shot count. During the retreat from Fort Mystic, John Underhill witnessed another example of the utility of marksmanship in keeping Indian attackers at bay: "The Pequeats playing upon our flanks, one Sergeant Davis, a pretty courageous soldier, spying something black upon the top of a rock, stepped forth from the body with a carbine of three feet long, and, at a venture, gave fire, supposing it to be an Indian's head, turning him over with his heels upward. The Indians observed this, and greatly admired that a man should shoot so directly. The Pequeats were much daunted at the shot, and forbore approaching so near upon us."[127] The significance of these episodes can easily be overemphasized. Since the settlers' smoothbore muskets were notoriously inaccurate even at short range, they tended not to rely on individual accuracy. Soldiers were not trained in marksmanship because their firearms were ill-suited for sniping. Without rifling, musketeers had only limited control over the direction of their projectiles. Thus, one has to judge incidents of individual accuracy as accidental.

A truly important innovation, relied on more heavily in later years, was the use of small shot. Describing how his company was charged by a Pequot force at the Fairfield Swamp Fight, John Mason adds, "but we sent them back by our small Shot."[128] Similarly, Lion Gardiner's gunners once fired two cannons loaded "with Carthages of Musket Bullets" at hostile Indians outside Saybrook's walls, effectively dispersing them.[129] Firing several small bullets rather than one larger projectile increased the firepower of each musketeer or gunner (as well as compensated for his lack of marksmanship).[130] Thus, the use of small shot strengthened the defense by increasing firepower—inhibiting the enemy's mobility, rather than mimicking enemy tactics.

FOLLOWING THEIR DEFEAT at Mystic, the Pequots disbanded and dispersed. One group, led by Sassacus and Chief Mononotto, headed west, killing, capturing, and torturing any Europeans they encountered.[131] Sassacus was desperate and on the run. "The Pequots now became a Prey to all Indians. Happy were they that could bring in their Heads to the English: of which there came almost daily to Winsor, or Hartford."[132] Sassacus found shelter in a swamp located near today's Fairfield, Connecticut. The Massachusetts General Court commissioned Captain Israel Stoughton (who had served in Dorchester under Mason) to end the war and capture Sassacus. Landing at Pequot Bay, Stoughton's force (120 men) marched west, capturing Pequot stragglers along the way and obtaining intelligence on Sassacus's whereabouts.[133]

Finally, Sassacus was surrounded by the armies of John Mason and Israel Stoughton at the Fairfield swamp (July 12, 1637). Firing rounds into the swamp paved the way for negotiations. One hundred eighty noncombatants accepted Mason's offer and were allowed to leave the swamp as captives. Roughly one hundred warriors remained with Sassacus in the swamp. The English surrounded the swamp, as they had done at Fort Mystic, standing about four yards apart. When several Englishmen broke independently toward the Indians in the interior, the mud impeded their progress, leaving them vulnerable to Indian fire. They were rescued with great difficulty.[134] Throughout the night the English remained on the perimeter, discharging their muskets into the swamp, hoping to force the Indians into action or surrender.[135] At daybreak, taking advantage of the morning fog, the Pequots assaulted the English line. They charged the section under Captain Daniel Patrick's command, but Mason reinforced Patrick and Sassacus was repulsed.[136] The Indians then quickly charged another section of the line, were rebuffed, and returned immediately to Captain Patrick. By stretching the English defenses (as the Duke of Marlborough often did), Sassacus weakened Patrick's position and was able to break through the English defensive line. Seventy warriors escaped the swamp.[137]

The Fairfield Swamp Fight provides a good case study for the interplay between offensive and defensive tactics. Sassacus and his men were initially on the defensive in the interior. When the Englishmen charged the swamp, the thickets and the mud inhibited their mobility, thus diminishing the effectiveness of their assault. The Pequots, relying on firepower, took advantage of the attackers' slow advance. Thereafter, the English took a positional, defensive stance on the perimeter and the Indians took the offensive, hoping to break through the English line. Enhancing the firepower of the defense (by reinforcing Captain Patrick's section of the line and by using small shot) enabled the English to keep the Indians at a distance, disabling their assault. However, the Pequots' mobility eventually caused the defense to break down. Attacking a different section of the line stretched the defense by drawing men away from Patrick's section. Quickly turning back to assault Patrick's men, Sassacus caught Patrick defensively unprepared (that is, surprised and undermanned).

SASSACUS ESCAPED to Mohawk territory, where he was hunted down by the Mohawks in fall 1638. His scalp and those of five of his chiefs were presented to the Governor's Council in Boston. Cotton Mather wrote that the surviving Pequots "submitted themselves to English mercy, and the rest of the Indians who saw a little handful of Englishmen massacre and capture seven hundred adversaries and kill no less than thirteen Sachems in one short expedition; such a terror from God fell upon them that after, for near forty years together, the land rested from war, even unto the time when the sins of the land called for a new scourge, and Indians, being taught the use of guns, were capable of being made instruments of inflicting it."[138]

CHAPTER THREE /
Military Degeneration and Victory

BY THE MID-SEVENTEENTH CENTURY, the New England colonists were engaged in an extensive exchange with local Indians, trading guns and ammunition for furs. Explicit imperial prohibitions against this arms trade did little to curb the Indians' acquisition of firearms from the English.[1] As Cotton Mather observed, proficiency in the use of firearms enabled the Indians to inflict heavy casualties on the settlers during King Philip's War (1675–76).[2]

During the first half of the seventeenth century, however, English victories over their Indian neighbors had cleared the way for English settlement in western Connecticut and Massachusetts (see Fig. 5). At the outbreak of King Philip's War, the English population in New England numbered roughly forty thousand. By the end of the war, approximately eleven hundred settlers had lost their lives (over five hundred of them soldiers; approximately 10 percent of the four colonies' fighting strength), twelve hundred houses and barns had been razed, and thirteen settlements evacuated or ruined.[3]

Successful Indian attacks on colonial forces during the war, combined with the celebrated exploits of Benjamin Church (who adopted characteristics of Indian warfare), have led some to conclude that the combination of firearms and Indian tactics was too potent for English forces, relying on conventional European tactics. Consequently, it has been argued that exposure to Indian tactics (during King Philip's War, King William's War, and Queen Anne's War) improved the efficiency of English military forces.[4] Battlefield experience forced colonial commanders to "unlearn" what their European military man-

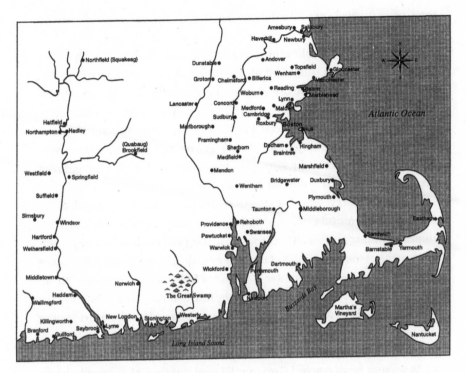

5. Southern New England, 1675.

uals had taught them. Only by utilizing the Indians' method of fighting against them were colonial commanders able to stem the tide, achieve tactical success against Indian forces and, consequently, win these wars.

This argument, however, is not supported by the evidence. King Philip's War, as well as the later colonial wars in the early-eighteenth century, were *not* won through a succession of tactical victories, but through a campaign of attrition. Furthermore, on a tactical level, a comparison of the first generation of New England's military commanders (conventional-minded European veterans) with the Americanized commanders of the later colonial wars reflects very poorly on the latter. The colonial wars of the late-seventeenth and early-eighteenth centuries demonstrated not only that the effectiveness of colonial forces was on the decline, but also that Colonial commanders, as a group, were not Americanized; they were simply remarkably inexperienced and unprofessional. Thus, they were ill-prepared for combat and, consequently, were often tricked into abandoning the tactical defense, with disastrous results.

The war broke out following a running dispute between the Plymouth colony and Metacom (King Philip), the leader of the Wampanoag Indians. Philip was reported to have been conspiring against the English. An informant who warned the Plymouth authorities of Philip's conspiracy (Sassamon, a Christian Indian who had served as Philip's counselor) was subsequently murdered. Three of Philip's men, (including his son and one of his counselors) were arrested by the Plymouth authorities, tried, and found guilty of the murder.[5] Their execution led Philip to attack.

Philip's first target was obvious—Swansea was situated at the neck of the Mount Hope peninsula, where he and his men were located (see Fig. 6). Hostilities in Swansea began on June 19, with looting and random violence in outlying areas of the town. Inhabitants living on the perimeter left their homes and joined families at the center of town. As Indian violence intensified, all the inhabitants of Swansea moved into the town's three garrison houses. The garrison houses, fortified private homes, were situated too far apart to offer any protection to other homes and public buildings. Thus, Philip could attack targets throughout the town at will and unharmed.[6]

As soon as news reached Governor Edward Winslow of Plymouth, he ordered the towns closest to Swansea, Bridgewater and Taunton, each to conscript seventy men and send them that very day, June 21, 1675, to relieve Swansea and to send a second force of equal strength the next day. Winslow then informed Governor John Leverett of Massachusetts of the military operations undertaken by Plymouth, warning him of the inclination of the Nipmucks and the Narragansetts, under the jurisdiction of Massachusetts, to join Philip's rebellion. After deliberating with his council, Leverett replied quickly, promising Winslow military support.[7]

The first relief force reached Swansea late on June 21. It reinforced the town's three garrisons. Meanwhile, the second relief force assembled at Taunton, under the command of Captain James Cudworth. Benjamin Church refused a commission from Governor Winslow, but agreed to join this force as a volunteer. His assignment was to lead the advance guard (composed of English and Indian soldiers) from Taunton, scouting ahead of the secondary relief force on its way to Swansea. On this first assignment, Church demonstrated the enthusiastic overaggressiveness that characterized his conduct throughout his career. By advancing too quickly and too far ahead of the main

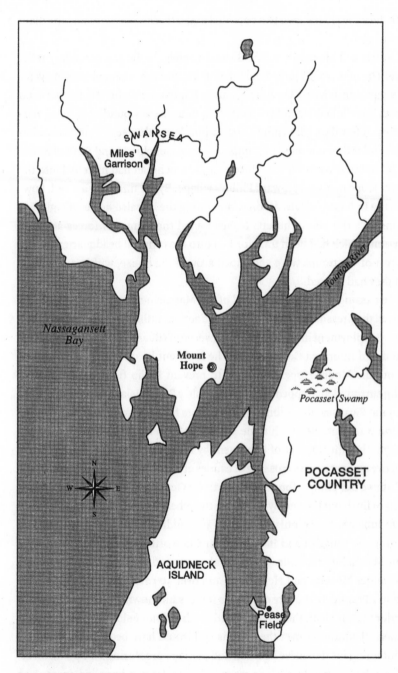

6. The Mount Hope vicinity.

force, he exposed his men to a potential ambush, thus jeopardizing the main force as well.[8]

Church and his men reached Swansea safely, as did the secondary relief force. The new troops joined the inhabitants and the other soldiers in Swansea's garrison houses. On June 24, nine Englishmen who left the garrison houses were killed by Philip's men. Two more were wounded in these skirmishes. A few days later (June 28), two hundred volunteers from Massachusetts, under the command of Captains Daniel Henchman and Samuel Moseley, joined Cudworth's force. Moseley and Henchman had marched into the Mount Hope peninsula toward Philip's village. By the time they arrived, however, the Indians had left. All they found were the impaled heads of eight Englishmen.[9] The Massachusetts troops joined the Plymouth forces at Mile's garrison, which had been transformed into the officers' headquarters, while the rest of the troops were encamped around the house, within a barricade that they had erected.

The passing time and the arrival of the Massachusetts reinforcements increased the pressure on Cudworth to take action, rather than maintain the defensive deployment in the garrisons. Governor William Coddington of Rhode Island had informed Cudworth that he had sent boats to patrol the waters around the Mount Hope peninsula, to prevent Philip from escaping. With Philip surrounded, trapped between the paltry Rhode Island fleet and the land troops at Swansea, the colonial governments felt relatively secure that the rebellion was contained within the peninsula.[10] It should have been obvious, though, that the number of boats sent by Rhode Island was too small to be effective against a mass crossing of canoes at night. Rather than bide his time and starve out Philip's forces, Cudworth (at Governor Winslow's urging) decided to flush out the enemy and bring the rebellion to an abrupt end.

On June 28, the colonists had over 350 soldiers stationed in Swansea—roughly 100 (English and Indian) under Cudworth's command and the rest from Massachusetts under the general command of Major Thomas Savage (200 under Moseley and Henchman and over 50 cavalrymen under Captain Thomas Prentice). The size of Philip's force is unknown but estimated at 500 warriors.[11] It is clear, though, that Cudworth did not enjoy an overwhelming numerical advantage over the Indians and would have been better served by maintaining his defensive position and perhaps pressuring Philip into an attack on the fortified English forces in Swansea. He was impelled, instead, to pursue.

Captain Prentice set out with twelve of his cavalrymen to scout the peninsula and locate the Indians. Benjamin Church, who had already grown impatient with Cudworth's conservative handling of the situation, joined Prentice's scouting mission. They quickly found themselves under ambush by an Indian force. A few Englishmen were killed by the first Indian burst of fire, while the rest scampered quickly back to town.[12] The next day, a much larger force went into the field with the same purpose in mind. When they reached the site of the previous day's ambush, they broke into smaller units to form a broad scouting line, advancing with cavalry units flanking them, protecting the infantrymen from encirclement. Not seeing any action (except for a minor skirmish between two English units that mistook each other for the enemy), the scouting party returned to Swansea. The following day's mission produced similar results. The absence of any canoes in the Indian villages clarified that Philip and his men had escaped the peninsula.[13] By pressuring Philip overland, Cudworth and Savage forced him to challenge Rhode Island's porous naval blockade.

Church urged his superiors to pursue Philip immediately in the Pocasset country to the east.[14] Instead, Cudworth and Savage decided to sweep the peninsula once more and then to build a fort on the eastern shore, near the mouth of the Kickamuit River, to insure the security of the region. While most of the force was busy erecting fortifications there, Captains Henchman and Prentice conducted patrol and scouting operations north of Swansea in case Philip was determined to destroy the town and was planning another attack on it.[15]

As hostilities spread throughout New England, a discernible pattern emerged. English settlements were repeatedly surprised, suffering considerable casualties. When towns were prepared for an attack, however, they were able, with great regularity, to repel the attackers with very few casualties. Throughout the war, Indian attackers, lacking the necessary degree of discipline, coordination between subunits, and logistical preparedness, repeatedly displayed their incompetence against a fortified and well-armed enemy.

On March 16, 1676, for example, a large Indian force, three hundred strong, attacked Northampton. The town's population, concentrated in its garrison houses, repelled the Indians with ease, inflicting heavy casualties on them. The houses within the town's palisade were unharmed, whereas the four outside the wall were looted and destroyed. Similar assaults on Hatfield and Hadley brought similar results.[16]

Especially instructive in this respect was the battle that took place in Brookfield (Quabaug), on August 3–5, 1675. Captain Edward Hutchinson, of Massachusetts, was returning from a failed peace mission to the Nipmucks. Not expecting an attack, his small force was not set up defensively on their march. A large force of Nipmucks hiding in a nearby swamp surprised the group near Brookfield, killing eight and injuring many more. Guided by his Indian scouts, Hutchinson was able to lead the remainder of his force, under fire, back to Brookfield. On their arrival, the soldiers and the town's inhabitants gathered in the town's garrison house. The Nipmucks pursued Hutchinson to Brookfield and surrounded the garrison. They looted and burned the vacant houses throughout the town and killed Englishmen that they encountered in their homes and fields. When they turned their attention to the fortified house, the defenders (twenty-six men and approximately fifty women) fended them off with musket fire and quelled their efforts to set fire to the house. The fighting continued for three days, until a relief force of fifty mounted troops, under the command of Major Simon Willard, reached Brookfield, routing the Nipmucks, who were unprepared for an attack from the rear.[17]

Aided by the element of surprise, as well as the incompetence of English defenders, Indian raiding parties were often very effective in their assaults against New England towns and villages. In many instances, despite strict orders from the colonial governments, town watches were lax, defenses were left unmanned, and garrison houses were not properly utilized. This lack of vigilance was exacerbated by imprudence. Repeatedly settlers were fooled into leaving their fortified defensive positions and giving chase. Feigning retreat, Indian forces were able consistently to surprise and ambush these pursuing English forces.

The perplexing proclivity of English forces to repeat their mistakes was demonstrated yet again in Groton, Massachusetts, on March 2, 1676. In a midnight attack on the town, a number of houses were looted and a few cows stolen. Retreating to the safety of their garrison houses, the inhabitants were all saved. One week later, two settlers were attacked on the outskirts of town. One was captured, tortured, killed, and mutilated, but the other managed to escape and warn the townspeople, who again gathered in their five garrison houses.[18]

On March 13, the defenders of one of the central garrison houses detected two Indians not far away. Impetuously, the men left the house to pursue and capture the Indians. The pair did not budge until the English drew very near, when a group of Indians rose from behind cover and fired at the approaching settlers. Four men were hit immediately. The rest scattered and fled toward the garrison house. In the meantime, however, a second group of Indians rose from its hiding place and situated itself between the English attackers and the garrison house where only women and children remained.[19] As the two Indian forces were concentrating on firing at the panicking men, the women and children were able to escape the house and reach one of the other garrison houses. The Indians, led by John Monoco, "one-eyed John," took all the food they could find in the town and burned the vacated houses. The only dwellings that remained unharmed were the town's garrison houses.[20]

The characteristic imprudence of the English was compounded by their failure to learn from their own experience. That same afternoon (March 13), the Indians attempted to trick the defenders once again with the same stratagem. An old Indian was spotted at a distance from one of the garrison houses, just beyond musket range. When musket fire failed, a large force exited the house to capture the man. Luckily for them, the pursuing Englishmen caught a glimpse of an Indian force lying in hiding and quickly withdrew back into the garrison house.[21]

The colonial governments reacted to successful Indian attacks by issuing admonitions to all towns to be vigilant at all times and to make use of their garrison houses (that is, for all families to spend every night in the garrison houses, rather than in their own homes).[22] These repeated admonitions were indeed required, since towns were too often caught off guard, with devastating results. A surprise attack on Lancaster (February 10, 1676), for example, was so devastating and crippling that the town was consequently abandoned.[23]

The English follies during King Philip's War are too numerous to recount. One blatant example occurred during Philip's assault on Hatfield, October 19, 1675. A force of a few hundred Wampanoags lit a bonfire in the woods near the town and lay in wait for townspeople to approach. Just as Philip had anticipated, the town dispatched ten men to attack the Indians in the woods. Philip's men ambushed the men, killing nine. The subsequent attack on the town itself was unsuccessful, however, because of the settlers' ability to defend their garrison houses. The town was saved by the arrival of two relief forces that attacked Philip's rear, dispersing his army.[24]

Even without the benefit of strong artificial fortifications, English troops were able to defend themselves successfully against larger Indian forces whenever they maintained a defensive stance, as they did in the battle of Pease Field. On July 8, 1675, a detachment of Plymouth soldiers (thirty-five men, led by Captain Matthew Fuller and Benjamin Church) set out on an armed peace mission to the Pocassets. As the English reached the Pocasset Neck, they split into two groups, each one supported by a number of boats operating along the shore. Fuller's detachment encountered a band of enemy Indians and withdrew to the safety of an abandoned house near the water, where they defended themselves until rescued by their boats.[25]

Believing that he could find enemy Indians to the south, Church led his detachment of twenty men to the southern point of Tiverton, toward Narragansett Bay. There he came across more Indians than he had hoped to find—he was attacked by three hundred warriors, under Philip's command. Fearing encirclement, Church ordered his tiny force to retreat toward the shore (Pease Field). Church calmed his men and instructed them to erect minor fortifications out of stones. His boats attempted to sail across from Aquidneck Island, but Indian fire prevented them from approaching the shore. Church signaled to the boats to withdraw and send back a sloop with a canoe (a smaller boat could slip through more easily). Before evening, the sloop appeared and the men were evacuated with the canoe, two by two and under heavy fire.[26] The Wampanoags were unimpressive in this battle in terms of both tactics and marksmanship. Church and his men were besieged on the shore for more than six hours and outnumbered fifteen to one; yet all of them escaped safely and unharmed.

Despite the effectiveness of defensive tactics against Indian troops, inexperienced and overenthusiastic commanders were often tricked into abandoning the tactical defense. One such commander was Captain Michael Pierce, commissioned by Plymouth in spring 1676 to lead a company of sixty-three Englishmen and twenty Indians on a search-and-destroy mission against Narragansett war bands that had been attacking villages throughout the southern part of the colony. Pierce received intelligence that a large enemy war band led by Canonchet, the Narragansett sachem, was camping near Patuxet. He led his men there immediately. When he arrived, he spotted a small Indian force, which he pursued without delay. Soon, however, Pierce and his men were surrounded by five hundred Narragansett warriors. They retreated toward a nearby river, believing it would protect them from encirclement. To their misfortune, though, the river was narrow enough to allow effective musket fire from the opposite bank. When a contingent Canonchet had dispatched there began firing at the English force, Pierce was forced to divide his already small force. Outnumbered, surrounded, and engaged in two fire fights without shelter or fortifications, Pierce and his men had no chance of winning. In the late stages of the battle, after decimating the English force, the Narragansetts to charged their line. In the midst of the melee, thirteen Englishmen escaped.[27] The relief force that arrived from Providence had nothing to do but bury the dead.[28]

Captain Wadsworth, sent from Marlborough with fifty men to relieve Sudbury, April 21, 1676, was also routed when he abandoned the tactical defense. On his arrival he encountered a small body of Indians, who immediately took flight. Believing this was the main force fleeing before him, Wadsworth ordered his men to follow in pursuit. The English were drawn away from the road into the woods, where they were surrounded by the entire Indian force of over four hundred men. Despite heavy fire from all directions, they managed to reestablish formation and return fire, while retreating toward an elevation. From there they kept the Indians at bay for over four hours, suffering only five fatalities. The settlers' firepower and their superior position were sufficient to counter the Indians' mobility—the English killed and wounded enough Indians to prevent a charge toward them. In response, the Indians set fire to the woods, letting the wind carry the fire toward the small hill commanded by Wadsworth and his men. The English were thus forced to vacate their position. They panicked, broke formation, and were summarily routed. Only thirteen of the fifty escaped.[29]

James Cudworth's conduct at Swansea also exemplifies the struggle between conservative faith in defensive tactics and enthusiastic aggressiveness and offensive-mindedness bred by inexperience. This tension manifested itself even more strongly in Cudworth's next assignment. Soon after Church's misadventure at Pease Field, Cudworth was dispatched with a large military force composed of Plymouth and Massachusetts companies to the Pocasset country to engage this Wampanoag war band. Philip and his men, aware of the English approach, withdrew into the Pocasset swamp. Cudworth was confident that he had finally trapped Philip and was enthusiastic about the prospect of capturing him. Philip took advantage of Cudworth's enthusiasm and sent a small force to intercept the English troops. On July 19, 1675, a brief fire fight between the two forces resulted in two English fatalities. The Indian group then withdrew toward the swamp, drawing the overeager English in pursuit. Cudworth's men pushed forward under fire, as the Indians drew them still deeper into the swamp. Despite their efforts, the English could not catch up to the retreating Indians. They were then ambushed by Philip's main force. The English troops panicked and fired in all directions, including at one another. They eventually managed, with a great deal of luck, to retreat to the perimeter of the swamp.[30]

This experience cured Cudworth of his enthusiasm. He decided to take the tactical defense on the perimeter and starve out the Indians, forcing them to leave the swamp and attack the English. He built a fort southwest of the swamp (thus blocking Philip's route to open water) and put together a small mobile force of "flying dragoons" to harass and cut off the Indians whenever they were spotted at the edge of the swamp.[31]

Just as he had done at the Mount Hope peninsula, Cudworth had Philip trapped and under siege. Benjamin Church again was outraged by Cudworth's patience and conservatism. He urged his superiors to pursue Philip, rather than wait behind a palisade for an enemy attack (he viewed forts as "nests for destruction" rather than tactical and strategic strongholds).[32] And once again, Cudworth's poor execution of a sound plan enabled Philip to escape. Instead of strengthening English deployment around the swamp, thus tightening the siege, Cudworth diluted his forces. First, dwindling supplies and the mounting costs of maintaining the army in the field brought about the evacuation of four of the five Massachusetts companies from Plymouth. Then Cudworth led a hundred of his remaining troops to a quick mission in nearby Dartmouth, which had been attacked a few days previously. With the swamp left unguarded, Philip and his men escaped easily and undetected.[33]

The colonies' main concern in the early stages of the war was the suspected belligerence of the Narragansetts. Philip and the Wampanoags (with a fighting strength of roughly five hundred) posed no serious threat to the colonies as long as they were politically isolated. However, an alliance between Philip and the Narragansetts, the largest and strongest Indian tribe in the region, threatened to draw many other Indian tribes into the circle of violence (most alarmingly, the Nipmucks, with a fighting force of one thousand).[34] For this reason, Massachusetts authorities decided to pursue negotiations with the Narragansetts, rather than chase and capture Philip's fugitive army after his escape from Mount Hope. On July 5, 1675, Captain Edward Hutchinson arrived at Swansea with instructions from Boston to take the Massachusetts units with him on a peace mission to the Narragansetts. (This mission was ordered by Governor Leverett in accordance with Governor Winslow and at his request.) The Plymouth forces remained on the peninsula to keep watch and ensure that Philip did not return.[35] Captain Hutchinson's armed peace mission was successful, and by mid-July the Narragansetts had signed a peace treaty with the English colonies, delivering hostages to the English as a guarantee of their neutrality.[36]

Within a few months of this accord, however, the colonial governments were moved by the Bloody Brook Massacre to mobilize their resources for a major campaign against the Narragansetts. Following a devastating attack on Deerfield in which the Indians razed all of the town's houses but the garrison houses, Captain Thomas Lothrop was instructed to accompany and defend a supply train headed for Hadley. The force made its way south on September 18, 1675, through the meadows south of Deerfield. Because Indians had not been seen in the area since the assault on Deerfield, the soldiers placed their weapons on the supply wagons and began gathering berries as they walked. They were attacked by an Indian force that was hiding in a marsh near Muddy Brook (renamed Bloody Brook by that evening). Many of the soldiers, including Captain Lothrop, were hit in the first volley of fire. The rest rushed to collect their firearms or attempted to escape. Fifty-four men of Lothrop's company and all the teamsters were killed in the rout.[37] When it was discovered that the Indian band that attacked Captain Lothrop were sheltered by the nominally peaceful Narragansetts, the Commissioners of the United Colonies (Massachusetts, Plymouth, and Connecticut) met in Boston and decided to mobilize an army to force the Narragansetts to honor their promise of neutrality. In time, the authorities received more reports about the Narragansetts' direct and indirect participation in the fighting. The commissioners met once more and resolved to mobilize one thousand men for service in the Narragansett country. Governor Winslow was named as commander in chief of this army, with Major Robert Treat, of Connecticut, as his second in command.[38]

The campaign against the Narragansetts' main fort, near Kingston, Rhode Island, was the most hazardous and difficult campaign in the history of New England up to that point. The Narragansetts could field approximately thirty-five hundred warriors and were the most formidable and feared tribe in New England. Such a momentous and large-scale expedition, especially in winter, required logistical planning and preparation on a massive scale. The General Courts put a great financial and administrative effort into furnishing the army with sufficient supplies. More important, they labored to provide an effective transportation system and secure supply routes. Wickford, on the western shore of Narragansett Bay, was chosen to be the army's advance base. Wickford's proximity to the ports of Newport and Portsmouth, that is, the facility with which the colonial governments could keep the town well-supplied, was the critical factor in this decision. By orders of the Commissioners of the United Colonies, each colony organized a crude depot system—magazines where supplies (ammunition, food, clothing, building materials, and so forth) for the army's base of operations would be collected. Furthermore, colonial governments provided subsidies for the purchase of supplies and services in anticipation of the expedition.[39]

On November 16, 1675, Massachusetts recalled the army of the west (under the command of Major Appleton) from the Connecticut Valley in anticipation of the Narragansett campaign. The ranks were filled with new recruits to form six infantry companies and one cavalry squadron.[40] On December 16, the Massachusetts troops joined the forces sent from Connecticut and Plymouth at the army's base of operations, Smith's Garrison, in Wickford.[41] While men and supplies were assembled in Wickford, Benjamin Church and others scouted the area, taking many captives, who provided the English with useful intelligence about the Narragansetts and their fort.[42]

These scouting expeditions, combined with the mobilization for war and the continuing attacks by the Narragansetts and their tributaries, made peaceful negotiations nearly impossible, and certainly improbable. Thus, when General Winslow led the colonial army from Wickford on December 18, it was prepared to repel an Indian attack. Captains Moseley and Davenport, with their Narragansett informant, led the march. Major Appleton and Captain Oliver followed, and General Winslow, with the Plymouth companies, held the center. The Connecticut troops secured the rear.[43]

The Narragansett fort was an impressive and imposing structure. It enclosed several acres and stood on high ground in the midst of a swamp. The fort was defended by rows of heavy palisades enclosed by a thick hedge composed of a mass of lumber and brush several yards thick. These fortifications were supported by a number of small block houses surrounding the fort. The only entrance to the fort was a long bridge guarded by a block house.[44] As Winslow and his army approached the fort the following day (December 19), they commandeered or destroyed any Indian corn stores they came upon.[45] In the afternoon, Moseley's advance force encountered a small group of Indians north of the Great Swamp. After a brief fire fight, the Indians took flight.

Characteristically, the English commander pursued the Indians into the swamp before the rest of the army could catch up with him to provide support in case of an ambush. Luckily for Moseley, his overaggressiveness went unpunished. In fact, by following the Indians to the fort (or perhaps with the guidance of his Indian informant), his force was led to the weakest section of the palisade, where the breastwork was only five feet high.[46]

When Winslow arrived at the fort, he divided his men into two units, stationed to attack the fort from the front and the rear. The Massachusetts companies, attacking from the front, charged the weak section of the palisade. They climbed over the breastwork but were repelled by heavy defensive fire. The number of English casualties mounted as more soldiers rushed the gap in the wall, some falling victims of friendly fire).[47] The English troops withdrew, but in a second assault they pushed the Indian defenders back. The Indians then stabilized their defensive line and repelled the attackers back to the swamp. Yet, the Massachusetts soldiers repeated their frontal assaults for nearly three hours. Meanwhile, the second contingent (the Plymouth and Connecticut companies, led by Benjamin Church), attacking from the rear, created a breach in the wall and fired on the Indians. The Narragansetts, engaged in a fierce battle with the Massachusetts companies, were completely surprised by the heavy fire from their rear. They continued to fight, firing from their wigwams and from behind cover, but broke formation and suffered heavy casualties.[48] In order to avoid further casualties and bring the battle to a speedy conclusion, General Winslow ordered his troops to set fire to the wigwams and withdraw from the fort.[49]

Benjamin Church urged Winslow not to set fire to the fort. He suggested that when the battle was over the English army might camp in the fort, relying on the shelter and provisions that it provided. The fact that Winslow ignored Church's advice sheds light on the inadequacies that characterized English military operations. Despite the elaborate logistical planning, Winslow's army was poorly supplied. By the time the battle began, the army's food supplies were already depleted.[50] Taking this into account, Winslow could not afford to let the fighting drag on. Had the battle continued into the night (had he not resorted to the use of fire), the English might have been forced to camp there for the night and lay siege to the fort. Without food supplies, however, Winslow would not have been able to maintain a siege and would have had to withdraw his hungry and exhausted men back to Wickford that night, without achieving his goal and with the Narragansetts at his heels.[51]

Winslow's logistical weakness made him desperately aggressive. Under optimal conditions (that is, with sufficient supplies), Winslow's army could have besieged the fort, rather than storming it. However, because of poor logistical support, Winslow did not have the time necessary to "conquer the enemy with famine."[52] Lack of provisions allowed Winslow only the narrowest window of opportunity for success. Consequently, he took a chance on a frontal assault that nearly failed.[53]

Thus, even in the most impressive military victory of the war, the settlers displayed a shocking degree of amateurism and artlessness. Despite months of preparations, the colonies could not organize an adequate supply system for one thousand men for more than a two-day expedition. Just as this logistical planning and execution in anticipation of the Narragansett expedition reflected poorly on civilian magistrates, so did the strategic planning (despite its eventual success) reflect poorly on the military leaders of the expedition. Even if the English knew beforehand about the weak section of the Narragansett fortifications, one has to condemn General Winslow and his officers for criminal optimism. By launching a winter campaign against such a strong fort deep in enemy territory, without numerical superiority and without adequate provisions for a lengthy siege, English magistrates and generals were flirting with disaster, gambling impulsively with their men's lives. The army's logistical vulnerability led to an unsound plan of action, making the Great Swamp Fight much more difficult than it should have been. Such recklessness would have been unfathomable and shocking for military professionals in Europe. In New England, however, the inexperience and amateurism of military leaders bred strategic adventurousness and inconstancy, as well as a crippling lack of logistical foresight (or at the very least, logistical competence).

The English suffered 240 casualties, including 80 fatalities, in the Great Swamp Fight, whereas the Narragansetts lost up to 1,000 warriors and noncombatants. The Narragansetts' real loss, however, was the fort itself. In the midst of winter they were driven out to the forests, without shelter and provisions. Hundreds of Narragansetts are estimated to have perished in the months following the Great Swamp Fight from starvation and disease.[54] The Great Swamp Fight broke the power of the Narragansetts as a major military force in the region, though they were still able to launch effective raids against New England towns and small English forces in the field.

As was the case following the battle of Mystic, the English force was still in grave danger after the destruction of the Indian fort. The English were exhausted, weakened by injuries, and low on supplies deep in enemy territory, with enemy war bands still roaming the area. Because they were unable to camp for the night in the fort they had burned, Winslow marched his men through the snow back to the safety of Wickford. By dawn, when they reached their base of operations, twenty men had died from their injuries. Most of the remaining men were no longer fit for service for the remainder of the campaigning season.[55]

Following the English victory in the Great Swamp Fight, hostilities continued. Philip's rebellion had already spread throughout New England and become a general uprising, far beyond Philip's control or command.[56] During winter and early spring 1676, Philip continued his campaign with attacks in Plymouth, while the Nipmucks and other tribes farther north attacked settlements in Massachusetts. In contrast, English forces were unable to curb the movement of Indian troops throughout southern New England and recorded few tactical achievements during that period. One notable exception occurred in late April 1676. Captain George Dennison had been commissioned to hunt down and punish the Narragansett war band that had ambushed and decimated Captain Wadsworth's company near Sudbury April 21, 1676. The same Indian force, under the command of Canonchet, was responsible for the devastating attack on Captain Michael Pierce's company in March.[57] Captain Dennison tracked Canonchet's men to their camp, at Seekonk, where he caught them by surprise in a nocturnal attack. The Indians awoke in panic and fled toward a nearby stream. More than fifty of them were killed in the rout.[58]

Despite successes in winter and spring 1676, Indian forces throughout New England clearly were suffering the ravages of war after almost a year of campaigning. In fact, it has been argued that the Indians were driven by hunger and desperation to launch such audacious attacks on English farms and villages. By summer, the Indian uprising was quickly winding down. Weakened more by disease and starvation than by English bullets, a growing number of Indian groups surrendered to colonial authorities, bringing with them useful intelligence about the movements and intentions of more stubborn war bands.[59] Consequently, colonial forces were much more successful in launching surprise attacks on enemy camps during July and August 1676. It was in these raids, after the outcome of the war had already been decided, that Benjamin Church achieved his fame and reputation as a skilled and accomplished Indian fighter. Philip became a fugitive, hunted by both English and Indian forces. He was eventually killed in one of Church's raids.[60] In time, all the region's Indians tribes were pressured into signing peace treaties with the colonial governments.

THROUGHOUT King Philip's War, Indian forces were not particularly impressive from a tactical perspective. Against fortified houses they were practically useless, but even in the field they were remarkably mediocre. The Indians' individualistic style of combat limited the potency of their armed forces. Their effectiveness was further limited by the fact that they fought in loose formations. Not only were Indian combatants unable to utilize massed fire but their reliance on individual marksmanship was unrealistic, considering the limitations of their firearms (smoothbore muskets).[61] On several occasions, including the battles at Pease Field (July 8, 1675) and against Captain Wadsworth's company, near Sudbury (April 21, 1676), despite outnumbering colonial forces, Indian troops were unable to capitalize on their advantage and defeat the English convincingly.[62]

When Indian troops were successful against forces in the field, it was usually as the result of an ambush, leading to a rout (that is, catching an enemy force by surprise and firing at the fleeing panicking men), rather than a battle that involved actual combat and required tactical skill. Whenever the surprised force did not panic and flee, Indian attacks usually settled into inconclusive and ineffective exchanges of musket fire that ended with nightfall. A series of Mohawk attacks on Wampanoag and Nipmuck war bands in 1676 illustrates this point. In February, a force of three hundred Mohawks (allies of the English colonies) attacked five hundred of Philip's warriors in their winter camp, forty miles east of Albany, near the Hoosick River. The Wampanoags were caught by surprise and vanquished. On June 12, the Mohawks surprised a Wampanoag camp once again, with similar results.[63] In March, however, when this Mohawk force stumbled upon a band of Nipmucks and Pocumtucks on its way to Canada, the Mohawks killed only two men.[64]

These and other battles during King Philip's war demonstrate that, contrary to popular belief, Indian troops were not more accomplished tactically than English forces. English forces were just as devastating as Indian war bands when, in the late stages of the war, aided by informants, they were able to surprise Indian war bands in camp. Taking an enemy by surprise was not a novel concept for European commanders. It was simply much more difficult to surprise military forces in Europe because of the terrain, the size of European armies, and the defensive conservatism of Europe's professional military commanders. The vulnerability of both English and Indian forces in New England to surprise attacks was symptomatic of their characteristically unprofessional approach to defensive preparations. With their lack of vigilance and lack of attention to detail, English and Indian commanders failed to take steps to protect themselves from surprise attacks.[65] It is misleading, however, to draw conclusions about tactics and battle skills from the aforementioned Mohawk raids, the Bloody Brook Massacre, Captain Dennison's raid on Canonchet's camp in late April 1676, and other such routs. Scouting and stealth, rather than battle skills (combat skills), were the critical factors, especially in attacks on enemy troops not noted for their vigilance. This explains the growing success of English forces in the late stages of the war, when they were guided to enemy camps by a growing number of individual informants and newly acquired allies.

Thus, although Indians were not particularly valuable to the English as soldiers,[66] they were indispensable as scouts. So much so, that on a number of occasions English officers refused to accept command over their companies unless they were supplied with Indians to serve as "guides," "pilots," or "scouts."[67] English companies were usually either so noisy and obvious in their approach that Indian troops escaped without notice or they were simply unable to find enemy war bands in order to engage them in battle.[68] As John Pynchon explained to Governor Leverett: "We are endeavoring to discover the enemy; daily we send out scouts but little is effected; we sometimes discover a few Indians and sometimes fires, but not the body of them, and we have no Indian friends here (though we have sent to Hartford for some) to help us. Our English are somewhat awkward and fearful in scouting out and spying, though we do the best we can. We find the Indians have their scouts out."[69]

The assumption that the Indians' military success against the settlers was the product of a more effective tactical doctrine cannot be substantiated. Nevertheless, that assumption has led some contemporaries (as well as some historians) to argue that the defensive-minded Englishmen were forced to emulate Indian tactics in order to compete with, and defeat, their Indian adversaries.[70] Historians have indeed produced spotty evidence suggesting that repeated debacles in King Philip's War convinced the New England colonies of the need to Americanize their tactics by making marksmanship training an integral component of soldiers' military education.[71] A close examination, however, indicates that throughout the colonial period, American soldiers were not exceptional in their marksmanship training or ability.

A number of American editions of British military manuals (European manuals edited for the use of colonial armed forces)[72] did instruct soldiers to take "good aim by leaning the head to the right, and looking along the barrel."[73] This fleeting and brief exhortation should not be perceived, however, as evidence that colonial militias were Americanizing their training procedures and fighting methods. Throughout the colonial wars of the seventeenth and early eighteenth centuries, colonial troops in New England never distinguished themselves as able marksmen.[74] Moreover, European military manuals also mention aiming as part of the firing procedure. In the American edition of Humphrey Bland's military manual, *Abstract of Military Discipline*, the standard manual used in New England, soldiers are instructed to handle the musket with the "muzzle a little lower than the butt in order to take Aim at the Centre of the Body."[75] Bland's *Treatise of Military Discipline*—originally published in 1727 and easily the most influential military text of its time—includes the very same instructions for English soldiers in Europe. A similar command is given in one of the most popular and prominent military manuals of the seventeenth century, William Barriffe's *Militarie Discipline*.[76]

Despite these instructions, one need not conclude that European and colonial officers valued individual marksmanship. These manuals never instructed soldiers to take precise aim at individual targets; aiming merely meant leveling the musket with the "muzzle a little lower than the butt" and giving "fire brest-high," to prevent firing into the ground or over the opposition's heads.[77] Furthermore, whereas aiming instructions were brief and perfunctory—one sentence at most—both European and American editions of military manuals repeatedly and in great detail instructed soldiers to fire uniformly and by ranks. To insure uniformity and rhythm of fire, the firing instructions called on colonial soldiers to draw the trigger "strongly and at once."[78] Even Nicholas Boone's *Military Discipline: The Compleat Soldier* (published after King Philip's War), a typically American manual, written in a very simple style and plain language,[79] emphasizes uniformity: "Here you must keep true motion in drawing the Trigger, doing it all together, so that the Fire of a Battalion may give but one Report, or appear to be no more than one Flash."[80]

The emphasis on uniformity of fire and firing by ranks precluded individual aiming and effective marksmanship,[81] indicating that in the decades following King Philip's War, the colonies' military leadership was not moved by the actions and writings of Benjamin Church and his admirers to reevaluate accepted military conventions. In America, as in Europe, constancy and volume of fire continued to be more valued and valuable than individual accuracy.

Military manuals and treatises were widely read by officers and laymen in the American colonies. An integral part of officers' military training, they reflected the military doctrine of the colonial militias.[82] Nothing in American military manuals published in the colonial era indicates that the men and institutions in charge of military training in the colonies were won over by a new philosophy of war through exposure to Indian tactics. Furthermore, the American editions were not necessarily more popular or influential than the British originals. Colonial troops were not instructed to fire at individual targets or to fight in loose formation. Like European manuals, the American editions emphasized the importance of maintaining close, rigid formation during marching, deployment, and combat.[83] Even after the American Revolution, military training in the United States Army reflected a conventional European doctrine, with a heavy emphasis on rapid uniform fire (by ranks), rather than individual accuracy.[84]

Rather than counting on enhanced individual accuracy to compensate for the small size of colonial forces, English troops in New England increased their volume of fire by loading their firearms with shot, rather than a single large bullet.[85] Loaded with small shot, a musket loses range and power, because the velocity of shot decreases much faster than that of a large bullet. But smaller shot produces a better pattern and more hits.[86] Thus, small shot increased the close-range effectiveness of the musketeers.

The practice of loading smoothbore firearms with small shot long predates the seventeenth century.[87] For the New England settlers, however, the use of small shot was particularly effective and important. European commanders never had to resort to the use of small shot, because they compensated for the inaccuracy of the muskets and the musketeers by deploying numerous musketeers on the line. Colonial forces were tiny by comparison and they faced enemy forces that were more scattered in their deployment (that is, more difficult to hit). Unable to ensure a higher hit ratio by deploying more musketeers, colonial forces often did so by increasing the number of projectiles each musketeer fired. Thus, the English forces in the colonies responded to the tactical challenge of wilderness warfare with enhanced firepower, rather than through a greater emphasis on individual marksmanship. The loss of range resulting from the use of small shot was not as damaging in New England as it would have been in Europe, since long-range fire was rarely necessary in wilderness warfare.

Taking into consideration the Indians' offensive tactics, it is not surprising that the settlers were most consistently successful when they maintained a defensive position. Throughout the wars of the late seventeenth and early eighteenth centuries, the colonists could rely on their ability to repel Indian attacks on their forts and garrison houses. Time and time again during King Philip's War, English villagers were forced to evacuate their homes and congregate in their garrison houses. Time and time again they survived these attacks thanks to the Indians' impotence against fortified positions. During the war, Indian forces captured very few garrison houses. Nearly all of the ones they did capture had been abandoned by the time of the attack.[88]

Most garrison houses were fortified private dwellings, although some were public buildings, such as churches or meeting houses. The fortification of private homes was usually financed by the towns, although some garrison houses were financed by private funds or as neighborhood enterprises. In some frontier communities, in times of need, colonial governments contributed as well to the erection of garrison houses and block houses, which were usually fortified log houses constructed strictly for military purposes. In many block houses and some garrison houses, the second floor projected beyond the first, forming an overhanging gallery that enabled defenders to fire on attackers storming the doors and windows below. From the second floor, the defenders could also put out fires lit by attackers below. Sometimes, a stockade provided these fortified houses with an added measure of defense.[89] To help eliminate the element of surprise and provide the settler communities with yet another dimension of defense, colonial governments urged towns to maintain a continuous watch and send out scouts to patrol their surroundings.[90]

The Indians' ability to successfully attack English towns and forces in the field depended on their ability to *surprise*. One of the factors that figured most prominently in the Indians' early success against the English was the lack of strategic cooperation between the four colonies.[91] The inability of the colonies to coordinate the actions of their military forces enabled the Indians to approach English settlements in secrecy and take full advantage of the element of surprise. Their high mobility enabled them to close in quickly on English forces and, taking advantage of the settlers' deplorable state of vigilance, induce panic and confusion. Thus, the defensive measures New

England towns adopted (fortified houses, stockades, watches, guard dogs, and patrols) were designed to curtail the element of surprise and slow down the Indians' advance. And though the settlers were generally unsuccessful at gathering intelligence on the movements of nearby Indian forces, they were consistently successful in countering the mobility of Indian attackers with firepower from behind their fortifications. Similarly, in the Great Swamp Fight, the Narragansetts—in defensive formation—were able to repel recurring English assaults, inflicting heavy casualties. They were finally defeated only after they were forced by an attack from the rear to break formation.

In a defensive posture, massed fire was very effective in keeping the enemy at bay, inflicting casualties on the attackers while maintaining a protective gap between them and the defenders. Conversely, by closing this gap, offensive tactics did not utilize to the fullest the potential of the musket (that is, range). This characteristic of projectile weapons, in contrast to shock weapons, such as swords and bayonets, makes them extremely effective in defensive formations, because they enable defenders to maintain the protective gap between themselves and the opposing army. Thus, when a musketeer chose to pursue, he utilized offensive tactics, rather than relying on the defensive characteristics of his weapon. The success of defensive tactics, however, required a large number of musketeers producing a sustained volume of fire. Most English forces were too small to produce sufficient firepower to inhibit mobility. With fortifications and the use of small shot they were able to compensate for their limited numbers.

Indian attackers usually attempted to draw English defenders away from their garrison houses to avoid costly and ineffective frontal assaults on fortified positions. Similarly, they preferred to draw large companies in the field into lengthy pursuits, rather than engage them head on. When successful, the Indians impelled the English to break formation and assume an offensive role to close the gap between the forces. Consequently, when surrounded, these forces were not set to defend themselves adequately by producing a massive volley of fire. By taking the offensive (drawing closer to the enemy, targeting enemy troops rather than a strategic position), English forces lost the primary advantages offered by projectile weapons and, consequently, became less potent.

The settlers' supposedly outdated European military manuals cautioned against being drawn into such reckless adventures: "great Care must be taken by the Officers to prevent their Men from Breaking after [fleeing enemy troops]; neither must they pursue them faster than the Line advances: For if a Battalion advances out of the Line, it may be attack'd on the Flanks." "Restrictions of this kind are not only proper, but absolutely necessary; without which, the party so detached may not be only lost, but the regiment thereby involved in insuperable difficulties."[92] Humphrey Bland learned these lessons not on American battlefields but on campaign in Europe. The fact that Indian forces in New England repeatedly tricked the English into assuming an offensive posture testifies not to the unique challenges of warfare in America but to the amateurism, poor discipline, and recklessness of colonial commanders and their men (and their disregard for their manuals).

American military manuals published between King Philip's War and the Seven Years' War illustrate that the colonies' military leadership understood these dynamics. The training of provincial soldiers and the education of their commanders indicated that the lessons taught by Benjamin Church and his ideological successors went unheeded by those in positions of high military command. Appreciation for European military conventions was not limited to a small ring of military insiders, however. The Reverend William Hubbard, for example, criticized English commanders who did adopt an offensive doctrine fashioned after Indian tactics. He maintained that by fighting in loose formation, "taking their aim at single persons, which is the usual manner of the Indians fighting one with another," English troops were reducing the military potency of their units and failing to utilize the increased effectiveness of coordinated fire.[93]

The assumption that accurate fire is more effective than massed fire is questionable even when soldiers are armed with modern rifles. In the early modern era, when troops were armed with smoothbore muskets, accurate fire was nearly impossible.[94] Since no degree of enthusiasm or dedication to the cause could have transformed the smoothbore musket into a sniping weapon, it did not lend itself to open-order tactics. Conversely, a medium-sized company of musketeers could generate a formidable production of fire when ordered in close formation and relying on coordinated fire—two or three volleys by an entire company could clear a patch of forest of enemy troops, whereas the same number of shots fired individually could not. Since the Indians were armed with smoothbore muskets as well, they had to advance to within musket range of English formations in order to be effective. Thus, whenever English troops maintained formation under attack, their assailants were vulnerable to devastating massed fire. Educated by experience, Indian troops rarely chose to take part in such battles. However, as Hubbard argued, when English troops mimicked Indian tactics, they could not capitalize on the defensive characteristics of their weapons and fought merely as a collection of individuals. Since the English were usually outnumbered in the field, this practice made it nearly impossible for them to survive a lengthy engagement, unless they managed to reestablish a defensive formation.[95]

It is important to realize that beyond being poorly trained in marksmanship, colonial troops were poorly trained in most other aspects of soldiery. Colonial forces were so undistinguished in the field, repeating their mistakes over and over again, not because they were hampered by their military manuals, but because both the officers and the men were lacking in proper European instruction and training. As Francis Parkman remarks about colonial forces in King William's War, "Massachusetts had made her usual mistake. She had confidently believed that ignorance and inexperience could match the skill of a tried veteran, and that the rude courage of her fishermen and farmers could triumph without discipline or leadership."[96]

Most of the fighting during the war was performed by civilians forced to defend their towns or conscripted for military service. The militia training days were the only form of military instruction they had ever received. By the time King Philip's War broke out, general training days, those dedicated to the training and drilling of militia companies, were being held "four dayes annually, and no more."[97] Regimental training days took place once every three years. Training consisted of roll call, performance of the manual exercise and other small unit drills, review and inspection by officers and public officials, and mock battles. Yet all accounts of colonial training days illustrate that the main attractions in these assemblages were drinking, eating, smoking, dancing, and public games.[98] The constant threat of Indian violence did little to change settlers' attitudes toward military training, and truancy was a persistent problem. The law books reflect the continual attempts by colonial assemblies throughout the colonial period to force attendance at training days by imposing fines, as well as harsher penalties, such as riding the wooden horse.[99]

The settlers' military skills were not honed, therefore, by practice and drilling. To make things worse, the units that the men trained in were not fighting units; the militia company was an administrative unit, rather than a tactical one.[100] The purpose of militia training days was to arm and train men, rather than produce cohesive military units for combat missions. In times of need, new combat companies and regiments were formed, usually of volunteers. Thus, as ill-trained as they were, soldiers in combat units were not instructed and drilled together. Moreover, combat units were not permanent establishments—provincials usually enlisted for one campaigning season, rather than for the duration of the war. As a result, the ranks were continually filled with new recruits, who were unaccustomed to combat, to working and fighting together, and to relying on one another for protection. Furthermore, discontinuity of service was also rampant among the officers.[101] Consequently, the unprofessionalism that characterized colonial armed forces made them uniquely inept and unreliable.

Many examples of battlefield routs attest to the amateurism and unreliability of colonial troops. The inability of officers to rely on their men to perform their assignments repeatedly crippled colonial forces. Coordinated action between units was difficult because commanders were unable to count on subunits to follow the plans, perform their tasks, and provide support for other subunits. Despite the impressively forceful rhetoric of the courts, it is clear that commanders in colonial New England could not coerce and punish their men effectively. Unlike European soldiers, colonial troops were not professional, disciplined soldiers; they were civilians, with highly politicized representatives in colonial assemblies.[102] An incident that took place on November 1, 1675, exemplifies the tactical and logistical plight of colonial commanders. On that day, Captain Daniel Henchman left Boston to attack an Indian war band at Hassanemesit (now Grafton). As usual, the English failed to find the Indians. At Mendham they learned of the location of another nearby Indian band. When they located the Indian camp, Captain Henchman devised a plan for a two-pronged attack. He divided his company, one force under his command and the other under the command of his lieutenant, Philip Curtice. He stealthily led his force toward the camp. When the Indians' dogs picked up the scent and began barking, Henchman gave the signal to his men to open fire. The ensuing silence made Henchman turn, only to discover that all his men had deserted him. Meanwhile, Curtice's force attacked the Indian camp as planned. However, unsupported by Henchman's contingent, this force was too small to do much damage or to maintain its position. When the Indians returned their fire, killing Lieutenant Curtice and one of his men, the rest of the men immediately turned away to make their escape.[103]

As the argument goes, English troops were ineffective against Indian forces in the early stages of King Philip's War because they were trained in

European tactics that were ill-suited for "Indian fighting" in the New England wilderness. They were hampered and handicapped by their "text-book knowledge of European tactics." As the war dragged on, English commanders learned from experience what they could never have learned from their European drill books and manuals—fighting in loose formation, relying on individual accuracy of fire, and targeting enemy troops rather than taking strong defensible positions. Consequently, thanks to their reeducation on the battlefield, English commanders, beginning with Benjamin Church, were able to stem the tide, enjoy greater success against Indian forces, and ultimately win the war.[104]

This assessment is misleading in two respects. The war was not won through tactical victories of Americanized commanders leading scouting and raiding parties in search-and-destroy missions against the Indians.[105] Nor were English commanders, as a group, Americanized. English forces achieved their few significant tactical victories by employing a defensive style of war, relying on massed fire. English raiding parties were indeed responsible, to a considerable degree, for the settlers' eventual victory over the New England tribes. However, it was not tactical victories over Indian troops (victories which these ranger units were hard to come by) that led to the Indians' material and political exhaustion and final collapse. Rather, it was the rangers' campaign of attrition, executed against Indian fields, fisheries, and stores.

Defensive forces in the towns, behind fortifications, were consistently successful in fending off the attacks of Indian raiding parties. This system of defense was costly, however, because every town at risk required its own garrison (provided by the government to bolster the ranks of the local defenders).[106] Furthermore, town fortifications were designed to protect the lives of the townspeople, rather than to defend the towns themselves. Thus, although the garrison houses saved many English lives, Indian raids produced extensive damage to public and private property, including agricultural fields and grain stores. The heavy financial burden of providing numerous towns with militarily and material support led the colonial governments to seek an alternative or complementary solution. By sending English raiding parties against Indian villages and Indian raiding parties, the governments hoped to prevent these attacks on the towns.

Unfortunately, the attacks did not subside. Until the late stages of the war, offensive forces in the field enjoyed very little success against Indian war bands. They were rarely able to locate Indian forces, and when they did locate enemy troops, they were slow in pursuit, unable to force the Indians into an all-out confrontation. Nevertheless, the governments continued to commission officers to lead ranger units on seek-and-destroy missions against Indian forces and villages.

Although they consistently failed to produce even a mediocre toll of Indian casualties, these raiding expeditions achieved a valuable, though long-term, objective for the settlers. As mythically terrifying as the New England Indians were, they were also quite vulnerable as military adversaries. Indian tribes were usually small, and their military establishments lacked training and discipline, as well as large-scale cooperation and coordination between forces. Their inconsistent and uneven political organization and the unauthoritative sovereignty of their sachems further hampered their ability to coordinate their operations, to form reliable alliances, and to commit themselves to a long-term war.[107] Even more important, their economies were fragile. The economic and social frailty of the New England tribes severely hampered their ability to sustain the war effort in long, drawn-out military contests.

The settlers' political and military leaders understood this weakness of Indian society and consistently targeted the enemy's material resources, especially their food supplies. Thus, despite being a tactical failure, raiding expeditions served an important logistical function by impoverishing and weakening the Indians. English commanders were very much aware of the long-term objectives of this scorched-earth policy they were instructed to apply; they recognized that they were waging a war of attrition against their enemies. Commenting on their conduct at the Great Swamp Fight, for example, one English soldier related, "we having burnt down almost all their Wigwams, as also all their Corn that we could find, they thereby have less Shelter and less Subsistance left them, which Misery of theirs is much aggravated by [the] great Snow."[108] The English army destroyed Indian corn stores on their way to the Narragansett fort. During the Great Swamp Fight itself, English destroyed the Narragansetts' food stores, but also took care to kill their only blacksmith, demolish his forge, and carry away his tools.[109] Throughout King Philip's War, English forces continued this policy, destroying Indian provisions and property wherever they came upon them. Failing to locate enemy troops, English ranger units often resorted to raiding Indian food and grain stores, as well as Indian crops.[110] These raids, along with the Indians' own raids on English towns and forces in the field, combined to drain the resources of the New England tribes.

By the end of winter 1676, the New England tribes were feeling the effects of the war. The patrolling ranger units, as well as the planned expeditions of regular English forces, forced Indian warriors and their families to remain on the move and without shelter. Cold weather, starvation, and disease led to low morale and a waning commitment to the war. As the war progressed through the spring, the nearly united Indian front began to unravel. Some Indian groups splintered off, conducting independent negotiations with English authorities, first about exchanges of prisoners, and subsequently about peace settlements. Disagreements arose within Indian tribes about the wisdom of remaining in rebellion.[111] As more Indian bands surrendered, the remaining tribes were forced to reevaluate their position. The peaceful tribes were supplying the English with information about active war bands, and the English could commit more resources to target fewer enemy tribes. It was clear to every Indian leader that terms of surrender would grow harsher and more vengeful as the war wore on. Thus, Indian morale abated and the number of peace agreements increased steadily throughout spring and summer 1676.

Contemporary, as well as modern, accounts detail the futility of English efforts to coerce the Indians into field battles by attempting to corner them, as they had done at the Great Swamp Fight, and forcing them to hold their ground and defend their position. According to these accounts, the Indians refused to be drawn by such "European nonsense" and continued to employ their own successful methods, avoiding meeting the English in open combat.[112] This explanation is true but misleading. Although the Indians succeeded in avoiding English forces, and although they achieved tactical victories, they were losing the war. As frustrated as the English became over their inability to locate and destroy Indian war bands, their long-term strategy won the war for them. They attempted to force the Indians to take the field or else forfeit their possessions. Because Indian troops refused to take the field against the English, their villages and fields were left undefended. Consequently, the Indian war effort collapsed from physical, social, and political exhaustion.

The battle of Turner Falls (May 19, 1676) was instructive in this respect. On May 12, a band of starving Indians stampeded about seventy head of cattle from the Hatfield meadows into the woods. The inhabitants organized a retaliatory expedition. Captain William Turner gathered together 150 volunteers and led them north on May 18. He had received information about the location of a large Indian band nearby, busy fishing and planting corn on the bank of the Connecticut River. The Indians did not keep a watch, and so the English soldiers simply crept into the camp at dawn and opened fire on the sleeping Indians. Roughly 100 Indians (warriors and others) were killed in this "battle," and 140 more died in the river, trying to escape.[113]

Still, the tactical victory that day belonged to the Indians: nearby Indian forces rushed to the falls and routed Turner's men, killing Turner and thirty-seven others). Despite their tactical victory, however, the massacre of Turner Falls was very demoralizing for the region's Indian tribes. Their food supplies were depleted, they were suffering from hunger and disease, were forced by English harassment to stay on the move. These Indian bands were unable to fish or plant their crops. When they did manage to plant, their fields were often pillaged by English forces. Consequently, disagreements began to emerge between tribes regarding their commitment to the war. As soon as the Massachusetts authorities learned of this discord, they offered to negotiate for exchange of prisoners and for peace. The Narragansetts refused the offer, but a growing number of their tributaries and other smaller tribes accepted.[114]

Thus, despite attempting to defeat the Indians on the battlefield (that is, to win the war through a succession of tactical victories), the English actually won the war by wearing down their opponents in a war of attrition. English forces in the field were usually unsuccessful tactically against the Indians early on. Their offensive operations were crippled by poor soldiery, poor organization, poor scouting, and poor vigilance.[115] Nevertheless, by adopting a scorched-earth policy from the earliest stages of the war, the English set the wheels in motion for the Indians' exhaustion and eventual collapse.

Unlike the Indians, the English were forced by the imperatives of town defense to wage war somewhat conservatively. The Indians, on the other hand, exhausted their resources and energies on relentless—and perhaps strategically reckless—offensive operations. They were successful in their offensive raids, but that was not enough. As Lion Gardiner had stated, after the Pequot War, "war is a three-footed stool, want one foot and down comes all; and these three feet are men, victuals, and ammunition."[116] Without adequate provisions, the Indians could not sustain their war effort.

Like most wars, King Philip's War was not won on the battlefield. The critical factor in determining victory and defeat has always been each side's ability to outlast the enemy in sustaining the fighting with men, matériel, and morale. For the New England tribes, sustaining morale (that is, the willingness to continue persevering and sacrificing) grew increasingly more difficult as their reserves of men and matériel withered during the harsh New England winter. Thus, the colonial wars of the seventeenth and early eighteenth centuries repeatedly reaffirmed Machiavelli's Rules of War: "It is better to conquer the enemy with famine than with yron. . . . He that prepareth not necessary victuals to live upon, is overcome without yron."[117]

The misadventures of English forces during King Philip's War demonstrated that English soldiery did not improve when "text-book knowledge of European tactics" was complemented by experience in wilderness warfare. Rather than revitalizing colonial armed forces, exposure to Indian tactics brought to light the ongoing degeneration of English soldiery. The war demonstrated that English commanders and their men were hampered by their ignorance of European military conventions, as outlined in contemporary military textbooks.

This second generation of colonial commanders differed in education and training from the first generation. Unlike Miles Standish, Lion Gardiner, and John Mason, most of the colonial commanders during King Philip's War were not professional soldiers trained and seasoned on the battlefields of Europe. The vigilance and conservatism of Standish, Gardiner, and Mason (demonstrated, for example, by John Mason's unwillingness to be drawn into offensive pursuits following the destruction of Mystic) were much rarer in the later colonial wars. English commanders during the colonial wars of the late seventeenth and early eighteenth centuries consistently displayed shocking imprudence and recklessness on both offensive expeditions and garrison duty. They consistently neglected to maintain watch when on the defense and to maintain advance and rear guards on the march.[118] They misjudged their own strengths and weaknesses and misunderstood the situations they found themselves in and consequently were drawn into abandoning the tactical defense. Repeating their own blunders and miscalculations time and time again, colonial commanders and their men displayed the type of military amateurism one would expect from civilians. Naturally, the absence of a military tradition and a standing army in New England lent itself to military incompetence.

Contemporary and modern admirers of Benjamin Church, following Church's own lead, have portrayed him as the hero of King Philip's War and indeed the conqueror of Philip and his cohorts. These admirers assume that Church and other students of Indian tactics made a significant difference in the war by improving the military performance of English forces. If only other commanders had followed Church's example, the argument goes, the English could have defeated their enemies much earlier and avoided many of the war's hardships.[119]

Benjamin Church learned from Indian captives and from his own Indian troops about their military tactics. Concluding that marching in close formation made English forces vulnerable to ambushes and to enemy fire, he marched his troops in loose formation, "thin and scatter," making it more difficult for enemy troops to encircle and fire accurately at his men.[120] He took care to advance silently, stealthily, and quickly, taking the offensive whenever possible. However, since most of his victories were surprise raids on enemy camps, intelligence and stealth were the most critical factors contributing to his military successes (the surprised Indians rarely engaged Church's men in combat). In this respect, Church was not different from other, more conventional commanders. He was simply more aggressive in acquiring intelligence and patrolling the countryside.

English commanders grew more successful in their raids on enemy forces during spring and summer 1676, as increasing numbers of Indian groups and individuals surrendered to the English and provided them with intelligence on enemy forces. Benjamin Church himself enjoyed a string of successful raids on enemy camps from July to September. In these attacks he was able to inflicted a high number of casualties on the Indians, while suffering very few casualties.[121] However, when he and other commanders of ranger units started to accumulate tactical victories over Indian forces in the summer 1676, the remaining mutinous tribes were already starving, weakened, politically isolated, and on the run. Desperate and demoralized, they had already lost the war and were merely postponing the inevitable.

Yet Church's victories were conspicuous. After more than a year of being the hunted, the English public enjoyed hearing and reading about an English force taking the war to the enemy, assuming the role of the hunter, and operating successfully against Indian forces in the woods. This fascination with Church's tactical victories (a fascination shared by some historians) has led many to overstate Church's contribution to the English victory in the war.

Church's memoirs did much to present these operations as the turning point of the war and as a demonstration of the value of his Indian-like tactics. Yet, Church never distinguished himself as a competent wilderness warrior until that summer. The groups of Indian fugitives that Church targeted in 1676 were exhausted, slow, and demoralized.[122] Moreover, other Indian groups were eager to provide Church and his colleagues with information about the movements of these fugitives.

Church's summer expeditions were a welcome change for the English, but they were mostly hollow victories from a strategic perspective, taking place after victory had already been secured. They were the finishing blow, not the turning point in the war. In actuality, there was no turning point in the war. The war was won through the continuous campaign of attrition waged by the colonial governments from the earliest stages of the war. The true conquerors of Philip were colonial magistrates who took care to maintain an English civilian and military presence on the frontiers, to transport supplies and provide subsidies for outlying communities, and to enlist sufficient troops for garrison and patrolling duties. Benjamin Church's victories demonstrated the importance of good intelligence and an exhausted, isolated, and desperate enemy. They did little to validate his tactical doctrine. Indeed, the lessons offered by Church and by enemy war bands during the wars of the late seventeenth and early eighteenth centuries went unheeded by the military leadership of the colonies.

KING PHILIP'S WAR was a local affair. During the late seventeenth and early eighteenth centuries, the New England settlers took part in England's imperial wars, facing French and Indian forces on England's North American front. Nevertheless, the military confrontations in the Northeast during King William's War (the War of the Grand Alliance, 1688–97) and Queen Anne's War (the War of Spanish Succession, 1701–13) were reminiscent of King Philip's War, taking the form of small-scale raids and counter-raids of English, French, and Indian forces.[1]

The English governments faced military challenges with which they were all too familiar—amateurism, limited funds, shortage of troops, defensive carelessness, a faulty logistical support system, and the consequent impotence of English forces in offensive operations. One factor that worked in the New England colonies' favor during King William's War and Queen Anne's War was the geographical distance separating the settlers and their adversaries. Unlike the hostile Indians of King Philip's War, the settlers' enemies during the later colonial wars came from New France or from the perimeter of New England. Thus, although the region's borders were porous, they still provided the English settlements on the interior with a protective frontier. Meanwhile, life in all of New England's frontier settlements was much more hazardous than it had been during King Philip's War.

The colonies relied on traditional defensive measures, hoping to outlast their Indian adversaries, as they had done in King Philip's War. However, since military inadequacies had not been addressed since King Philip's War, settlements on the frontier were repeatedly ravaged by enemy attacks. In order to counter their defensive liabilities, the colonial governments attempted to carry the war deep into enemy territory. However, colonial forces did not distinguish themselves in such large-scale and far-reaching offensive expeditions. Only when Britain involved itself in the planning and execution of these offensive campaigns were the colonies able to effectively threaten French centers of military and administrative power.

The rivers flowing south from Canada (the Penobscot, Kennebec, Merrimack, and Connecticut Rivers) made the northern and western frontiers of New England vulnerable to enemy raids. These rivers, as well as scores of smaller waterways, provided French and Indian forces with invasion routes deep into English territory. Colonial governments attempted to address this challenge through defensive fortification. During the wars of the late seventeenth and early eighteenth centuries, the Massachusetts and New Hampshire assemblies repeatedly voted for funds for the construction and maintenance of forts on the northern and western frontiers.[2] The most impressive of these was the fort at Pemaquid (renamed William Henry when it was rebuilt in 1692).

Provincial forts were much like Indian forts and the privately owned garrison houses in the towns. They were usually small, made primarily of wood, and surrounded by a round or rectangular stockade or palisade.[3] Rarely did this outer fortification serve the settlers as a first line of defense. Whereas in European forts, bastions created "lines of fire" along the walls, the simple construction of these frontier forts made it impossible for defenders to enfilade, or rake, the outer walls from within the enclosure (that is, to fire along the length of the walls, sweeping them clean of enemy troops).[4] Furthermore, the palisades enclosing colonial forts or towns were not necessarily a continuous wall. Often the wooden vertical planks (or logs) were placed side by side but not touching. Thus, the palisade did not form a wall behind which the defenders could find shelter. Instead, it was an obstacle that slowed the enemy's approach. Consequently, in all enclosed towns and most colonial forts of the seventeenth and early eighteenth centuries, defensive fire was offered not from behind the stockade or palisade but from the garrison houses, block houses, and barracks that were enclosed within it.

The English responded to the participation of French forces (including heavy gun boats) in the hostilities by constructing strong forts, made of stone, along the Maine coast at Pemaquid and Saco Falls. Fort William Henry, for example, rebuilt at King William's command, had a circumference of 737 feet (the wall fronting the sea was 22 feet high and 6 feet thick), twenty-eight gun ports, and a 20-foot tower. It was armed with eighteen mounted heavy guns (including six eighteen-pounders) and a strong garrison (between sixty and a hundred provincial soldiers).[5]

Although the stronger provincial forts adhered to European conventions, they were simple and rudimentary compared with European fortresses. Furthermore, many of the forts in New England and upper New York were still in an advanced state of disrepair even as late as Queen Anne's War.[6] To make matters worse, the forts' permanent garrisons were usually undermanned.

Limited numbers had been a constant problem for colonial forces in both offensive and defensive assignments. In *On Fortifications*, John Muller explains that even in stronger forts than the ones in the American colonies, fortifications can never replace large garrisons. Successful defense of fortified places requires the deployment of a large number of defenders.

> It appears to me a vain imagination to think, that a fortification ever so strong, with a small garrison, can resist long a numerous army; for if their loss is ever so inconsiderable, in respect to that of the besiegers, it must nevertheless prove a great detriment to them in the end; on the contrary, nothing, in my opinion, but a proportionable number of troops in a garrison, to that of the besieger's army, can make a proper defence according to the bigness of the place.[7]

It was the colonists' good fortune that the Indians were rarely willing or able to sustain a siege for a considerable length of time.

The colonies built forts on their frontiers to attract enemy attacks and cut off French and Indian advances toward the interior, as well as to create bases of operations for expeditions deep into enemy territory. Indeed, when Count Frontenac, the governor of Canada, learned of the erection of Fort William Henry, he planned an immediate attack on it.[8] An English captive held in Quebec (a Boston merchant named John Nelson) managed, however, to alert English authorities in Albany and Boston with the aid of a messenger, and the garrison at William Henry was fortified in time. When the attacking French forces arrived at Pemaquid, in October 1692, the commander, Pierre le Moyne d'Iberville, felt that the fort was too strong and turned back.[9] Ten months later, following this failure to take William Henry and the erection of another English stone fort, at Saco Falls, Sir William Phips, then governor of Massachusetts, signed a peace treaty (August 11, 1693) with thirteen of the principal sachems of the eastern Abenakis.[10]

It is evident that strong English forts did attract enemy attacks and did impress the Indians as attributes of regional military power. Nevertheless, the English forts on the frontiers did not seal off the English countryside to enemy raids. French and Indian raiding parties easily penetrated English territory through New England's porous first line of defense. Because New England's frontier stretched from the Hudson to the Penobscot (from Albany to Pemaquid) and was only sparsely settled, the avenues to the English settlements were wide open to enemy troops. The frontier was too vast to patrol effectively. Similarly, the English forts on the perimeter were too small and too few to block traffic on the rivers and rivulets flowing south from Canada. The primary factor limiting the effectiveness of patrolling ranger units and of the line of forts on the frontier was financing—in order to block access to English settlements, colonial governments would have had to invest heavily in the deployment of more men, the construction of more fortresses, and the creation of an effective supply and transport system to serve these garrisons and forces in the field. Even if such a financial commitment were within the capabilities of the colonies, its benefit did not outweigh the costs. Thus, the northern borders were left virtually undefended, enabling enemy forces to quickly and secretly penetrate deep into English territory and catch English towns by surprise.

The second line of defense were the garrisons placed within the frontier towns (bolstering the local defenders). Although the garrisons were effective in protecting the inhabitants, troops assigned to garrison duties diverted men from the colonies' offensive operations in enemy territory. More important, maintaining garrisons in every frontier town was a costly solution to the problems posed by Indian raids. For this reason, colonial governments always preferred to direct their limited funds toward offensive expeditions, rather than toward the financing of garrisons. From a military perspective, offensive operations in enemy territory held the prospect of preventing Indian raids and "convincing" them to abandon the war effort. From a financial perspective, offensive campaigns were more cost-effective than defensive deployment of garrisons because militiamen were not called away from their occupations until the expedition was prepared to get under way (saving the treasuries the expenses of compensation for lost income),[11] and, unlike garrisons, offensive forces on campaign were usually employed for relatively short terms (weeks, rather than months).

Colonial governments and assemblies responded to pressure from frontier communities protesting against the redirection of troops from garrison duties. Because devoting colonial troops to offensive campaigns left frontier towns undefended, the colonial governments employed flying dragoons to serve frontier settlements. Rather than station defenders in every town, the authorities used these ranger units as patrol and rescue forces for a county or region (that is, for a group of settlements). But just as in King Philip's War, Indian raiding parties rarely lay siege to English settlements and were usually gone by the time English troops came to the rescue.

False alarms further hampered the effectiveness of the flying dragoons as a defensive force. Settlers would send messengers to their neighbors when they feared an impending attack, but often relief forces arrived to find that they had been summoned in vain. During Queen Anne's War, Governor Fitz-John Winthrop of Connecticut wrote to Governor Joseph Dudley of Massachusetts, complaining about false alarms issued by the Massachusetts settlements in the upper Connecticut Valley (Hampshire County): "the late alarm made by your scout (frightened with Jack in the Lantern) put us to a great deal of trouble and £400, and he deserves to be cashiered and punished. It has so much disobliged our soldiers that it will be difficult to get them into a good disposition to your service." As long as settlements were not furnished with permanent garrisons, however, the colonies' system of defense depended on the quick dispatch of relief expeditions whenever alarms were sounded. Since speed was essential to the success of this system, refusing to come to the rescue, or even taking the time to verify the emergency of calls for help, could have been disastrous for the inhabitants, as Governor Dudley pointed out to Governor Winthrop: "otherwise, I only expect your people will come to their funeral, as has been sometimes done heretofore."[12]

Based on the miserable performance of these relief forces during King William's War, commanders of local trainbands and representatives in colonial assemblies asserted that this defensive system was ineffective and irresponsible. Their complaints went unheeded until the stunning Indian attack on Deerfield, Massachusetts, February 24, 1704. In March 1704, the Connecticut General Assembly issued orders for the fortification of the colony's frontier towns. Two months later, the assembly ordered the enlistment of four hundred men for the garrisoning of frontier towns in Connecticut and western Massachusetts (the Hampshire County towns of the upper Connecticut Valley served as a buffer for Connecticut towns).[13]

Throughout King William's War and Queen Anne's War, the colonial governments' commitment to town defense fluctuated as the intensity of Indian attacks and the settlers' panic level oscillated. The towns relied on their traditional fortifications (garrison houses and block houses) for self-defense[14] but were too often surprised by raiding parties. Poor vigilance compounded the challenge of defending the vast frontiers with isolated settlements. The towns were separated by up to twenty or thirty miles of wilderness and connected only by occasional patrol units. Relief forces rarely arrived in time to engage the attackers.[15]

The preference of the governments to invest in offensive operations, rather than in garrisons, seriously compromised the security of their settlements. Frontier towns, such as Northampton, Hadley, Hatfield, Deerfield, Springfield, Haverhill, Kittery, York, and Wells, suffered devastating and recurring attacks.[16] Indian attacks during King William's War nearly destroyed the system of settlements in Maine. At the outbreak of Queen Anne's War, the Maine settlements formed a fragile line along the shore, from Kittery to Casco. Understandably, this state of affairs led many families to leave their homes and seek a safer existence in the interior.

Because frontier settlements served towns on the interior as a buffer, the depopulation of the northern and western frontiers posed a serious threat to the security and productivity of the colonies' more established towns. Soon after the start of King William's War, the General Courts responded by issuing strict prohibitions against the evacuation of frontier towns. They informed the inhabitants that any family that left its home without authorization from the assembly would risk the forfeiture of its property, adding the incentive of lower taxation rates for frontier settlements, as well as garrisons to help out with defensive duties.[17] Nonetheless, the townspeople were left with the prospect of captivity or death if they stayed and governmental disciplining if they left.

The imperatives of town defense at times of heightened Indian activity hampered the governments' offensive operations. For example, during Queen Anne's War, the towns of the upper Connecticut Valley (Northampton, Hadley, Hatfield, Deerfield, and Springfield) could field roughly seven hundred men of fighting age for military service. They were supported by troops from Connecticut and Massachusetts. Only half of the men could take the field, however, the rest were required for garrison duties.[18]

From King Philip's War to Queen Anne's War, frontier towns were instructed to contribute substantial numbers of men to offensive operations, at the expense of local defense. A letter from Colonel John Pynchon of Springfield, commander of the Hampshire County militia regiment, to the authorities in Boston (October 8, 1675) reflects the tensions between the government's preference for offensive operations and the settlers' commitment to town defense: "Honored Gentlemen, It is not for me to find fault with the Providence of God, or to blame in the least that strict order, that we should leave no soldiers in garrison, but call out all. In the day of it, it was my rule and a ground for my action, though very much against my mind, had I been left to myself."[19] Fifteen years later, on February 24, 1690, Colonel Pynchon wrote to Colonel John Allyn of Connecticut, again complaining about the ill-advised policy of drawing troops for campaigns in the north from the garrisons of frontier towns in the upper Connecticut Valley: "begging your serious thoughts about it, . . . knowing that the quitting of those places will but draw the enemy lower and may bring them upon us and yourselves, which is necessary to prevent. . . . If the upper places should be deserted, . . . it will advantage and animate the enemy.[20]

The divergence of strategic imperatives between different colonies in New England—even different counties within colonies—was a major military stumbling block. Since colonial governments could not overcome this problem on their own, the Crown attempted to address it in 1685 by uniting New England and New York under one administrative system, the Dominion of New England, with New York governor Sir Edmund Andros as governor general. The objective of this project was to provide the settlers in the northeast with a stronger, wealthier government that would be able to serve the interests of the region (and the Crown), rather than those of local elites.

In 1677, the Five Iroquois Nations and the English had forged the Covenant Chain, a bond of friendship, alliance, mutual support, and cooperation. This alliance was of critical importance in shaping Anglo-French relations in North America. As the Anglo-Iroquois alliance drew the English colonies into the traditional rivalry between the Iroquois and the "Far Indians," or "Upper Indians" (the tribes of the Great Lakes region, such as the Ottawas, Pottawattamies, Sacs, Foxes, and Sioux), their relations with the French in New France—the allies and trading partners of the Far Indians—deteriorated, intensifying the need for the New York and the New England colonies to better defend their western and northern frontiers.[21]

The dissolution of the Dominion of New England (when news of the Glorious Revolution reached America, in spring of 1689) exacerbated the administrative fragmentation of New England.[22] Through the administration of the Dominion of New England, Governor Andros had given coherence to military affairs in the region. As hostilities with the eastern Abenakis intensified that spring, and especially after news arrived from Europe about the outbreak of hostilities between England and France, the Massachusetts government sought to recreate that administrative and strategic coherence by attempting to recreate the United Colonies of New England.

Sir William Phips's commission as royal governor of Massachusetts in May 1692 stipulated that he would command not only the Massachusetts militia but also the militia of Rhode Island, Connecticut, and New Hampshire.[23] Whereas New Hampshire, because of its exposed position on the frontier, was pleased with the prospect of a partial revival of the Dominion of New England, Connecticut and Rhode Island were reluctant to recreate the "domination" of the Dominion. During King William's War, Massachusetts found that the commissioners Connecticut sent to Boston were not as willing as expected "to yield all necessary assistance when desired according to the rules of [the] ancient union and confederation" (the United Colonies of New England) for the common defense of New England.[24] The continuous bickering between the colonies subsided in 1693, when command over the Connecticut militia was transferred by royal decree from Governor Phips to Governor Benjamin Fletcher of New York.[25]

Governor Phips sought to compensate for New England's weak defensive system through coordination of military action and better logistical and tactical cooperation. The new governor of Massachusetts, Joseph Dudley, tried to follow up on this effort during Queen Anne's War. Dudley had been expelled from Massachusetts during New England's Glorious Revolution, for his support of Governor Andros and the Dominion of New England. In 1702, with the assistance of influential friends in London, he was appointed as the colony's new governor.[26] Dudley's responsibilities as colony's wartime governor (his attempts to recreate the "tyranny" of the Dominion of New England), as well as his personal history with the New England social and political elite, made him very unpopular in New England once again. A running feud with the Winthrops was renewed when he and Governor Fitz-John Winthrop repeatedly clashed over Connecticut's wartime responsibilities toward its neighbors.[27]

This tension between the colonies, as well as between frontier communities and the more established and secure settlements on the interior, highlighted the most critical strategic weakness of the New England colonies—

the absence of a coherent regional strategy and of regional execution. Whereas the more protected population on the interior preferred investing in offensive operations, which were cheaper and held the prospect of shortening the war, frontier towns supported mass deployment of forces as garrisons. To make things worse, throughout King William's War and Queen Anne's War, Connecticut and Rhode Island were reluctant and slow to support the war effort of Massachusetts with money and men. Flanked by Massachusetts and New York, these colonies were less threatened by Indian attacks from the north and west. In October 1703, for example, the Connecticut General Assembly relented to Dudley's threatening pleas and authorized the Council of War to send relief forces to the Hampshire County settlements in western Massachusetts that served Connecticut settlements as a protective buffer.[28] These relief forces, however, were not to exceed sixty men, unless Connecticut itself were invaded. Throughout Queen Anne's War, Governors Dudley and Winthrop repeatedly clashed over Connecticut's position regarding its responsibilities toward the Massachusetts towns of the upper Connecticut Valley.[29]

As the sacrifices required of the settlers differed from region to region, so did the strategic imperatives. Consequently, the financial burden of the execution of the war differed from colony to colony. During King William's War, Connecticut towns were never attacked, manpower losses were slight, and the entire cost of the war has been estimated at £12,000. Meanwhile, towns in Massachusetts and its territories were constantly ravaged by Indian attacks. The immense costs of the war (upward of £150,000) forced Massachusetts to increase taxation and issue paper bills of credit.[30] Similarly, during Queen Anne's War, no Connecticut towns were attacked and Connecticut seldom had more than two hundred men serving in the field.[31] And as in the previous war, Massachusetts bore the brunt. In 1711, for example, 20 percent of Massachusetts' eligible manpower—estimated at ten thousand—was performing military service.[32]

This administrative and military fragmentation of New England into autarchic components hampered offensive and defensive operations during the colonial wars of the late seventeenth and early eighteenth centuries. The weak coercive powers of the English governments played into the hands of the French by limiting large-scale strategic and logistical cooperation and by hindering coordination between forces.

King William's War began in America before King William assumed the

English throne. English relations with the eastern Abenakis of Maine had been unstable and sometimes violent since the 1670s. A fresh round of hostilities broke out in 1686 when Governor Andros decided to establish English control over the territory east of the Kennebec River. On three occasions between 1686 and 1688, English forces plundered a French trading post and mission (Castine) at the mouth of the Penobscot River. The settlement's founder and commander, St. Castin, was a French gentleman and soldier of fortune. When his regiment was disbanded, he took up trading in furs, ammunition, and other commodities. Through trade, wealth, and marriage, he achieved considerable influence among the Penobscot Indians, establishing his trading post in their territory. Andros tried in vain to bully and cajole St. Castin and the Penobscots into switching alliances. In fall 1688, English farmers near Casco (Falmouth) began suffering retaliatory raids at the hands of New France's Indian allies.[33]

Once hostilities broke out in Europe (the War of the Grand Alliance), French authorities in New France increased their material support of the eastern Abenaki tribes. They provided the Indians on the northern frontier with weapons and ammunition, as well as soldiers and military commanders. Yet, like King Philip's War, King William's War was less a war in the European sense than a continuous series of small-scale local attacks. French and Indian forces were limited in size, relying on guerrilla or mobile tactics. Once French and Indian violence was unleashed on the English settlements on the frontier, the traditional defenses were employed—establishing watches, maintaining the fortifications around and within towns (stockades and garrison houses), congregating in the garrison houses in anticipation of or reaction to Indian attacks, and sending out ranger units to patrol the countryside as scouts and relief forces.[34]

In spring 1688, soon after the third English attack on St. Castin's settlement, a small Indian band killed a number of heads of cattle in North Yarmouth, Maine. In response, a small English force, led by Benjamin Blackman, captured sixteen Indians at Saco. Immediately, English settlements in the region suffered reprisals. The Kennebec Indians descended on New Dartmouth (Newcastle), destroying property and taking two families captive. Egeremet, the chief Sagamore, told his captives that this attack was launched in retaliation for the outrages that were perpetrated at Saco and at St. Castin's mission.[35]

In response to these Indian attacks in 1688, Governor Andros led a force of

700 men on an expedition to the northern frontier (November, 1688). As he progressed eastward, Andros left redcoats and provincial soldiers along the way as garrisons in frontier settlements and fortresses. After leaving 60 men in Casco, Andros ended his trek in Pemaquid, where he placed his remaining 120 men as a garrison at the fort.[36] This expedition lasted four months, ending early in 1689. Andros took steps to secure the safety of the settlers on the frontier, but finding no enemy Indian troops along the way, he took no offensive measures. When he arrived at Boston, on his return, he discovered that his absence enabled his political rivals to carry out a coup d'état (coming on the heels of the Glorious Revolution in England). In April he was arrested and imprisoned.

The first defensive measure taken by the restored government of Massachusetts (following the dissolution of the Dominion of New England) was to reduce the garrisons established by Andros along the northern frontier and recall officers suspected of Catholicism. These garrisons had already suffered significant losses to desertion, as soon as news of the Glorious Revolution in Boston reached the settlements in Maine.[37]

The dwindling English presence in the north exposed the frontier to attack. On August 1, 1689, St. Castin and Moxus (an Abenaki sachem) led an expedition against the English fort at Pemaquid. They landed undetected on August 2, while all the inhabitants were in the fields. The assailants positioned one group of warriors between the fort and the main village (a quarter of a mile away), cutting off access to the fort. A second group was situated between the village and the fields, three miles farther away from the fort. Accounts of the events indicate that when the village was attacked, panic ensued and no resistance was offered.

> [We] tarried near the farm-house in which we had dined till about one of the clock, at which time we heard the report of several great guns at the fort. My father said he hoped it was a signal of good news, and that the great council had sent back the soldiers to cover the inhabitants (for on report of the revolution they had deserted). But to our great surprise, about thirty or forty Indians at that moment discharged a volley of shot at us from behind a rising ground near our barn.[38]

The people in the village and in the fields fled pall mall toward the security of the fort. Only a few were able to reach the fort safely and bolster the garrison there. The fort was already undermanned because many of the men who had been posted there as a permanent garrison had deserted their post following the Glorious Revolution in Massachusetts.

The assailants then turned to the fort itself. Some of them positioned themselves in the houses near the fort and from there fired at the defenders. By August 3, the fort's commander, Lieutenant Weems, had only thirteen able-bodied men left for the defense of the fort. Weems himself was injured. He surrendered the fort on condition that the garrison be allowed to leave unharmed. The Indians burned the fort and left with their loot and captives, making their way to New Harbor, a small settlement of twelve households. However, by the time they arrived, the settlers had already evacuated the village, having learned of the attack on Pemaquid.[39]

During winter 1689–90, Count Frontenac, who had begun his second term as Canada's governor-general, continued to support Indian attacks against the English frontier.[40] Indian and French forces attacked settlements throughout the English lengthy and scantily defended northern frontier when the characteristically lax English expected a respite for the season. A war party from Montreal attacked Albany and then surprised and destroyed Schenectady, killing sixty and capturing over eighty English prisoners (February 8, 1690). Another force, under the command of Joseph François Hertel, was sent from Three Rivers to attack settlements in New Hampshire. In a surprise attack on March 18 it destroyed the village of Salmon Falls, killing twenty-seven and capturing fifty. Meanwhile, a war party from Quebec, commanded by Captain Portneuf, was directed against Casco and the Maine frontier.[41]

The fall of Pemaquid was a significant setback for the English. It effectively pushed the English frontier south and made Casco of critical importance to English presence and government in eastern Maine (all settlements east of Casco had been evacuated). Casco was a small settlement, supported by the small and lightly fortified Fort Loyal and the four blockhouses surrounding it. Although the fort had a few light guns to defend the approach from land or sea, its defensive works were in a state of disrepair. Furthermore, when the fort was attacked, Captain Sylvanus Davis had under his command only one hundred able-bodied men (soldiers, civilian inhabitants, and civilian refugees from other towns), as some of his troops were away on a scouting expedition.[42]

After the destruction of Salmon Falls, Hertel's force joined Captain Portneuf and his men (forming an army of over five hundred men) in preparation for the attack on Casco. Undetected by the English, Portneuf positioned his force on an elevation on the northeastern corner of the peninsula (Munjoy Hill). On May 25, 1690, the French force attacked the village but was unable to capture the blockhouses. During the night, the defenders quietly abandoned the blockhouses and joined their comrades in the fort. In the morning, the French took control of the blockhouses, from which they fired at the fort. The siege lasted two days, during which Portneuf's men continued firing at the English troops while also diligently digging a trench zigzagging toward the stockade (the French fire on the fort protected the men working in the trench).[43]

On the third day, when the trench had nearly reached the wall, Portneuf offered Davis terms of surrender. Davis requested a six-day truce (hoping for the return of his scouting party) but was denied. When the fighting renewed, the French intensified their fire from the blockhouses and from the trench. The offensive fire became more deadly when the soldiers in the trench began throwing grenades over the wall. When the men in the trench wheeled a barrel filled with tar and other combustibles up against the fort wall, Davis surrendered the fort, having received assurances from the French officers that all his wards—soldiers and civilians—would be allowed to leave the fort unharmed and retreat to the south. They were all killed or carried off as prisoners.[44]

The fall of Casco led to the near depopulation of Maine. Indian forces were then able to attack the New Hampshire frontier repeatedly and without fear of harassment from the east. Meanwhile, in the east, Massachusetts was organizing the first English large-scale campaign of the war—an attack on the French fort of Port Royal and on the French fisheries in Acadia. Despite the English presence in Newfoundland, the English could not establish control over the fisheries of the Gulf of Saint Lawrence. For this reason, they were unable to prevent French attacks on New England fishing fleets. The expedition was proposed by a group of merchants from eastern Massachusetts, but it was endorsed and supported by the General Court (February 6, 1690).[45]

On April 28, 1690, Phips, the colony's provost marshal, led his army (500 militiamen, 228 sailors, and seven sailing vessels) out of Boston. His instructions were to take Port Royal, capture or destroy French shipping, and then seize other French settlements along the coast. Phips returned a month later, after having captured Port Royal and most French posts to the south.[46]

Phips and his men reached Port Royal on May 11, catching the French garrison off guard. Since the fort was in poor battle condition and its garrison numbered only seventy men, its commander decided to surrender his post without giving battle. Contrary to the terms of surrender, Phips's troops plundered merchants' property, seized the fort's stores, and desecrated the church, smashing its images and destroying the altar.[47] Phips then destroyed the fort and seized its guns. Before returning to Boston, with his plunder and sixty prisoners, Phips commissioned a president and six councilors to govern French Acadia (Nova Scotia) by the grace of Massachusetts. Back in Boston, he began planning his next campaign—against Quebec.

Phips and Major John Walley took command of an army of twenty-three hundred men, mobilized for the monumental strike against the center of French power in New France. A second army (mobilized by New York and Connecticut) was to simultaneously invade Canada overland and attack Montreal, thus stretching the French defenses and facilitating English success on both fronts. By the time Phips and his men set sail, however, the overland expedition had already disintegrated; due to slow recruitment, poor provisioning, and an outbreak of smallpox, the army from New York returned to Albany without reaching its destination.[48]

Phips's army sailed from Massachusetts on August 9, 1690, unaware of the disintegration of New York's overland expedition. The Massachusetts army was supplied with provisions for only four months and with insufficient stores of ammunition (requests for assistance from England were denied). To complicate matters further, the English did not have an experienced pilot to navigate through the Saint Lawrence.[49] This ill-conceived expedition was reminiscent in some ways of the planning for the Great Swamp Fight: Phips's army set sail too late in the summer toward a destination fifteen hundred miles away (a voyage of over two months). Thus, by supplying the army for only four months, the government of Massachusetts committed it to capturing Quebec quickly—*without a siege*—and wintering there. If English troops failed to take the heavily fortified and well-supplied city upon arrival, as they had managed to do in Port Royal, they would be stranded deep in enemy territory, without supplies in the midst of the harsh Canadian winter.

The magistrates in Boston ignored these tremendous risks. Moreover, even though they committed the army to storming the city, rather than laying siege to it, they did not provide it with a sufficient number of men to overwhelm the French defenders and overcome the city's formidable natural and artificial fortifications, as well as its artillery.[50] To make matters worse, this limited number of men was supplied with an even more limited supply of ammunition.

With such deplorable logistical and strategic planning, the expedition was doomed before it was launched.[51] Yet, despite these insurmountable odds, Phips attempted to take the city. His army arrived at Quebec on October 15. By then, Frontenac had already completed the city's fortifications and mobilized the militia in the surrounding countryside to bolster the city's defenders.[52] Phips wasted his limited supply of ammunition by first bombarding the city without assaulting it. Major Walley's force was meant to launch such an overland attack. But by the time Walley's men reached their position across the Saint Charles, having skirmished for two days with local troops, they were too battle-worn to launch a significant attack across an unbridged river without artillery support, while charging uphill in the face of cannon and musketry.[53]

Faced with this collapse, Phips finally decided to cut his losses and return home as quickly as possible before the onset of winter and before exhausting his supplies. The English fleet's withdrawal was hasty and disorganized. Some of the vessels did not return to Boston until February 1691. Four of the vessels have yet to return.[54]

In November, the French recaptured Port Royal without having fired one shot, as the English failed to garrison the fort adequately. In summer 1692, the French evicted the English from Newfoundland. Four years later, Governor Frontenac dispatched two war ships to attack Fort William Henry. On August 14, 1696, the two ships, commanded by Pierre le Moyne d'Iberville, anchored at Pemaquid. An Indian force landed and advanced on foot behind the fort, cutting off overland communications. Iberville quickly established batteries of heavy guns on the adjacent islands, encircling the fort and isolating it by land and sea. At first the fort's commander, Captain Pascho Chubb, boldly and defiantly refused Iberville's terms of surrender. After the French fired a few shells toward the fort, however, Chubb was persuaded to surrender his post. Fort William Henry was razed and its cannon carried off.[55]

The strong French presence in the Gulf of Saint Lawrence and the Bay of Fundy continually challenged Massachusetts's ability to wage war effectively. French war ships and French privateers preyed on English shipping, placing a heavy financial burden on the people and government of Massachusetts.[56]

While this fortress-oriented campaigning took place to the north, more conventional violence persisted throughout New England's frontier. Following the English debacles in Montreal and Quebec in 1690–91, Indian war parties continuously harassed English settlements along the northern frontier. English garrisons and forces in the field were repeatedly caught by surprise, drawn into unproductive pursuits, and ambushed.[57] Just as in King Philip's War, English commanders failed to learn from experience.

Benjamin Church took part in the war, but like most of his colleagues, he could not boast an impressive military record by war's end. Authorities in Boston felt that Phips's advance toward Quebec would expose the eastern Abenakis to English offensives. The assumption was that as long as Montreal and Quebec were in danger, the French could not offer adequate support to the Indians tribes in the east. Consequently, Church was commissioned to lead an expedition against the eastern Abenaki tribes that had brought about the depopulation of Maine.

In the light of his poor showing during a previous campaign near Casco (an expedition in which Church's men arrived at the battlefield with bullets that were too large for their muskets),[58] Church was not enthusiastic about setting out on a new mission. Eventually, he acquiesced and recruited three hundred of his veterans for the expedition. His plan was to attack the Indian villages along the upper Androscoggin. His force landed at Casco Bay on September 11, 1690, and made its way forty miles up the river, toward the Androscoggins' principal village. As soon as the English force was discovered, the few men that were present in the village fled. Church rescued five English captives that were held there. After burning the Androscoggin fort and its stores and killing a number of his Indian prisoners for good measure, Church set sail again with nine women and children—the wives and children of Chiefs Kankamagus and Worombo—as his captives.[59]

Church learned from his prisoners that the Androscoggin warriors were gathering provisions along the Saco River for an expedition. Church was determined to attack them. His scouts came across a small number of enemy Indians. They killed two and rescued one English captive, who informed Church where the Indians had hidden their beaver pelts. Church and his men sailed there and took the pelts but found no Indians.[60] Church then complied with his men's demands, and began the journey home. On the first night they camped at Purpooduc Point, on Cape Elizabeth, where they were attacked by the Indians they were pursuing.

The Androscoggins attacked at dawn. Although still in enemy territory, the English were lax in their defensive preparations and totally unprepared for an attack. The three companies that were encamped on the shore were pinned to the riverbank until Benjamin Church and the troops from the boat came to their rescue. The English force suffered seven fatalities and twenty-four wounded.[61] They finally returned to Portsmouth on September 26, to a cool reception.[62]

Nevertheless, the high-profile prisoners taken from Fort Androscoggin yielded a bountiful reward. In October 1690, a number of sachems arrived at Wells to negotiate with the English about a settlement. The Indian leaders agreed to sign a peace agreement on November 23, at Sagadahoc. However, news of the disastrous English campaigns against Montreal and Quebec resulted in a resumption of hostilities.[63]

As the war wore on, French and Indian raids continued. An Abenaki attack on Oyster Bay (Durham, New Hampshire), in 1694, was somewhat typical. The attack took place on July 18. After more than six months of relative calm— the result on Governor Phips's short-lived peace treaty with the Eastern Abenakis—the settlers were characteristically lax defensively. Not expecting an attack, they kept only a loose watch and did not congregate in the garrison houses for the night. The Indian troops—a group of over 250 Penobscots, Norridgewocks, and Maquoits—were led by Captain de Villeu (a French commandant at Penobscot), Moxus, and Madockawando. They arrived on the evening of July 17 and divided into roughly eighteen smaller units, set to attack as many homes as possible simultaneously, at dawn. When the attack began, some inhabitants attempted to defend their homes, while others fled to the garrison houses. Of the town's twelve garrison houses, seven survived the attack. Two of the remaining five surrendered peacefully after the Indians promised not to harm the defenders (sixteen of them were killed immediately thereafter). Three more garrison houses were abandoned at the moment of attack. The attack on Oyster Bay yielded eighty fatalities and thirty captives.[64]

On the way back to Canada, Moxus and his men broke away from the rest of the force. They crossed the Merrimack undetected and, after a long march, attacked Groton (thirty-two miles east of Boston) at dawn on July 27. The town was caught by surprise. Fortified defenders were, nevertheless, able to repel Indian attackers. Moxus and his men left town after killing twenty-two and capturing thirteen.[65]

The violence persisted—with varying degrees of intensity—throughout the 1690s, despite the fact that on December 10, 1697, the Peace of Rijswijk (signed on September 30, 1697) was proclaimed in Boston. With the resumption of the war in Europe, this violence was legitimized by a name—Queen Anne's War (the War of Spanish Succession).

The central figure during Queen Anne's War was Joseph Dudley. On June 11,

1702, he arrived in Boston to take his position as the new governor of Massachusetts. Despite his personal and political feud with the New England elite, Dudley was relatively well received by the Council and the Assembly. Contending simultaneously with the exigencies of war and the financial pressures imposed on the treasury by the war forced Dudley to adopt what his opponents condemned as an "absolutist" personal rule.[66] As Sir William Phips had done, Dudley attempted to recreate the administrative and strategic cohesion of the Dominion of New England by assuming responsibility for the military affairs of all the New England colonies. Dudley's authority over the New England colonies was as poorly defined as Phips's had been during the previous war. And like Phips, Dudley discovered that Connecticut and Rhode Island were usually resentful and reluctant to cooperate. New Hampshire, in contrast, weak and exposed to attacks from Canada, was eager to submit to Dudley's leadership.

Queen Anne's War can be divided into two stages. The first four years (1703–7) were characterized by raids and counterraids like those of King Philip's War and King William's War. During the second phase of the war, this violence persisted, but was complemented by large-scale offensive operations by colonial and British forces.

At the start of the war, Dudley was eager to placate the eastern Abenakis. To ensure their neutrality in the war between the English and the French, he invited Abenaki representatives to a council at Fort Casco (built on the ruins of Fort Loyal in 1700). Representatives from most enemy tribes (such as the Penobscots, Norridgwocks, Androscoggins, and Pennacooks), as well as Dudley himself, participated in the negotiations at Casco in June 1703. The meeting went well, though no peace treaty was signed. The Indian representatives were not impressed by Dudley's boasts about English military might and refused to cooperate with the English. They were courteous to Dudley and his men, however, and proclaimed their neutrality.[67]

The governor of New France, Philippe de Regaude de Vaudreuil, was very much perturbed by Dudley's diplomatic efforts. Vaudreuil took advantage of the lack of unanimity among the eastern Abenakis and their weak, non-coercive form of government to draw them into the circle of violence during Queen Anne's War. Following the hardships of the war, most of the established Indian leaders favored a policy of neutrality. They were unable, however, to impose their will on younger and more adventurous leaders, who preferred to wage war against the English. Thus, by recruiting *some* Abenakis to participate in raids carried out by European and Micmac troops, Vaudreuil impelled Dudley to ignore the proclamation of neutrality and declare war on all the eastern Abenaki tribes.[68]

The French were easily able to undermine Dudley's efforts to secure Indian inactivity in the war. Charlevoix, the Jesuit historian, explains that Vaudreuil had two objectives in initiating the slew of attacks in Maine in summer 1703, following Dudley's peace talks at Casco. The secondary objective was to check the progress of English settlement along the Anglo-French frontier. "The essential point was to commit the Abenakis in such a manner that they could not draw back."[69] While harassing the English on the New England front, Vaudreuil diligently pursued peace along the New York border: "I have sent no war party toward Albany, because we must not do nothing that might cause a rupture between us and the Iroquois; but we must keep things astir in the direction of Boston, or else the Abenakis will declare for the English."[70]

The Iroquois' neutrality and the resulting passivity of New York and Pennsylvania exposed the New England frontier to enemy attacks. Since most French offensives took place in Maine and New Hampshire, Dudley's forces dealt harshly with the Indians on the eastern frontier. As the commander-in-chief of the Massachusetts and New Hampshire military establishments, Dudley was able to create and implement a strategic plan for eastern New England. Protecting the Connecticut Valley, however, was a more difficult task. Throughout the war, Dudley clashed with Connecticut and Rhode Island authorities over their responsibilities toward English settlements in western Massachusetts. Financial reasoning, considerations of local—rather than regional—defense, and personal animosity toward Joseph Dudley led Fitz-John Winthrop and his council to reject Dudley's requests for assistance in defending western Massachusetts.

The "Deerfield Massacre" (February 28, 1704) convinced Winthrop that it was in his best interest, as the governor of Connecticut, to support the English settlements of western Massachusetts. In 1704, Connecticut supplied Massachusetts with sixty English troops for service in western Massachusetts, as well as one hundred Indian troops (Pequots, Mohegans, and Niantics) for service on the eastern front.[71] Nevertheless, Connecticut's contribution to regional defense was limited and inconsistent throughout the war.

Hostilities began with a French offensive soon after the conclusion of Dudley's peace conference. A force of 500 men, under the command of Beaubassin, sacked Wells on August 10, 1703. Subsequent attacks on Cape

Porpoise, Winter Harbor, Saco, Spurwink, Scarborough, and Fort Casco yielded roughly 150 English captives and fatalities (as well as terrifying tales of captivity and torture). The French troops encountered no substantial opposition other than a few garrison houses and blockhouses that were not overrun and could not be forced to surrender (in most of these settlements only the garrison houses remained standing). The forts at Saco, Blackpoint, and Casco were assaulted in August but not taken.[72]

Beaubassin's final target was Casco. He began by inviting the fort's commander, Captain John March, to a conference outside the walls. Soon after negotiations began, however, the French killed three of March's companions. March himself was able to escape safely to the fort. The French captured and burned the houses surrounding the fort and then attacked the fort itself. For six days the defenders were able to fend off the besiegers, despite the fact that Beaubassin's force was reinforced by fresh troops. During the last two days of the siege, Beaubassin advanced troops toward the wall to undermine the fortifications on the bank on which the fort stood. The arrival of the British *Province Galley* prevented the French from capitalizing on their advantage. The vessel's guns targeted the French party that was working on the fort's wall, forcing Beaubassin and his men to leave Casco by nightfall.[73]

Throughout the war, the French raided the New England frontier in the usual manner. The frontier towns of Maine, New Hampshire, and Massachusetts (towns such as Wells, Kittery, Blackpoint, York, Berwick, Casco, Oyster River, Dover, Exeter, Northampton, Haverhill, Groton, Deerfield, Amesbury, Dunstable, and Lancaster) suffered repeated attacks.[74] The most famous of these attacks took place in Deerfield. An isolated frontier town, Deerfield had always been a very attractive target for enemy raiding parties. It had endured thirty Indian attacks during King Philip's War, King William's War, and Queen Anne's War. On February 28, 1704, a French and Indian force of over three hundred men launched another, devastating attack, on the town. In what became known as the Meadow Fight, an English posse set out to pursue the attackers and liberate the captives. As the posse gave chase, the men broke formation, were ambushed, and chased back to the town's fortifications.[75]

These episodes demonstrate that little had changed on the frontier. The troops' experience could not counteract poor training. Similarly, English commanders demonstrated their habitual lack of restraint and discipline in both offensive and defensive assignments—lack of vigilance and an eagerness to take the tactical offensive were the recurring theme of military activity on the frontier. Relief forces usually arrived too late to give assistance. Ranger units were unable to locate enemy forces but did their best to destroy or confiscate as much property and provisions as they could.[76] As in King Philip's War and King William's War, these offensive operations yielded few Indian casualties. They were effective, however, in harassing and impoverishing the eastern tribes, leading—toward the later stages of the war—to their migration north.

A critical factor that contributed to the effectiveness of offensive operations in this respect (that is, in making the war a contest of attrition) was the inauguration of winter raids by Governor Dudley. As early as the fall of 1703, Dudley proposed equipping and dispatching forces for winter expeditions, as the French had done during the previous war. The Massachusetts Assembly objected that such service would be too rough, imposing too much on troops that had already served for most of the summer.[77] The Massachusetts Council also opposed Dudley's initiative, but the New Hampshire Council and Assembly supported it: "it ever hath been judged the best season in the winter to go to the enemy's headquarters; they cannot be pursued so well in the Spring."[78]

Winter expeditions were a difficult undertaking for the colonial governments—military forces in the field were more dependent on their supplies in winter than during the campaigning season. Thus, in order to enable winter raiding parties to travel to their prospective targets and return safely, governments had to purchase sufficient provisions well in advance, as well as coordinate the movements of the troops and the transportation of their supplies. Because of this complication the Massachusetts Assembly preferred to follow what had been the custom for generations and disband most of the provincial soldiers for the winter.[79]

Despite the disincentives, Dudley was able to force his will on the Massachusetts Assembly on a number of occasions, selling the concept of winter expeditions with the privatization of military activity, through enhanced scalp bounties. Scalp bounties—for both Englishmen and their Indian allies—had been a constant feature of warfare in New England as early as King Philip's War. Although the governments of Massachusetts and New Hampshire offered bounties to contracted soldiers, they now offered larger rewards to irregulars—men who were not on the colony's payroll.[80] Unlike regular soldiers (whether draftees or volunteers),[81] who were supplied by the government with provisions and guaranteed income, civilians who organized themselves as bounty hunters were paid only if, and to the degree that, they were successful; irregulars were paid only for their accomplishments, not their service.

Imperial officials often complained that because of their short-term contracts, colonial soldiers cost four times as much as European soldiers, limiting the number of troops the colonies could finance.[82] By attracting civilians to military activity with scalp bounties, the colonial governments could put armed ranger units on the frontier and avoid the financial and political costs of drafting and financing large numbers of enlisted men.

Despite Dudley's innovations, however, the activities of New England's regular and irregular ranger units did not yield significant numbers of Indian casualties. Although they did contribute to the slow exhaustion of the Indians' material and political reserves that eventually forced the Indians to withdraw from the war, they could not provide a crushing blow against the Indians or hurt the French centers of power in Canada. To achieve these objectives, Dudley designed and organized a series of campaigns against French strongholds.

Unlike the poorly managed King William's War, Queen Anne's War was well organized, with efficient recruiting, centralized command, and effective logistical support for garrisons and forces in the field. By the end of August 1703, Dudley had nine hundred men under contract (only five hundred of them were available for offensive assignments, as the rest were required for garrison duties).[83] By the middle of September, Dudley had eleven hundred men under his command, half of whom he intended to march with on the enemy's headquarters.[84] As soon as Dudley declared war on the eastern Abenakis,[85] the newly created office of commissary-general (held throughout the war by Andrew Belcher) arranged for the purchase and manufacture of equipment, ammunition, firearms, and provisions for the troops. The Garrison at Fort Hill (in Boston) was designated as the central supply depot for the armies of Massachusetts, while Pepperell's garrison at Kittery, Maine, was appointed as the supply depot for forces on the frontier. By appointing a commissary-general, as well as subcommissaries in most garrisoned forts and depots, Dudley not only established a more efficient, streamlined, and professional logistical infrastructure for Massachusetts armed forces but also increased his personal control over the military, at the expense of the colonial assembly.[86]

Governor Dudley planned to use this infrastructure for expeditions against the eastern Indians and campaigns against Port Royal and Quebec. In anticipation of an expedition against Port Royal in 1707, Dudley's Council of War—through a hierarchy of committees—tended to the purchase, storage, and transport of supplies (from banners and clothes, to entrenchment equipment, ammunition, and transports). Colonel John March, former commander of Fort Casco, was commissioned to lead the campaign, with Francis Wainright as his lieutenant. March's force was formed of two regiments numbering 1,150 in total (including 100 Indian rangers, under the command of Benjamin Church).[87] Despite meticulous preparations, however, this campaign failed miserably.

March and his men set sail on May 13, led by the *Deptford*, a British fifty-gun ship. The English force arrived at the Port Royal basin on May 26. Despite outnumbering the defenders four to one, and despite catching them by surprise, the English were unable to capitalize on their advantage. The disarray in the camps and on the ships, coupled with the constant disagreements among the officers, crippled the English army. Colonel March was slow to attack, allowing Subercase—the fort's commander—time to store supplies for a potential siege, repair a breach in the wall, and drill his men on their defensive assignments. Furthermore, because of the difficult terrain and heavy brush surrounding the fort, English artillery was positioned slowly, thus preventing the infantry from charging the fort. Eventually, Colonel John Redknap, a professional military engineer sent from England, lost his temper trying to position the artillery batteries, declaring that "it was not for him to venture his reputation with such ungovernable and undisciplined men and inconstant officers." He refused to set the guns in place, since other English units did not give adequate cover to his men; the fire from the fort was too effective. The captain of the *Deptford*, also blamed the English failure on the poor soldiery of the men. The fort was too strong, he said, to be threatened by "raw men."[88]

As the blunders, miscommunications, and disagreements mounted, the men became increasingly demoralized. English troops were repeatedly harassed by French skirmishers. Although the English suffered few casualties and were able to keep the French at bay, exaggerated rumors spread through the ranks regarding the strength of the French garrison. Meanwhile, the officers' indecision and bickering brought about a total collapse in morale. The men had lost confidence in their commanders and in the feasibility of the mission. After a quick council, Colonel March and his officers decided to withdraw. They returned to Casco to await new orders from Boston.[89]

As Dudley's critics grew more vociferous in Boston, Dudley felt compelled to recommit his troops.[90] Three commissioners from Boston made their way to Casco and informed the English officers that the force was to return to Port Royal. The English force again set sail for Port Royal but once again did little harm and returned to Boston safely.[91]

In March 1709, the British government, with the recommendation of the Board of Trade, approved a plan to recreate Phips's disastrous two-pronged attack on New France in 1690—overland from New York to Montreal, and by sea from New England to Quebec. A squadron was to be sent from Britain with five regiments of regular troops. Massachusetts and Rhode Island were required by Her Majesty's council in London to supply fifteen hundred men for the naval expedition, and all the remaining colonies north of Virginia were to contribute quotas of men for the overland expedition by mid-May.[92] The Five Nations were to be pledged for service as well. Orders were issued in London regarding the establishment of supply depots and the purchase of firearms, ammunition, and other provisions.[93]

These royal orders reached Boston on April 28, 1709. On April 29, an embargo was imposed on all shipping north of Virginia (excepting shipping along the coastline) in order to deny the French access to provisions and prevent them from gathering any intelligence about the upcoming expedition. Scouting units were scattered densely along the northern frontier the same purpose, in an effort to deter the Abenakis from launching attacks against English settlements, by which they could gather information about English preparations for the ambitious campaign.

Responding to royal orders, colonial administrators invested considerable time, effort, and money in preparing plans, purchasing supplies, and coordinating the transportation of men and matériel from the various colonies to the front. However, military emergencies in Europe in summer 1709 prevented the Crown from dispatching the vessels and troops that were promised (it was decided to divert these troops to service in Portugal). Consequently, the entire enterprise was discarded.[94]

A year later, when successive French defeats in Europe, as well as the British blockade of Canada, had already taken their toll on New France, Samuel Vetch and Francis Nicholson initiated yet another expedition against Port Royal, which had been a safe harbor for French privateers who raided English shipping and the New England coast. In anticipation of the joint expedition with the British Navy, the colonial governments imposed another embargo, and tended to recruitment and to the purchase and storage of provisions. A force of nineteen hundred colonial and British soldiers, commanded by Colonels Vetch and Nicholson, arrived at Port Royal and lay siege to the fort on September 24. Under fire from the fort, the English troops entrenched their positions and methodically unloaded and deployed their artillery. On October 1, the English bombardment began. On October 2, Subercase, in command of a small, exhausted, and hungry garrison, surrendered the fort. Port Royal was renamed Annapolis Royal, and Samuel Vetch was named governor of Nova Scotia. The residents of French Acadia were given two years to swear allegiance to the English Crown or be evicted.[95]

Following the capture of Port Royal, Dudley petitioned the Crown to launch an attack against Quebec. The plans for the aborted 1709 expedition were revived and expanded upon. This time the British government pledged fifteen ships of war, forty transports and store ships, and seven infantry regiments (five of which consisted of the Duke of Marlborough's veterans). However, planning by remote control proved to be a difficult task, as preparations on the American side were repeatedly delayed. As time wore on, anger and consternation of British commanders rose to a fever pitch. So much so, that accusations of an anti-Tory plot—an attempt to embarrass the new Tory government in London by sabotaging the expedition—were leveled against the colonial assemblies.[96]

In August 1711, the English fleet (under the command of Sir Hovenden Walker) was finally ready to depart. On the night of August 22, however, the joint expedition was brought to an abrupt halt. Weather conditions in the Gulf of Saint Lawrence (near Egg Island) and human error combined to create one of the worst disasters in the history of the British Navy—eight of the British transports, one store ship, and one sloop were destroyed on the breakers. Although all the war ships survived, 705 men were lost, as well as a valuable cargo of provisions and ammunition.[97] As reports regarding Walker's expedition made their way west, the forces advancing from Albany to Montreal disintegrated. The joint attack on Quebec and Montreal had to be abandoned once again.

By the beginning of the campaigning season of 1713, the war had ended. According to the Peace of Utrecht, signed April 11, 1713, Britain retained Nova Scotia and Newfoundland, while France retained possession of Cape Breton Island (Isle Royale) with permission to fortify there.[98] Following the peace settlement between France and Britain, separate peace treaties were signed with the Indian tribes of the northeast.[99] During the next thirty years, small-scale hostilities with Indian tribes continued along the English frontier.[100] Meanwhile, Anglo-French relations suffered—flaring into violence on occasion—because of competition over an alliance with the eastern Abenakis, as well as border disputes in Nova Scotia, the Great Lakes region, and the Mississippi Valley.[101]

DURING THE SUCCESSION of military contests between King Philip's War and King George's War, few innovations can be discerned in the settlers' military conduct. The significant military developments—winter expeditions, cooperation with British forces, a stronger emphasis on fort building, and strategic and logistical preparations on a grand scale—took place during Joseph Dudley's tenure as governor of Massachusetts and New Hampshire.

As soon as hostilities erupted, the New England colonies fell back on the tested measures of King Philip's War: reliance on scouting expeditions, garrison houses and watches, and dragoon units as relief forces. Since the settlers repeatedly demonstrated their vulnerability to surprise attacks, these measures were designed mostly to restrict the mobility of the Indian attackers, allowing the settlers time to prepare for attacks.[102] When English defenders were ready in their garrison houses to repel their assailants, they were never dislodged from their positions by force.[103]

Nevertheless, the settlers consistently displayed what to colonial magistrates was a perplexing and aggravating tendency to disregard the threats of Indian attacks. Time and again, defenders were caught off guard and, consequently, routed. The settlers' defensive lethargy impelled the authorities to enact legislation in recurring attempts to force townspeople to carry their firearms with them at all times, keep vigorous town watches, send out patrol units, and spend their nights in the garrison houses, especially during the campaigning season.[104]

The constant conflict between colonial governments and frontier settlements reflected the diverging interests of settlers on the frontier and those in the more established and secure towns of the interior. As both sides understood, flying dragoons were not effective defensive forces.[105] In order to be effective, provincial troops had to be on the spot at the time of attack.[106] Thus, reeling from the succession of Indian attacks, frontier settlements demanded that their governments provide the towns with permanent garrisons of provincial troops.[107] The governments, however, were reluctant to adopt this policy. The men who were sent to garrison the towns (from the more populous and better protected communities in the interior) were drawn away from their farms, businesses, and families. They had to be compensated, fed, and equipped by the taxpayers. Since hundreds of men served in the colonies' military establishments during these lengthy wars, garrison assignments placed a heavy burden on colonial economies, translating into higher tax rates, supply shortages, and inflation.[108]

Heavy expenditure on defense would commit the colonies to long, drawn out wars. At times of great danger, when public pressure swelled, colonial governments relented and placed provincial troops as garrisons in the towns to prevent the depopulation of the frontiers. However, they preferred to rely on flying dragoons for town defense and devoted as many resources as possible to offensive operations geared to shortening the war by draining enemies' resources and hampering their ability or willingness to attack.

When engaged in small-scale offensive operations, English troops were rarely effective from a tactical perspective. They hardly ever located enemy war bands, except when attacked. These units were very effective, however, strategically and logistically, when attacking stationary targets—the vacated Indian villages, corn fields, and fisheries. The English governments were very much aware, as they had been during King Philip's War, of the long-term importance of attrition in determining the outcome of a war. Counting on the habitual inability of English troops to draw or corner the Indians into open combat, ranger units were instructed to "Kill, Take and Destroy to the utmost of your power all the Enemy Indians you can meet on your March, and Search for their Corn, destroying all you can find."[109] It was hoped that with these raiding missions, "the Indians might be kept from their usual Retreats, both for Planting, and for fishing, and lye open also to perpetual Incursions from the English . . . : And it was Thought by the most sensible, this method would in a little while compel the Enemy to Submit unto any Terms."[110] With these attacks the English were eventually able to keep the Indians on the move, "to distress them farther against winter," and drive them north to Canada.[111]

Like Indian war bands, English ranger units (whether provincial troops or independent bounty hunters) were unencumbered by defensive imperatives.[112] Unlike town defenders and large armies in the field, ranger units were not forced to defend and hold their ground. This freedom, coupled with the unprofessional and undisciplined conduct of commanders and their men, was detrimental to their success. When rangers did encounter enemy troops, they were too often drawn into reckless pursuits, induced to break formation, and then ambushed and routed. On the rare occasions in which the English maintained formation on offensive operations, their massed fire forced their opponents to either charge the English lines or withdraw from the battlefield.[113] Often, however, amateurism and lack of discipline, exemplified by the Deerfield "Massacre" and the subsequent Meadow Fight, ensured that English field units followed the dysfunctional pattern established during King Philip's War.[114]

The New England colonies faced a daunting challenge in their attempt to prevent the penetration of their northern and western frontiers. A lack of men and funds made it impossible for the settlers to seal off the borders. Thus, other than garrisoning every town at all times, the only way to force enemy troops to remain on the defensive, far away from English settlements, was to maintain the pressure on the enemy's civilian and manufacturing centers.

The few English accomplishments in offensive assignments, however, were unimpressive. Prior to Queen Anne's War, the colonial governments were usually unable to prepare provisions and coordinate the purchase and movements of men and supplies in anticipation of large-scale and far-reaching expeditions. Governor Dudley invested considerable resources and political capital in preparing the infrastructure for successful small-scale expeditions against Indian villages, crops, and fisheries, as well as large-scale campaigns against French military strongholds. To achieve offensive success, Dudley followed the lead of his mentor and predecessor, Sir Edmund Andros.

At the outbreak of hostilities in King William's War, Governor Andros applied his troops to the construction, fortification, and garrisoning of frontier strongholds. He predicted that "Good Forts, being thus Garrison'd with Stout Hearts, in several Convenient places" would enable English forces to set out on short incursions into Indian territory, thus keeping the Indians away from their crops and fisheries. Furthermore, by garrisoning these fortresses year-round, English forces would be able to harass the Indian tribes during the winter months, when they were most vulnerable to the ravages of war and surprise attacks.[115] Andros's foresight and logistical prudence were lost on his immediate successors. The garrisons he established were reduced, and the strong English presence along the northern frontier quickly withered.

To achieve his first offensive goal—effective harassment of Indian war bands and noncombatants—Governor Dudley fortified the garrisons in the front-line fortresses. At the start of the war, backed by Her Majesty's government, he tried in vain to persuade the Massachusetts Assembly to finance the rebuilding of the fort at Pemaquid.[116] Like Phips and Andros before him, Dudley was anxious to advance the English front line of military strongholds closer to enemy territory. By maintaining a strong English military presence on the frontier and by defending front-line settlements, Dudley hoped not only to draw Indian attacks away from settlements in the interior but also to provide bases of operations for English raids on enemy Indian tribes, their villages, corn fields, and fisheries.[117]

After the destruction of Fort William Henry in 1696, the frontier fortresses proved resilient against enemy attacks.[118] Although they could not serve the colonies as a defensive barrier and prevent enemy war bands from reaching English settlements, these fortresses did provide English settlements and raiding parties with reserves of men, firearms, and supplies that drew the attention of enemy forces. Since the larger war parties targeted the forts, the settlements were harassed by smaller, less devastating forces.[119]

The frontier forts also supported English offensive operations against Indian targets, including winter raids. During the first winter of Queen Anne's War, Massachusetts launched three raiding parties against the eastern Abenakis. These attacks were renewed the following winter, and the practice was repeated during the military conflicts with the eastern Indians in the 1720s and 1730s. Although these units saw limited action, their activities deterred enemy war bands from raiding English settlements in winter, as their snowshoe trail could be easily traced by English forces.[120]

Offensive operations were directed toward French military strongholds, as well as Indian targets. In planning these missions, Dudley sought to avoid the mistakes and miscalculations committed by his predecessors. Like them, he had to contend with the traditional problems faced by colonial commanders—amateurism, small military establishments, limited resources, and a tradition of intercolonial discord. As he prepared to launch large-scale attacks against Port Royal and Quebec, Dudley addressed these problems through cooperation with regular British troops and increased taxation and by using influential friends in London and North America to bully colonial governors and assemblies.

By successfully petitioning the queen for joint Anglo-American operations, Dudley and his allies managed not only to significantly increase the funds and number of men at their disposal but also to gain access to a source of experienced, disciplined, and dependable soldiers. With England's support, Dudley's government also invested a great deal of time, energy, and funds in attempts to recreate the strategic and administrative coherence that characterized New England under Andros's "tyrannical" administration. During King William's War, little had changed from the time of King Philip's War in the military administration of the region—the authorities were incapable of preparing logistical support for even simple large-scale operations; commissary arrangements were defective or totally lacking. Conversely, under Dudley's demanding and aggressive command, colonial authorities consistently performed well in planning, financing, and coordinating logistical support for military operations on a grand scale.[121]

Although most of Dudley's ambitious campaigns eventually failed, failure was never due to ill-conceived plans, inadequate logistical arrangements, or poor logistical execution. Through a closer cooperation with London, and with aggressive support from the British navy and army, the New England colonies were finally in a position to bring their logistical advantages to bear.

In this respect, Queen Anne's War signified an important transformation in the New England colonies' military history. In the next large-scale military contests in the northeast, the guiding hand of British officials was even more pronounced. English military achievements in New England reflected the increasing degree of British participation, as well as British planning, administration, and command.

CHAPTER FIVE /
Administrators against the Wilderness

THE TACTICAL INEPTITUDE of provincial troops and their commanders has been attributed to the insurmountable challenges posed by the North American wilderness and by the offensive prowess of Indian combatants. A closer analysis indicates that colonial armed forces deserve a greater degree of responsibility for their failings and failures. The Seven Years' War offers military historians an opportunity to evaluate through comparison the performance of provincial forces and the administration of military affairs by provincial magistrates during the earlier colonial wars. The Seven Years' War showcased the strengths of British armed forces and especially of military administrators and policymakers. It demonstrated how a professional European army dealt with the challenges that the colonies had faced in their wars against the French and Indians.

Ever since the Revolutionary era, the historiographical debate over the virtues of "American tactics" has been colored by the political and cultural contest between the American rebels and their British rulers. The figure of Major General Edward Braddock—Britain's commander in chief of all regular and provincial forces in North America (1755)—has loomed large over this age-old transatlantic debate. An instructive American legend arose from Braddock's ill-fated expedition to Fort Duquesne at the start of the Seven Years' War in America. Legend has it that when Braddock's army was attacked, George Washington, who served as a junior officer on this expedition, pleaded with Braddock to allow him to head the army's provincial troops in a guerrilla assault on the enemy. The general refused Washington's request.[1]

This legend presents George Washington as an amateur warrior—fighting for his home, family, and neighbors—and Braddock as the stereotypical mercenary professional. From a military perspective, this legend posits Washington, the American champion of individual initiative and agency, squarely against Braddock, the Old World champion of regimentation. In American mythology, Braddock's defeat and death served not only as a personal punishment for his rejection of progress and the American way but also as a warning to the British empire and a sign of things to come.

British military misfortunes indeed abounded in the early stages of the war. However, the army's accomplishments during the war reflect well on Braddock and his colleagues. In fact, the United States Army learned from the experience of the British in its own campaigns in the wilderness. During the Seven Years' War, British military administrators were able—through effective logistical support and the construction of forts and secure roads—to bring Britain's logistical superiority to bear against the French and Indians. Thus, they set the stage for a string of British victories by creating battle situations that favored the larger, richer, and better-supplied army.

THE ERA OF GREATER British involvement in North American military affairs actually began with the brilliant success of a provincial expedition against the strong French fort of Louisburg. Following the signing of the Peace of Utrecht, the French government invested heavily in the fortification of the harbor of Louisburg, on the southeastern side of Cape Breton Island (Isle Royale). Construction on the town's elaborate fortifications, designed by Vauban and other eminent French military engineers, began in 1720 and ended only in the early 1740s. In time, Louisburg became a successful fishing town of roughly four thousand inhabitants, protected by a strong garrison (six hundred regular French troops and twelve hundred Canadians), heavy fortifications, and heavy guns. Thus, Louisburg served New France as a central fishing center, as well as an important supply center for Quebec and Montreal.[2]

France had created this stronghold—the strongest fort on the Atlantic coast—as a defensive measure against the British. Britain's naval command of the Atlantic, as well as its occupation of Nova Scotia and Newfoundland, threatened to seal access to New France from the east. Moreover, these factors allowed British subjects to assert themselves more aggressively in the rich fisheries of the north Atlantic. A secure port on Cape Breton Island (protected by the imposing fort of Louisburg) offered the French government a means by which to counter and check British power at the entrance to the Gulf of Saint Lawrence.

At the outbreak of King George's War (the War of Austrian Succession, 1744–48), New France had a distinct advantage over New England, since French authorities there received news of the declaration of war in Europe in late April 1744. English authorities in North America were informed about the war only a month later, when French forces commanded by Duquesnel, the military governor of Louisburg, attacked and overran the tiny British garrison at Canseau, Nova Scotia, opposite Cape Breton Island (May 24, 1744).[3] A subsequent attack on Annapolis Royal was repulsed. The besieged garrison of one hundred men was relieved eleven days later by a British fleet.[4]

Duquesnel attempted to reclaim Nova Scotia for New France with a quick preemptive strike against the enfeebled British garrisons of Nova Scotia.[5] He had hoped to loosen Britain's stranglehold over the entrance to the Gulf of Saint Lawrence. His failure, however, prompted Governor William Shirley and the Massachusetts General Court to launch a counterattack against Louisburg early in the next campaigning season.

Command of the expedition was given to William Pepperrell of Kitterry. Governor Shirley quickly orchestrated the acquisition and organization of supplies, transports, and troops.[6] He also sent a request for naval support to Commodore Warren, in Antigua (the colonies provided the expedition with only thirteen vessels, the largest of which was converted into a twenty-four-gun frigate). Without authorization from London, Warren refused Shirley's request. However, Shirley had sent a similar request to the government in London, and so the time colonial forces reached their base of operations in Canseau in March 1745, Commodore Warren had been directed from London to join the expedition.[7]

Pepperrell's army landed at Canseau on April 4. The troops fortified the town and prepared for the journey to Louisburg. They were joined by Warren's fleet on April 23. By the time the army set sail, one week later, three more war ships had arrived from Britain and three more from Newfoundland.[8] This strong naval force insured an air-tight blockade on Cape Breton Island. The fleet also offered effective cover for the landing of Pepperrell's land forces.

The inexperience of provincial commanders was evident in their plan to charge the city wall at night and seize the fort "while the enemy were asleep." This original plan was impracticable against such a formidable fortress as Louisburg. The army, therefore, was landed at a distance from the city. A detachment of four hundred men, under Colonel William Vaughan, was sent on a reconnaissance mission north of the town and harbor. North of the Royal Battery, Vaughan's force discovered undefended warehouses filled with naval and military stores. When Vaughan set fire to the warehouses, the explosions created a panic among the French troops on the Royal Battery. Assuming that a large English force was ready to attack, the French soldiers abandoned their position and fled to the fort. The next morning, the English took possession of the battery and turned its heavy guns against the city. With this artillery support, Pepperrell was able to construct new batteries closer and closer to the city walls.[9]

After the investment of Louisburg with naval and land forces, and as the British bombardment continued steadily, both sides were in dire need of munitions and supplies. Ironically, it was the arrival of French supply ships that sealed the city's fate. Headed for Louisburg, they were captured by Warren's fleet and used to replenish the waning English stores (only one French ship managed to run the blockade and reach the city). With no hope for relief, the fort was finally surrendered on June 16, 1745.[10]

The odds against a successful campaign of a colonial expedition against Louisburg were high. Francis Parkman calls the expedition "a mad scheme" and "a project of wild audacity."[11] It was planned by a lawyer with no military experience (Governor Shirley) and led by a merchant with little military experience.[12] Colonial troops were farmers and artisans, whereas the French defenders were professional soldiers, protected by the strongest fortifications in North America (second only, perhaps, to Quebec's). Nevertheless, the originators of the expedition—Vaughan and Shirley—were confident. They had good intelligence about the fort's rapidly diminishing supplies and mutinous garrison. Thus, they were able finally to convince colonial legislatures of the feasibility of the venture.[13]

Shirley's gamble paid high dividends. Louisburg's garrison was indeed weakened, resentful, and dispirited.[14] English forces, in contrast, were well supplied and well paid.[15] Although some colonies—Pennsylvania, New Jersey, and, of course, Rhode Island—did not deliver the men and matériel that they had promised, troops and supplies were mobilized quickly. Optimal weather conditions (an early spring) allowed Pepperrell's army to reach its target swiftly and safely. Most important, Commodore Warren's naval support facilitated Pepperrell's successful landing and, by blockading the port and keeping the besiegers well supplied, sealed the fate of the city.

The expedition against Louisburg, the only major campaign of the war, was the most successful military operation conducted by provincial troops in North America. Nevertheless, at the end of King George's War, Britain handed Louisburg back to France in return for the important trading post of Madras, in the Indian Ocean. The capture of Louisburg secured the New England fisheries but did not put an end to small-scale Indian raids against frontier towns in northern New England. These raids followed the all-too-familiar pattern of King Philip's War, King William's War, and Queen Anne's War— when English settlers and garrisons were prepared for an attack (when they were well-supplied and utilized fortifications and defensive fire), they consistently repulsed Indian attackers. English troops, however, were often caught unprepared or were drawn into reckless pursuits.[16]

As they had done during previous colonial wars, the ever-parsimonious colonial assemblies made liberal use of scalp bounties. Several young Englishmen took advantage of this opportunity for fortune and reputation, as the Reverend Thomas Smith of Falmouth observed: "People seem wonderfully spirited to go out after the Indians. Four companies in this town and many more in other towns are fitting for it; the government offer four hundred pounds for the scalp of a man to those who go out at their own expense."[17] English forces in the field—whether provincial troops or bounty hunters—were not tactically impressive or successful. They did, however, contribute to the Indians' material exhaustion and political collapse: "And although they had exceedingly annoyed and distressed the English settlers on all their borders, and were almost always successful in their forays against them, yet in the past five years of war they had . . . become amazingly reduced."[18] By the time the Peace of Aix la Chapelle was announced in North America in 1748, enemy Indian tribes were grateful for the cessation of hostilities.

King George's War seems to have been an insignificant military contest. At the end of the war, the northeast remained as it was before the war, since the only major military achievement—the capture of Louisburg—was reversed by the peace negotiators in Europe. Nevertheless, the events and outcome of King George's War set the wheels in motion for important developments along the English frontiers during the late 1740s and early 1750s, leading up to the Seven Years' War. Episodes of small-scale violence between English and French forces over the control of the valleys of the Great Lakes and the Mississippi occurred repeatedly during the thirty years following Queen Anne's War.[19] During the war, neither side expanded its frontier—English and French forces were no closer to one another in 1713 than they had been in 1690. Very few new outposts were established and no paths were forged in the wilderness to facilitate the transportation of men and matériel. Following King George's War, however, the northern and western frontiers of the English colonies were transformed into a theater of intense military activity.

The British government, always wary of the return of army veterans to British society, offered veterans of the War of Austrian Succession incentives for settlement in Nova Scotia in an effort to protect itself from this unstable caste of violent men but also to create a stronger British presence in Nova Scotia to control and deter its French, Micmac, and Abenaki inhabitants. To check and counteract the power of Louisburg over the Canseau fisheries, Britain constructed a strong naval base in Nova Scotia (Halifax), at a considerable cost to the Crown (see Fig. 7).[20] Following the strengthening of British presence in the east, French authorities—still smarting from the humiliating capture of Louisburg—responded with vigorous spending on fort construction in the west. French forts of varying sizes were strengthened and new ones built along the Great Lakes, as well as the Ohio and Mississippi Rivers and Mobile Bay, in an attempt to create effective and secure lines of communications between Louisiana and New France. Following the outbreak of hostilities—when a British naval blockade became likely—France dispatched several battalions of regulars to serve in these forts and secure them.[21]

The waterways connecting the Great Lakes with the Gulf of Mexico were Canada's only lifeline whenever the British navy was able to seal off the North Atlantic to French shipping. With a sense of desperation, France constructed impressive and expensive forts to protect this lifeline, employing the expertise of European military engineers.[22] Yet although the enhanced French military presence along the Great Lakes and in the west drew the attention of English colonial authorities, only limited funds were directed to the creation of a system of defensive structures to counter French encirclement. The English colonies were militarily and administratively disorganized and fragmented; they had no skilled engineers and were too poor—individually, and without significant British support—to construct fortified strongholds powerful enough to withstand even a feeble artillery barrage.

Along the northern frontier, Massachusetts and New Hampshire erected a system of forts (such as Forts Dummer, Number Four, Shirley, Sheldon, Morrison, Pelham, and Massachusetts) in the 1730s and 1740s. These structures usually consisted simply of wooden barracks or storehouses surrounded by a

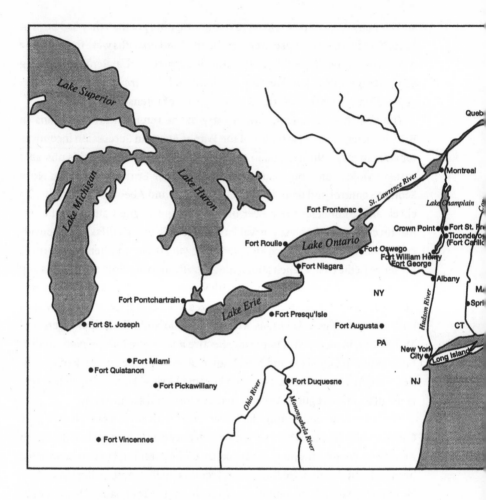

wooden stockade.[23] Without bastions or effective outer works, these stockades were indefensible against a disciplined military force, since they could not be enfiladed from within (defenders could not fire along the outer walls from behind their fortifications). Naturally, these structures had no means by which to defend against artillery.

By the mid-1740s, a chain of small forts stood as a first line of defense along New England's western and northern frontiers. In the west, only during the mid-1750s were new outposts built (by Virginia), but they were all small and supported by rudimentary and ineffective fortifications.[24] In 1754, Virginia commissioned Major George Washington to halt French progress in the west.

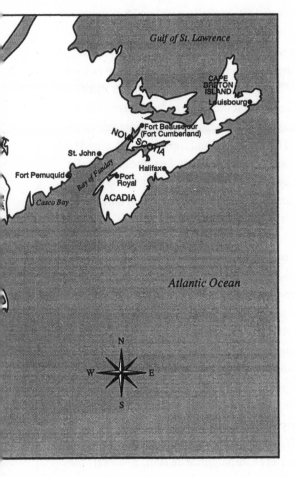

Gulf of St. Lawrence

CAPE
BRETON
ISLAND

Louisbourg

Fort Beausejour
(Fort Cumberland)

NOVA SCOTIA

St. John

Halifax

Fort Pemuquid

Bay of Fundy

Port
Royal

ACADIA

Casco Bay

Atlantic Ocean

N
W   E
S

7. The Anglo-French North
American frontier.

He began work on a fort at the forks of the Ohio but was driven off by the
French, who built Fort Duquesne on the same site. Another attempt by Washington to thwart the French ended in frustration, setting the stage for the appointment of General Edward Braddock as Britain's commander in chief in
North America, and for his infamous expedition against Fort Duquesne.

In June 1755, General Braddock instructed Governor William Shirley, his
second in command, to attack the French forts at the straits of Niagara as part
of four British offensives against the French. Braddock was to lead an expedition against Fort Duquesne, Lieutenant Colonel Robert Monckton was to attack Fort Beausejour in Acadia, and Major General William Johnson was

placed in command of an expedition against the strong French fortress at Crown Point (Fort Saint Frederic, on Lake Champlain).

Monckton easily occupied Fort Beausejour. Six thousand French Acadians who refused to take an oath of allegiance to the British Empire were evicted from the territory to Canada.[25] The other expeditions were much less successful. Johnson's campaign against Crown Point was designed to pave the way for future expeditions into Canada, toward the Saint Lawrence. William Johnson's army (3,000 provincial troops from New England and New York, supported by Mohawk troops) set out from Fort Edward in late August. En route to Fort Saint Frederic, Johnson's army was met by a French force (220 regulars, 600 provincials, and 700 Indians) under the command of Lieutenant General Baron Ludwig August von Dieskau in the Battle of Lake George. After easily brushing aside an attempt to ambush his force, Dieskau launched a frontal assault against Johnson's defensive position. Johnson's men eventually repulsed the French, inflicting heavy casualties. But they had suffered heavy casualties themselves and were unable to advance against the fort.[26] Johnson constructed fortifications for his men on the southern shore of the lake (Fort William Henry). By late November, the English troops, ravaged by disease and malnutrition, were ready to mutiny forcing Johnson to withdraw from the fort.[27]

Poor logistical support was also the undoing of Major General Shirley's expedition against Niagara.[28] Shirley was unable to supply his army with sufficient supplies and transportation for the campaign. He was forced to abandon the enterprise, leaving his troops to garrison Fort George (on the Oswego River and the southern shore of Lake Ontario) and prepare for next year's offensive operations. During the next campaigning season, however, the English garrison at Oswego was taken captive and carried off en masse to Canada by the Marquis de Montcalm, the newly appointed commander of French forces in Canada.

Oswego was the only English outpost on the Great Lakes. Future attacks on Forts Niagara and Frontenac depended on Oswego as a base of operations. Thus, Governor Shirley instructed Lieutenant Colonel John Bradstreet, the commander at Oswego, to build a small fleet strong enough to command traffic on the lake, thus preventing French transportation of artillery. He also instructed Bradstreet to improve Fort George's defensive works in anticipation of a French assault. On his arrival, Bradstreet determined that the fort—an unimpressive wooden structure that was more a trading house than a military stronghold—was poorly situated and poorly fortified. His men

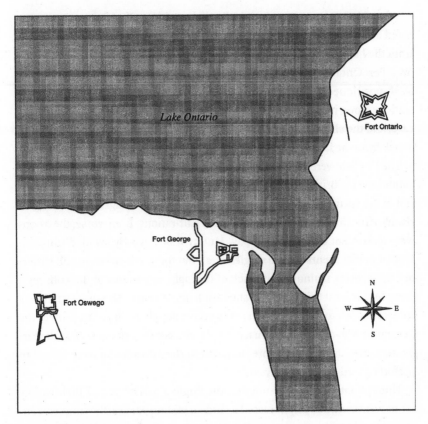

8. The English forts at Oswego.

constructed a palisade behind the fort and cleared the woods behind it but did not otherwise improve the fort's defenses. Instead, Bradstreet built two forts (Oswego and Ontario), on both banks of the Oswego, to support Fort George (see Fig. 8). Unfortunately, the forts were commanded by heights. Furthermore, Fort Oswego's fortifications had not been completed by summer 1756, and its garrison was withdrawn on June 13. The frail fortifications of Fort George were incomplete as well, defending it only from the west and south and leaving the entire lake front (to the north) exposed. The only available defense against an assault from the north were three cannons. On June 16, when these guns were fired against a group of enemy Indians, they collapsed the platform on which they were mounted and were rendered useless thereafter.[29]

When Montcalm approached the English positions, Fort Oswego was evacuated and Fort George was virtually defenseless. Fort Ontario was too far from the harbor and from Fort George to provide effective assistance. Moreover, Fort Ontario itself was facing serious defensive challenges: it was carelessly positioned only ninety yards west of an elevation, there were no firing stations along its stockade, its garrison was exhausted by starvation and disease, and the ships that Bradstreet was ordered to build to defend against an attack from the lake were uncompleted.[30]

The English were in no condition to oppose the French. The harsh living conditions for British soldiers on the shores of Lake Ontario led to a serious riot in the spring. During the entire winter, supply shortages forced the garrisons of the three forts to live on less than half-rations. Even worse, the troops were discontent over delays in pay. Mutiny was narrowly avoided (through lenient punishments for the ringleaders), but the garrisons were still suffering from severe malnutrition. Each of the eight companies of the 50th regiment lost at least thirty men to starvation and disease. The three garrisons were too weak to mobilize a guard to escort supply trains or to protect the carpenters who arrived in February to help with construction projects (the carpenters were unable, therefore, to perform their duties and were forced to perform guard duty themselves).[31]

Throughout spring and summer, the English garrisons and their supply trains were continuously harassed by Indian raiding parties. By summer, construction of fortifications and of Shirley's phantom fleet was halted because the troops could not or would not perform their duties. When Thomas Pownall replaced Shirley as governor of Massachusetts, the troops at Oswego were left without a patron and without pay, leading to a sharp rise in the number of desertions. Only when the troops learned of Montcalm's imminent attack did they agree to work on credit. Nevertheless, they were unable to save themselves. Estimates from June suggested that three months of work were needed—at 400 men per day—to complete the forts' fortifications. By the time work resumed, however, on July 23, only 220 soldiers per day were available for construction duties.[32] The French attacked less than three weeks later.

On August 11, Fort Ontario was invested by a vastly superior French force. Montcalm's force was not a raiding party relying on guerrilla tactics. Of his three thousand men, twenty-six hundred were regular troops sent from Montreal. They were supported by a powerful artillery train, which included the guns captured from Braddock's army in the previous campaigning season.

Fort Ontario's artillery was ineffective against the French, who bombarded the defenders from the elevation to the east. Since the fort's defenses could not withstand the French bombardment, it was evacuated on August 13. After a short siege and bombardment, Fort George fell to the French on August 14, 1756, and the entire English garrison—over sixteen hundred men, women, and children—was carried into captivity, as were the fort's provisions, munitions, and its treasure of eighteen thousand pounds.[33]

During the earlier colonial wars, colonial forts were practically invulnerable to attacks by enemy raiding parties. The early stages of the Seven Years' War, however, demonstrated that against regular troops, supported by supply trains and artillery, the shoddily constructed British forts were wholly ineffective. In March 1757, for example, Montcalm mobilized a raiding expedition against Fort William Henry. The French force numbered 1,400, of which only 150 were regulars. It was easily rebuffed.[34] In late July, Montcalm attempted to capture the fort once more, this time leading a force of 2,570 regulars, 2,546 militia, 1,800 Indians, and 200 artillerymen (operating thirty-six cannons and four mortars). A methodical investment of the fort, supported by massed cannon fire, brought about its surrender on August 9 after a week-long siege.[35]

British failures at Crown Point, Niagara, and Oswego in 1755 and 1756 left the French in control of the waterways to the Ohio Valley. A new, more advanced fort (Fort Ticonderoga, or Carillon) was erected on the narrow neck between Lake Champlain and Lake George, securing the route of invasion toward Crown Point, thus further frustrating Shirley's plans for 1756. Furthermore, the string of English failures in 1755 and 1756 led to an outbreak of Indian military activity against the colonies' frontiers.[36]

In summer 1756, William Shirley was replaced as commander in chief by John Campbell, Earl of Loudoun. Like Governors Phips and Dudley before him, Lord Loudoun believed that victory depended on a major strike against New France's center of military power, Quebec. By threatening as important an administrative and military center as Quebec, Loudoun hoped also to force the bulk of French forces to remain on the defense, rather than engaging in offensive operations along the English frontiers. He planned an expedition of fifty-five hundred men (four British regiments and one battalion of the 60th Royal Americans), supported by a fleet that would block the Saint Lawrence to French shipping. By summer 1757, however, Prime Minister William Pitt had dispatched new orders for Loudoun. Instructions from London for the campaigning season of 1757 called for a defensive deployment along the New

York frontier and a large-scale campaign against Louisburg. Prime Minister Pitt's strategy for the war in North America hinged on the ability of the British Navy to besiege New France by sealing off the Atlantic routes from France to Canada. By capturing Louisburg, Pitt hoped to command the entrance to the Saint Lawrence, effectively cutting off Canada's lines of communications with Europe.[37]

Pitt's plan was more methodical than Loudoun's—by capturing Louisburg and blocking the Saint Lawrence, Pitt hoped to weaken Quebec and Montreal over the winter in anticipation of a campaign against them during the next campaigning season. Pitt's course of action, however, allowed Montcalm a greater degree of freedom in conducting offensive operations farther west along the northern frontiers of New England and New York. Unencumbered by substantial defensive assignments, Montcalm launched two expeditions against Fort William Henry, as well as numerous small-scale raiding expeditions against English settlements, during spring and summer 1757.

Loudoun followed Pitt's directions, but after reaching Cape Breton Island (heading a force of fifteen thousand troops, seventeen war ships, and seventeen support vessels) he decided to abandon the attack against Louisburg, believing that conditions were unfavorable for an attack, since the main fleet was late arriving from England. Thus, the French were able to reinforce Louisburg and strengthen the French fleet on the Saint Lawrence. By the time Loudoun's army arrived at Louisburg, the town's port harbored a formidable fleet of French warships and smaller vessels.[38] When General Jeffery Amherst attacked the city one year later, Britain's naval blockade had already begun to take its toll—the absence of a strong French fleet there in 1758 enhanced the effectiveness of the British blockade and facilitated the landing of Amherst's forces around the city.

By the 1758 campaigning season, Loudoun was replaced as commander in chief by his second in command, Major General James Abercromby. Yet William Pitt appointed Amherst to lead the critical expedition against Louisburg and directed Abercromby to attack Fort Ticonderoga. Amherst enjoyed a manpower advantage of four to one over the defenders of Louisburg. Nevertheless, Louisburg posed a formidable challenge—it was defended by four thousand inhabitants and a garrison of three thousand troops (with 219 cannon and 17 mortars). The harbor was protected by five ships of the line and seven frigates, with roughly three thousand sailors and 544 guns. Escorted by a fleet of twenty-three war ships and several frigates and other smaller vessels, Amherst's army approached Louisburg and, after a nocturnal assault landing of infantry companies, slowly deployed its artillery. Attempts by mobile Indian relief forces to dislodge British units were unsuccessful. In time, the tightening of the siege and heavy British bombardment took their toll and on July 26 the city surrendered after a seven-week siege.[39]

Late in 1758, as the naval asphyxiation of New France intensified, an official in the French War Department commented on Canada's plight: "we must confine ourselves to treating Canada as a desperate disease is treated, in which the sick man is supported by cordials until he either sink or a crisis save him."[40] Indeed, as dramatic as the battle for Quebec was, the fall of Quebec (1759) and of Montreal (1760) should not be seen as decisive battles that changed the course of the war or decided its outcome. Rather, these battles were Canada's coup de grace, after its fate had already been decided. Slowly and consistently, from 1756 on, the British Navy denied French forces in Canada vital provisions, munitions, and reinforcements, while transporting to North America a well-supplied army capable of overpowering its enemies on the battlefield and, more important, of outlasting them through a succession of harsh winters. An immense but reliable supply system enabled the British, within a short period, to create and maintain in North America an overwhelmingly strong military establishment. Secure Atlantic routes and material support from the rich English colonies of North America provided this military establishment with the stability and staying power that the French lacked.

The battle of the Plains of Abraham (September 13, 1759), which led to the capitulation of Quebec, demonstrates how the army's mass deployment and enhanced firepower forced the enemy either to engage British forces on the battlefield in a European manner or forfeit the battle (see Fig. 9). As John Mason and John Underhill had done at Mystic and Pound Ridge, General Wolfe stationed his warships, infantry, and artillery around the town. By positioning a strong force on an elevation commanding the town's defenses, Wolfe threatened its inhabitants. Taking the strategic offensive, Wolfe induced Montcalm to take the *tactical* offensive, leading French forces from behind their fortifications in an attempt to dislodge the British troops. Wolfe's troops—a three-rank line of British regulars in the center, supported on the flanks and rear by auxiliaries—were set *defensively* to meet Montcalm's frontal assault on their position. Like Mason and Underhill, Wolfe relied on tested and established European conventions, counting on the superior firepower

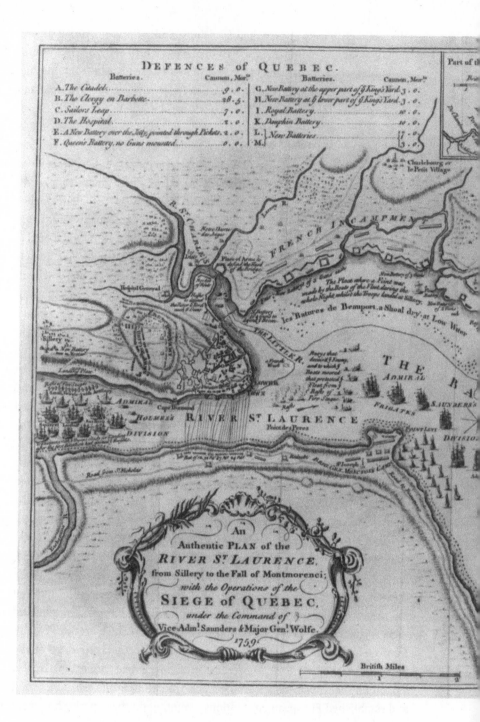

DEFENCES of QUEBEC.

Batteries.	Cannon, Mor.rs	Batteries.	Cannon, Mor.rs
A. The Citadel	9 . 0	G. New Battery at the upper part of ye King's Yard	3 . 0
B. The Clergy on Barbotte	28 . 5	H. New Battery at ye lower part of ye King's Yard	3 . 0
C. Sailors Leap	7 . 0	I. Royal Battery	10 . 0
D. The Hospital	5 . 0	K. Dauphin Battery	10 . 0
E. A New Battery over the Jetty, pointed through Pickets	2 . 0	L. } New Batteries	17 . 0
F. Queen's Battery, no Guns mounted	0 . 0	M. }	3 . 0

An Authentic PLAN of the RIVER St. LAURENCE, from Sillery to the Fall of Montmorenci; with the Operations of the SIEGE of QUEBEC, under the Command of Vice Adm.l Saunders & Major Gen.l Wolfe. 1759.

British Miles

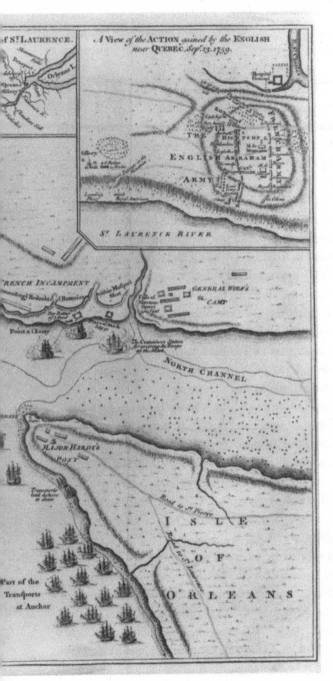

9. The siege of Quebec (courtesy of the Sterling Memorial Library, Yale University).

of the defense. As French troops approached, muskets blazing, Wolfe's men held their fire until the enemy drew closer. They then discharged their muskets, producing massive volleys at a steady rate of fire, exacting a heavy toll on their attackers.[41]

Adopting the tactical defense while taking the strategic offensive enables the stronger military force to capitalize on its advantages. General Abercromby's disastrous attack on Fort Ticonderoga (July 8, 1758) demonstrated that disregarding this axiom could be hazardous. Wolfe's sound battle plan at the Plains of Abraham highlighted Abercromby's folly. He led a force of twelve thousand men against the fort's thirty-five hundred defenders. The French garrison, under Montcalm's command, prepared itself for a siege, improving the fortifications facing the most obvious route of attack. Abercromby disregarded these defensive improvements. Rather than besieging the fort and bombarding it into submission from afar, he launched repeated frontal assaults on the defenders' field works. His men's slow advance—due to French obstructions—made them more vulnerable to defensive fire. They were repulsed with a loss of five hundred fatalities and fifteen hundred wounded.[42]

Whereas Amherst consistently brought Britain's numerical and material superiority to bear in his battles (as well as his campaigns), General Abercromby displayed a less disciplined and patient approach to strategic planning and battle tactics. Threatening the fort with artillery might have forced the defenders into an attack on the English lines or set the stage for a successful siege. Yet Abercromby chose a more direct and simple course of action; one that did not require the patience, meticulous logistical planning, and continuous subtle adjustments demanded by a long siege. His failure to employ a more conventional and conservative course of action drew the ire of a captain of his command, who complained that the use of cannon "must have occur'd to any blockhead who was not absolutely so far sunk in Idiotism as to be oblig'd to wear a bib and bells."[43]

Montcalm's successful defense of Ticonderoga was the last significant French victory of the war. Three weeks later, Amherst captured Louisburg. One month after that, on August 27, 1758, Lieutenant Colonel Bradstreet captured Fort Frontenac, on the northern shore of Lake Ontario. The fort was the principal French fur trading depot in the west, an important link in the supply system of France's western forts, and a base for French shipping on Lake Ontario. Yet it was defended only by a small garrison, since French authorities believed that its distance from English forts in the Great Lakes region offered it sufficient security. Bradstreet's attack, therefore, surprised the garrison; it could not recover from the initial English attack, nor could it withstand English artillery.[44]

With the vital provisions of Fort Frontenac in British hands, the French lake fleet and the western forts of the Great Lakes region, as well as the French forts along the Ohio, suffered severe shortages in rations, munitions, and other supplies. Thus, by the end of 1758, the French were gradually forced by British forces and low supplies to abandon their posts in the west. As the British blockade of the Gulf of Saint Lawrence continued to tighten, French strongholds in the heart of Canada as well began to show signs of financial and material exhaustion. Eventually, this siege of New France led to the collapse of Quebec and Montreal, and to the cession of Canada to Britain.

In confrontations with French regular troops, the British army demonstrated its effectiveness in siege tactics and in European linear tactics. Yet throughout the war, the army also had to contend with irregular troops—Canadian and Indian troops, serving as light infantry or conducting guerrilla-like raids on army posts, camps, and units in the field. During Amherst's siege of Louisburg, for example, a French relief force of roughly 300 Indians attacked the besiegers' backs in an attempt to create panic among British troops. A small force of 170 redcoats dispersed these attackers easily.[45]

Indian attacks against English settlements and military posts had been a constant feature of life in the northeast during the thirty years following Queen Anne's War.[46] Colonial governments of New England responded to the challenge by building a chain of small forts along their northern and western frontiers that proved too feeble to seal the frontier and stop Indian raiding parties from penetrating English territory. Nevertheless, they did provide a military presence—a concentration of men and matériel—and thus a compelling target for the enemy. By drawing the larger enemy raiding parties to them, these forts provided some degree of protection for frontier communities.

The construction and garrisoning of these strongholds also involved building roads and clearing trails through the wilderness that enabled large relief forces to travel more quickly to the aid of communities under attack. When the Pejobscot Company planned to settle communities in Brunswick and Topsham, Maine, for example, it was instructed by the provincial government not only to erect a fort there but also to construct a road for the transportation of supplies to the fort, "but most especially for facilitating the march of Forces to their relief in Times of War."[47]

Nevertheless, despite the usefulness of these measures in providing relief for settlements, provincial troops did not distinguish themselves in the field as able Indian fighters prior to the Seven Years' War. The first meeting between British regulars and Indian troops in an actual battle ended with Braddock's resounding defeat at the Monongahela in 1755. For some, this battle suggested that British units fighting in a European manner would be as incompetent against Indian forces as were provincial forces, if not more so. George Washington, for example, argued that the debacle demonstrated "the folly of and consequence of opposing compact bodies to the sparse manner of Indian fighting, in woods."[48] To Washington, therefore, this battle seemed to be a doctrinal contest between the Old World and the New. Not until his tenure as commander in chief during the American War of Independence did he reevaluate his position on the efficacy of "American tactics."

Major General Braddock arrived in North America in February 1755, with two undermanned Irish regiments, numbering roughly twelve hundred men. They were supported on the march to Fort Duquesne by eleven hundred provincial troops, deemed by Braddock to be "very indifferent men, this country affording no better." "With these I flatter myself to be able to drive the French from the Ohio."[49] The poor soldiery of the Irish and American troops has been used by some—most notably, Braddock's officers—to explain their poor performance against the Indian force that attacked them.[50] Indeed, the troops did act impulsively and eventually panic. A close analysis of contemporary accounts indicates, however, that the soldiers' misconduct was the result of poor positioning by Braddock's staff, as well as poor leadership.

Braddock's army made its way slowly toward Fort Duquesne, arrayed in a conventional manner—the main force, including an immense supply train and a force of artisans and road builders, was protected on its march by an advance guard of three hundred regulars, a rear guard, and small flanking parties. The vanguard was composed of a small group of guides, a grenadier company, and a group of reserves bringing up the rear. On the march, Braddock's army blazed its own trail while following the instructions of British military manuals regarding defense against surprise attacks. The crossing of the Monongahela was performed carefully and methodically, with great care to protect the army from attack as it forded the river. Braddock seemed to have assumed that since the French did not attack him when he was at his most vulnerable, they would not attack at all. When he proceeded toward Fort Duquesne, he neglected to take the necessary precautions recommended by European manuals. He sent no scouts to reconnoiter the territory ahead; nor did he dispatch detachments to occupy the heights commanding the route of the march, as he had done throughout the trek. Moreover, the column's three divisions marched much too close to one another to provide effective protection should one of the three be ambushed—the main body marched only 150 yards behind the advance guard, and the rear guard (one hundred Virginians) followed 20 yards or so behind the main body (see Fig. 10).[51]

Fort Duquesne was garrisoned by an inordinately small garrison of fewer than three hundred regulars and militia. It was supported only by light artillery. Under these circumstances, the fort's commander decided to launch a preemptive strike against Braddock's advancing army with the aid of Indian allies, rather than wait at the fort for the British siege to be deployed. As Braddock's advance guard made its way up an incline to the left of a small hill, a large Indian force took it by surprise, swooping down towards it (July 9). The grenadiers paused, formed a line of battle across the trail, and sent a volley of fire toward the Indians, who had opened fire on them. The Indians halted and took cover in the bushes to the right and left of the trail, flanking the British troops on both sides. The vanguard retreated to the road-making party, reformed and fired again, and then retreated once more, as the main body impulsively rushed forward to join the action. The advancing army entangled itself with the retreating guides, grenadiers, and workers. Afraid of being cut off once the fighting had begun, the weak flanking parties sought safety in numbers, rushing back to join this messy congregation. The trail quickly became congested with a mob of redcoats, provincials, artisans, and rangers. The confusion prevented the troops from maintaining or recreating their ordered formations. Thus, they were unable to produce massed and uniformly directed fire toward the enemy at a consistent rate.[52]

Because of the confusion and the clogging of the trail, Braddock's retreat was as confused and undisciplined as the battle had been, with infantry companies failing to protect the artillerymen who attempted to provide cover for the retreating army. French and Indian troops picked off the fleeing British troops, tomahawking the wounded and stragglers as they gave chase. The British suffered roughly one thousand casualties. They also abandoned to the French some of their artillery pieces and wagons, as well as a hundred head of cattle and over four hundred horses. Braddock was fatally wounded during the rout and perished soon after, during the long, wretched march back to Fort Cumberland. Fearing that the Indians would desecrate his body, Braddock's officers buried him in the dead of night, in the middle of the trail. The next day, the retreating army marched over the fresh grave, stamping it out.[53]

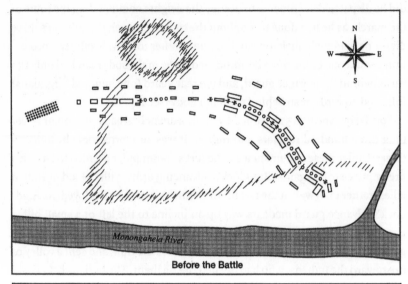

Before the Battle

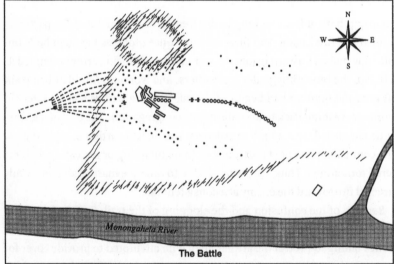

The Battle

10. Braddock's defeat.

Braddock's infamous defeat stemmed from a momentary neglect of the fundamentals of European military doctrine—his failure to occupy the heights commanding the trail and his impulsive and disorderly advance toward the fighting at the front. Throughout the expeditions, Braddock followed the accepted "principles" of war. A single careless act, on July 9, was his undoing. As Stanley Pargellis comments, "Any wise officer with a drill book, far better than a frontiersman, could point out the source of the trouble."[54]

Just as the Seven Years' War provides historians with the opportunity to compare the military conduct of American and British troops in the American wilderness, so does John Forbes's expedition against Fort Duquesne in 1758 illuminate Braddock's expedition. A comparison between the two campaigns provides insight regarding Britain's growing success against the French in North America. Such a comparison also belies accusations leveled against Braddock regarding his failure to adopt "American tactics."

General Loudoun meticulously planned the expedition in 1757. William Pitt chose Brigadier General Forbes to lead the expedition with Colonel Henry Bouquet, the founder of the 60th Royal Americans, as his second in command. Like Braddock, Forbes had to cooperate with colonial governments to provide his army—at the Crown's expense—with supplies, wagons, drivers, artisans, and additional troops. He arrived in Philadelphia on March 21, 1758, expecting to set out with seven thousand men before June. As late as early July, however, Forbes was still feuding with colonial legislators, magistrates, and administrators, chastising, threatening, and beseeching them to honor their agreements and supply him with the men, matériel, and services that they had promised.[55]

Forbes's plan was to build a series of fortified posts as he proceeded toward Fort Duquesne. This way, his army could be continuously resupplied, liberating him from the need to carry all his supplies for the entire expedition with him, as Braddock had done. Instead, Forbes could march with a less cumbersome supply train, carrying provisions for only two weeks at a time: "I am therefore lay'd under the necessity of having a stockaded camp with a block house and cover for our provisions at every forty miles distance, by which means, although I advance but gradually, yet I shall go more surely by lessening the number and immoderate long train of provision waggons &c."[56]

It is surprising that Forbes placed his life and the lives of his men in the slow fumbling hands of the colonial authorities that delayed his departure with their logistical ineptitude. Furthermore, traveling without as immense a supply train as Braddock's did not ensure that Forbes would reach Fort Duquesne more quickly than his predecessor; the construction of a new fort every forty miles was bound to prevent hasty progress. However, the forts built along "Forbes's road" were essential, since their garrisons could protect the movement of supply trains on the road by providing them with armed escorts. Forbes explained to Pitt that his plan would enable him to hold Fort Duquesne after its capture, whereas Braddock's plan would have forced him to destroy and abandon the fort due to a lack of supplies at the close of the campaign.[57]

Forbes's army proceeded slowly from one fortified post to another along the road that the working parties built. Forbes left garrisons behind him to protect the lines of communication with his base of operations against enemy raiding parties. He progressed slowly, taking great pains to improve the road and its defenses, but his defensive deployment proved very effective, as planned. The advancing army, the garrisons of the forts on Forbes' road, and the supply trains making their way west were all harassed by Indian forces. These attacks were all easily repulsed, however.[58] By conducting his army as a slow-moving fortress, Forbes prevented the enemy from harming his men. In fact, the main threat to the success of Forbes's expedition came not from the French and Indians but from the Pennsylvanians.

As expected, Forbes's decision to rely on a support system provided by provincial authorities came back to haunt him. His progress was continuously delayed by late arrival of supplies or the arrival of insufficient supplies. He was further hampered by the apathy, intractability, and willfulness of his civilian wagon drivers. As November approached, Forbes was still toiling to get to within striking distance of his objective. The onset of winter threatened to halt military operations, putting the army's efforts and sacrifices to naught. Forbes realized that he was paying for his cautious and methodical advance with valuable days and weeks. To speed up the army's progress, he reduced the size and strength of the forts that his men built along the way. This forced him to increase the precautions against surprise attack, since he could not rely on these small garrisons for relief in case of an ambush. To save more time, Forbes ordered that the morning meal be cooked the previous night. He was forced to rescind this order when provincial troops rebelled when confronted with the prospect of a cold breakfast.[59]

Forbes's army did not approach the vicinity of Fort Duquesne until November 24. The steady advance of the large British army convinced the fort's tiny and ill-provisioned garrison to abandon it, rather than attempt a defense with only two hundred men.[60] They withdrew with their provisions and artillery after demolishing the fort. Forbes occupied the fort's ruins, rebuilt it, and renamed it Pittsburgh, in honor of his benefactor.[61]

A comparison between the expeditions of Braddock and Forbes reveals a constancy in military doctrine. Although Forbes took a different route to Fort Duquesne and devised a different logistical system for his expedition, he did not reevaluate Braddock's overall conception of the campaign. Unlike Washington, who saw Braddock's defeat as a product of European tactics, Generals Loudoun and Forbes drew different conclusions from the 1755 expedition. Rather than relying on a smaller, more mobile force, trained in light infantry or American tactics, Loudoun and Forbes chose to send a larger army than the one Braddock led. Moreover, Forbes's army was even more dependent on a slow and cumbersome supply system than was Braddock's. On a tactical level, Loudoun and Forbes did not feel that Braddock's defeat discredited his tactical doctrine; quite the contrary. Thus, Forbes's plan was designed to take full advantage of the defensive prowess of his troops—their ability to repel enemy assaults on the army itself or its life line (Forbes's road). His sound and conservative defensive deployment along the march provided his men with a sense of security and dissuaded enemy forces from attempting a threatening assault.[62]

The conduct of the army during the Seven Years' War demonstrated that, unlike George Washington, British generals were convinced of the efficacy of European doctrine on the battlefields of North America. Nevertheless, they were very much aware of the value of light troops and rangers as auxiliaries. Throughout the war, high-ranking British officers attempted to create a reliable force of auxiliaries to perform special assignments for which British regulars were traditionally unsuited and untrained.

Robert Rogers, a New Hampshire frontiersman who had joined the army as an alternative to a prison sentence, rose to prominence in 1755 (under General William Johnson's command), as a commander of small skirmishing units and scouting expeditions. His missions involved the gathering intelligence, seizing captives for future negotiations, destroying supplies, and harassing small enemy units—missions described by Francis Parkman as the "hardy by-play of war."[63] In spring of 1756, General Shirley commissioned Rogers to raise his first "Independent Company of Rangers," a separate administrative and tactical unit attached to a regiment. His mission was "to make Discoveries of the proper Routes for our own Troops, procure Intelligence of the Enemy's strength and Motions, destroy (French) out Magazines and Settlements, pick up small Parties of their Battoes upon the Lakes, and keep them under continual alarm." They were unencumbered by uniforms and heavy gear and carried equipment for winter expeditions.[64]

In time, "Rogers's rangers" consisted of nine independent companies, conducting scouting missions for British garrisons and in support of British expeditions against French targets. At times, however, the rangers were sent on combat missions as well. Like Benjamin Church's independent companies, Rogers's rangers were a motley crew of Englishmen and Indians accustomed to frontier life and backwoods fighting. Like Church's units and Indian war bands, they enjoyed a somewhat undeserved martial reputation. Their most celebrated action was their attack on the Abenaki village of Saint Francis, at the head of the Connecticut River, between Quebec and Montreal, on October 6, 1759. A force of 220 rangers reached the village undetected, surrounded it, and attacked the sleeping Indians at dawn. Many were killed in their beds, and many more were killed trying to escape.[65]

Like most English victories against Indian forces during King Philip's War, King William's War, and Queen Anne's War, this victory required limited battle skills. Since the Indians offered no resistance, the "battle" started and ended as a rout. The retreat from Saint Francis provides a better appreciation of the rangers' soldiery. After taking as much corn from the village as they could carry, Rogers and his men quickly headed south, hoping to elude the French and Indian troops that were pursuing them. During that march back to safety, forty-nine men (nearly 25 percent of the force) perished. Thirty died of starvation; the other fatalities can be attributed to poor discipline and poor decision-making—defensive carelessness and lack of attention to conventional military practices enabled Abenaki pursuers to harass Rogers's men on their retreat and deplete their numbers.[66]

In contrast to the battle of Saint Francis, the Battle on Snowshoes (January 22, 1757) exhibited the rangers in a more flattering light, while discrediting their tactical doctrine. Rogers and 77 rangers arrived at Fort William Henry to scout the vicinity of Crown Point. They marched through the snow past Fort Ticonderoga without being detected by French and Indian forces. On January 22, they intercepted a group of Frenchmen. They captured 7 of them, but the others escaped to the safety of Fort Ticonderoga, alerting its 500 inhabitants to the presence of Rogers and his men. As the rangers hurriedly retreated south, they were ambushed by a force of roughly 150 French and Indian troops. The first volley of fire killed 7 Englishmen and was followed by an assault. The rangers returned fire and retreated, as the rear guard covered the retreat of the forward troops with steady volleys. The remnant of the English force gathered at the high ground behind them, forming a defensive line that repulsed a number of attempts to rush their position. Twice the French flanked the English line but were repulsed by a group of rangers who rushed to extend the defensive line in that direction. As darkness descended, the exchange of fire grew fainter and the rangers made their escape back to Fort William Henry.[67]

Like Abercromby's men at Ticonderoga in 1758, the French troops squandered their advantage with frontal assaults.[68] Like the Indians at the Narragansett fort during the Great Swamp Fight, Rogers's men were forced to stand their ground and defend their position, despite their martial tradition and instincts. What enabled them to defend their position and avoid a rout was not a reliance on guerrilla tactics; rather, it was the defensive line and the collective firepower of the musketeers.

Few of the rangers' encounters, however, involved such discipline and patience. Like ranger forces of earlier colonial wars, and like Indian war bands, Roger's men were often tactically ineffective, even in minor skirmishes and encounter battles (unplanned battles that break out when two forces come upon one another in the field). In early July 1759, for example, a small group of rangers (twenty-seven Englishmen and Indians) set out on a scouting mission sixty miles south of Crown Point. They came across a small group of nine Canadians and Indians with their two English captives. The rangers opened fire prematurely, enabling the Canadians to make their escape. During this brief melee, two rangers were hit by friendly fire while killing one Indian and wounding two others. Only one of the English captives managed to escape his captors. On their return, General Amherst expressed his disgust with the rangers' poor performance and, even more so, with their celebration over their exploits: "a very great noise for a very little they have done."[69] General Thomas Gage, in a letter to Amherst from the previous winter (February 18, 1759), expressed a similarly low opinion of the rangers.

> [we] will use all means to Chastise [the Indians] when they next make their appearance: But I despair of this being done by Rangers, judging from the many pursuits of those people after the Indians during my service in this Country, in which they have never once

come up with them. The Light Infantry of the Regiment headed by a briske Officer with some of the boldest Rangers mixed with Them, to prevent their being lost in the Woods, will be the most likely people to Effect this service.

Despite their limitations as a fighting force, ranger units were useful and effective—as they had been in previous wars—in gathering intelligence on the deployment and movement of enemy troops and in destroying the enemy's provisions.[70] For this reason, most generals used them in their expeditions during the Seven Years' War. But ranger units such as Rogers's tended to be unruly and, therefore, unreliable.[71] Often they simply dispersed before completing their missions, offered fabricated intelligence, consistently disregarded schedules set for them and refused to take part in the tedious business of camp construction and fortification.[72] These factors made it difficult for British commanders to involve rangers in missions that involved cooperation and concerted action between units.

Even more disturbing than the rangers' poor soldiery was the fact that they were exorbitantly expensive. In 1758, for example, Rogers's eight ranger companies cost the British army fifteen thousand pounds more than a full regiment of British regulars.[73] Nevertheless, during General Loudoun's tenure as commander in chief, Rogers's force was increased from one to eight companies. Yet Loudoun was distressed over the financial, military, and disciplinary challenges the rangers posed. He responded to these challenges by training British regulars in light-infantry tactics. He insisted that all British troops be trained and disciplined in the conventional European manner to prepare them to withstand enemy offensives and to attack fortified positions. He advised that following the complete course of their training, certain elite companies would also practice firing at targets and marching on different types of terrain, as well as loading and firing from the prone position—a distinct departure from the accepted practice of European regulars.[74]

The regular army was induced to take into its own hands a greater share of the prosecution of irregular activities because hopes that provincials might be relied on to perform these duties were not realized. In a letter from August 20, 1756, General Loudoun explained the creation of regular light-infantry companies as an attempt to gain self-sufficiency in such small-scale operations: "I am convinced, that till we have every thing necessary, for carrying on the War here, within ourselves, Independent of Aid from this Country, we shall go on very slowly."[75] He was disheartened by the poor sanitation and the level of disease in provincial camps, as well as provincials' high desertion rates, lack of discipline, and ignorance of military law and military training. General Wolfe described them as "the dirtiest, the most contemptible, cowardly dogs that you can conceive. There is no depending upon them in action. They fall down dead in their own dirt and desert by battalions, officers and all." Loudoun was appalled by officers' lack of control over their men, commenting especially on the fact that they did not punish their men for firing their pieces for sport during the march, wandering off in the woods with unloaded firearms, and withdrawing from their posts without permission.[76]

As soon as it became apparent that British regulars responded to ambushes and encounter battles in the wilderness better than did provincial soldiers, the army directed funds toward the creation of companies within the infantry regiments that would serve as light troops. In December 1757, Loudoun supported Lieutenant Colonel Gage's plan to form an entire regiment of five hundred men that would perform as light infantry. This regiment, the 80th, was the first of its kind in the history of the British army. Similarly, although Colonel Henry Bouquet's 60th regiment (the Royal Americans) was not designated as light infantry, Bouquet taught his men how to perform their duties and protect themselves in the woods. The instruction covered personal hygiene, carpentry, masonry, cooking, fishing, swimming, hunting, marksmanship, and more. Bouquet conditioned his men through competitions of endurance and taught them to progress quickly in open and close order and to flank the enemy while maintaining formation. He emphasized the importance of rapid loading and firing, and firing in the prone position.[77]

The reliance on light-infantry units for various aspects of the "hardy byplay of war"—raiding enemy supplies, harassing enemy forces, skirmishing, supply protection, scouting, and foraging—was not a novelty for European armies. Like most armies in Europe, the British army had employed such units—including rifle companies for sniping—as auxiliaries to regular troops long before the Seven Years' War.[78] It was an accepted European practice, borne of the dynamics and developments of warfare in Europe, rather than a response to the unique conditions imposed by the North American wilderness. As European armies increased in size and European wars increased in scope during the eighteenth century, so too did the size and scope of activity of these irregular units.[79]

Against a strong and disciplined defensive line—especially behind defensive works—such small and loosely deployed forces had little or no chances of success (barring mistakes in command). The defensive line's volleys were a remarkably destructive force, easily able to scatter a band of skirmishers whenever the defenders were set in their formations facing the direction of the attack. Attackers could counter the firepower of the defensive line by utilizing their mobility to flank the line and threaten its rear, capitalizing on the element of surprise. Light troops, acting in support of the defensive line, were used to keep track of the movements of the enemy and warn the main body of imminent flanking approaches. Moreover, they were expected to keep the flanking attackers occupied—to harass them and slow their progress—thus allowing the large formations more time to adjust their defensive position toward the new direction of attack.

The strength of large formations was devastating firepower. The strength of light troops was mobility and, therefore, the ability to surprise and disrupt the operations of the defense. Challenged by the attackers' mobility, the defense attempted to buy time and hamper the enemy's mobility through the annoying and disruptive tactics of their own light troops.[80] Thus, British commanders who had served on Britain's European battlefields before their service in America were familiar with such practices and tactics. Like New England's administrators and magistrates during the early colonial wars, they understood that through the actions of light troops, an army accumulated small advantages (captives, intelligence, booty, protection of one's own men and supplies, and harassment and impoverishment of the enemy), "and by multiplying small advantages, [one] procures, at length, a decisive one."[81] Lord Loudoun himself employed such practices to harass Scottish forces during the Scottish rebellion of 1745.[82] Success in conducting such small-scale operations against Canadian forces and in frustrating French petite guerre initiatives was the result of the application of lessons learned in Europe to warfare in America.

European armies did not usually utilize regular troops as light infantry and partisans (rangers). European generals on campaign usually hired locals or foreign mercenary war bands for such purposes.[83] In North America, however, the British relied more heavily on British regulars for light-infantry assignments, since the locals were not equal to the task.[84] As mentioned in a previous discussion, European warfare familiarized British troops with raids and ambushes. British officers, therefore, were educated by experience and by their military manuals in the methods by which to defend themselves and their supplies against the actions of light troops.

General Edward Braddock, for example, was instructed to enlist Indians for his expedition against Fort Duquesne to serve as scouts and flanking parties to warn his army of imminent attacks by enemy forces.[85] Unable to retain the Indians' services, Braddock deployed his own men as flanking units during his expedition.[86] He marched his army, as recommended by his European manuals, between advance and rear guards and the flanking parties.[87] Similarly, but for one fatal exception (July 9, 1755), he took care to occupy the heights commanding the route of the march in order to further protect his army and discourage enemy assaults. Indeed, the commandant of Fort Duquesne was repeatedly frustrated over his inability to surprise Braddock's army: "I have not ceased . . . to send out detachments of French [Canadians] and Indians to harry the English. . . . These troops kept on their guard so well, marching always in battle [order] that all efforts which the detachments made against them were useless."[88]

The futility of such attacks was a recurring theme during the war. Just as Indian troops had repeatedly demonstrated their impotence against New England's garrison houses and small forts during previous colonial wars, so did they fail against Britain's mobile fortresses—the large, slow armies advancing through the American wilderness—during the Seven Years' War. These failures demonstrated the inherent tactical weakness of guerrillas and other light troops.

British commanders were aware of the vulnerability of enemy light troops to strong defensive formations. Thus, British military manuals and drill books stressed that in response to the threat of an ambush or an encounter battle, British troops should send detachments to occupy places that would be advantageous to the enemy and to set up defensively, preferably behind makeshift defensive works that would hamper the attackers' mobility.[89]

Therein lay the critical difference between the operations of British light-infantry units—in America and in Europe—and those of Indian troops and colonial ranger units. For the most part, British commanders did not employ light troops as offensive fighting forces. Rather than targeting enemy troops, British military literature indicates, the objective of the army's light-infantry units was to gather intelligence and to secure advantageous positions for the benefit of larger formations of regular troops.

> The greatest Part of North-America consists of a thick woody Country, abounding with Mountains, Swamps, Rivers, Defile'es, &c. through which it is impossible for Troops to march, even by Files; without

being frequently thrown into the greatest Confusion; in particular, the heavy armed Troops . . . ; by this Means the Line of March is entirely broke, and if they should be attacked by light armed Troops in this Situation, they must be inevitably defeated and destroyed.

These Inconveniences are not to be remedied, without putting some of our Troops on such a Footing, as to be able to repel the Enemy's *Indians* and Irregulars, who are always lightly accoutered, and accustomed to the Woods.[90]

Whereas Rogers's rangers, English ranger companies of the early colonial wars, and Indian war bands could be described as guerrillas from a tactical perspective, British light-infantry units were not. Strategically, they were deployed to assist and *defend* the infantry battalions, allowing them to bring their full firepower to bear in any engagement. Tactically as well, light-infantry detachments usually employed defensive tactics in battle situations "to be able to *repel* the Enemy's *Indians* and Irregulars [my emphasis]." In the early stages of the siege of Louisburg, for example, light troops were deployed on the northern perimeter of the British camps and batteries (see Fig. 11). They were stationed in a loose chain of blockhouses and redoubts, situated close enough to one another to offer support in case of enemy attack or harassment.[91] Similarly, during the expeditions of Braddock and Forbes against Fort Duquesne, light troops served as scouting and flanking companies, assigned to occupy strategically strong positions along the route of the march and to protect the main body of the army as it advanced.

It is not surprising that British light troops usually took the tactical defense, rather than employing the tactics of Indian war bands. Their tactics were consistent with and dictated by their well-defined assignment as auxiliaries. As support troops to the fire producing units—the artillery and the large formations of the infantry battalions—light-infantry companies were instructed to protect other forces or positions that offered military advantages. Thus, they could not employ guerrilla tactics—a tactical doctrine that is predicated on abandoning territory in exchange for enemy lives.

Roger Stevenson's military manual underscores the conservative and defensive approach of the British army to small-scale operations. Stevenson's instructions indicate that British light-infantry units, unlike the independent-minded rangers and Indian troops, needed to be highly disciplined and well trained in order "to act in conformity with those around them" and maintain their position and formation under attack.[92]

Whereas the consistent and overwhelming firepower of the infantry battalions made close-quarters combat highly unlikely for them (especially against the light troops that usually opposed them in North America), the smaller light-infantry companies could generate only limited fire. They were, therefore, more vulnerable to frontal assaults. Thus, their tactical success stemmed from their limited assignments and from the security and support provided by the main body of infantry battalions. In Quebec, for example, General Wolfe directed his officers to fortify British camps and outposts in order to repel assaults by French light troops. More important, in case of enemy attack, he thought "it necessary to order some of the light troops to retire before the enemy . . . so as to draw them nearer the army . . . to engage them to fight at a disadvantage, or to cut off their retreat."[93] Similarly, during Abercromby's expedition against Ticonderoga, a company of Rogers's rangers, serving as an advance guard for the British column, stumbled upon an enemy detachment of roughly 350 men. A fire fight soon ensued between the rangers and the French force. Meanwhile, the main body advanced toward the fighting and opened fire, systematically decimating the French troops.[94]

When fighting independently (not as auxiliaries of larger infantry formations), light-infantry units could either assume the role of shock troops or settle into the lengthy and inconclusive fire fights that characterized Indian warfare (battles that usually produced few results because of the infamous inaccuracy of the musket). Determined to break this tactical stalemate and disperse enemy troops, Colonel Henry Bouquet asserted that small independent units in the field had to assume an offensive doctrine, since their strategic weakness (lack of numbers and firepower) prevented them from being as effective defensively as larger formations of musketeers. Rather than relying on the musket, as rangers and Indian troops did (disregarding the musket's defensive characteristics), Bouquet trained his men to rely on coordinated and controlled movement and on the use of the bayonet. With the bayonet charge, Bouquet meant to exploit the Indians' vulnerability to frontal assaults. Without the sense of security provided by a strong defensive line, and without the benefit of strong discipline and repetitive drilling, Indian troops hardly ever risked their lives in order to hold their ground in the face of a bayonet charge. Only in rare cases, when encirclement prevented a safe retreat (as had happened at the Great Swamp Fight), did Indian troops attempt to defend themselves by defending their position. Thus, the bayonet charge became an effective tactic against Indian troops in small-scale isolated actions (that is, in the absence of larger infantry formations that could provide

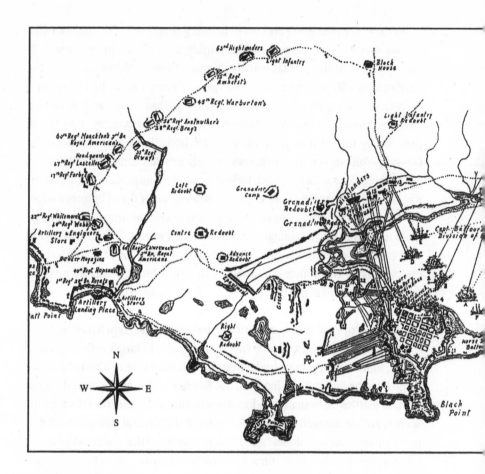

massive and deadly volleys of fire, thus preventing the need for risky frontal assaults).[95]

The early stages of the war did not inspire confidence in British armed forces. Yet by 1758, the army showed marked improvement. It was obvious that the British had found a formula for success against French and Indian troops. The fact that after one year of experience, no major body of troops suffered an ambush demonstrated how well British commanders adjusted to their new surroundings.[96] Yet, the army's achievements were not the result of a tactical or even a strategic reevaluation and adjustment. Rather, the army's swelling success rate stemmed from the sound logistical system that was built for it in London and in the administrative centers of British North America.

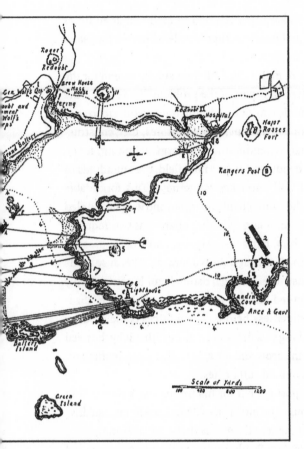

11. Light infantry deployment at Amherst's siege of Louisburg (reproduced from William Amherst, *Journal of William Amherst*, enfolded in back cover; courtesy of the Sterling Memorial Library, Yale University).

On his appointment as commander in chief, General Loudoun conducted a close study of the failed operations of his predecessors, Braddock and Shirley (especially the failure of the Oswego campaign). He concluded that British failures were primarily the products of a faulty supply system, rather than of misguided strategy or ineffective tactics. On Loudoun's recommendation, the government signed a long-term contract in March 1756 with the London trading firm of Baker, Kilby, and Baker for the supplying of all British troops in North America. The terms of the contract specified that one of the three contractors must be in North America at all times to handle the procurement and storage of provisions there. (To fulfill this requirement, Loudoun established three central depots in New York, Albany, and Halifax.)

The firm of Baker, Kilby, and Baker was obligated to maintain at all times enough provisions in these warehouses to supply at least twelve thousand men for six months.[97]

By creating a centralized, accountable, and efficient supply system for the army in America, Loudoun solved only part of the problem that retarded the progress of British forces in America. Military administrators still had to contend with transportation of supplies (rations, hospital stores, fuel, construction materials and tools, ordnance, ammunition, firearms, clothing, tents, and so forth) from the central depots to forces in the field, over hundreds of miles of unsettled, unmapped, and untracked wilderness. This formidable task required the services of skilled and reliable boatmen and wagon and sled drivers, as well as horses and oxen. A large number of artisans was required for the construction of ships, forts, barracks, wagons, and storehouses, as well as for the construction of roads through the wilderness.[98] Because roads and storehouses had to be constructed and garrisoned and because supply trains and working parties required military protection, a skeleton civilization had to be created in the wilderness before British forces could advance against Canada.[99] This undertaking was made even more difficult by the need for close cooperation between the army and navy, as well as slow, inefficient, and potentially uncooperative colonial authorities.

Creating a dependable transport system for his troops was a demanding and aggravating duty for Loudoun. The high prices demanded by civilian drivers and boatmen for their equipment and services drove the operating costs of the army to unacceptable heights. Furthermore, civilian drivers required armed escorts and could not be relied on to provide necessary services that were not specified in their personal contracts, such as fighting and constructing fortifications in times of hazard. In an attempt to liberate the army from its dependence on civilians, Loudoun created a military wagon corps. In 1757, the army built a central wagon center and stables at Albany. Wagons, horses, and oxen were purchased in bulk and drivers were supplied from the regiments. Loudoun estimated that this measure saved the army roughly seven thousand pounds annually.[100]

Under Loudoun's instruction and supervision, his quartermasters formed several companies of wagon drivers, boatmen, and artisans from within the ranks of the regiments.[101] Great care was taken to educate officers and civilians about the proper way to store and transport supplies, since on a number of occasions, provisions were spoiled en route to their destination, threatening the continuation of military operations on the front lines. Although Loudoun and his successors never achieved complete independence from civilian drivers and contractors, they did create a centralized and professional military transport system that could be relied upon to provide reliable, cost-effective, and timely service.[102]

During his short tenure as commander in chief, Loudoun made great strides in placing the army in America on a healthy footing, setting the stage for the conquest of the west and of Canada. The army's nearly continuous string of success from 1758 on testifies to his talent and ability as an administrator and a general. Yet Loudoun was no longer there to enjoy the fruits of his labor, due primarily to his failure at soliciting funds from hostile and unsympathetic colonial assemblies. His inflexibility and imperious demeanor made him an unpopular figure among provincial elites. His continuous attempts to streamline the bureaucracy and economy of the armed forces—to curb profiteering in the colonies—were in stark contrast to the administration of the popular William Shirley.[103] The creation of a centralized supply and transport system operated by the military, for example, deprived colonial merchants, artisans, and service-providers of valuable income. Moreover, Loudoun's endeavors to control and centralize the colonies' administrative and military activities were reminiscent of the policies instituted by Governors Andros and Dudley during the late seventeenth and early eighteenth centuries. Like Andros and Dudley, Loudoun triggered institutional and jurisdictional jealousy, as well as personal animosity, in provincial legislators and magistrates, and like them, he suffered for his commitment to the creation of regional military-administrative coherence. Provincial authorities opposed Loudoun at every turn, were slow to respond to his orders, and often denied him the funds and recruits that he demanded for regional defense and offensive operations.[104]

Nevertheless, despite the natural and political difficulties that beset him, Loudoun's administration was successful. During his nineteen months in command, British and provincial forces never experienced the supply shortages and backed wages that plagued the army under Shirley.[105] His administrative and logistical system overcame the vastness of the wilderness, inefficient and uncooperative provincial bureaucracies, and harassment of enemy troops to provide timely and secure transportation of men, matériel, and funds from Europe to America and from the eastern ports to the forces on the frontiers. In a relatively short time, he created a system that provided sustenance and security to over forty-four thousand soldiers.

William Pitt and Jeffery Amherst learned from Loudoun's harsh experience with colonial authorities. They took great care to deal respectfully and deferentially with the assemblies and to grease the wheels of provincial bureaucracy with generous subsidies for provincial forces. Inconsistent support from the provinces induced the British government to contribute a greater share of the army's expenses. In fact, most of the financing for provincial troops' wages and provisions came from the British treasury. Thus, whereas Britain's national debt rose from £76,000,000 to £132,000,000 during the war, provincial governments emerged from the war in a better financial state than they had entered it.[106]

Like Loudoun, Amherst recognized that military science involved not only recruitment, training, and the transportation of men, ordnance, and powder. And like Loudoun, his talents as a general were managerial, rather than tactical or inspirational. He immersed himself in the mundane details of the purchase and transportation of horses, wagons, drivers, foodstuff, bakers, butchers, and so forth. He spent significant time and money in the construction and repair of roads through the wilderness, as well as the construction and garrisoning of fortified supply depots along these routes.[107]

His methodical, conservative, and defensive-minded approach manifested itself repeatedly in 1759, when he captured Ticonderoga and Crown Point. When Ticonderoga's small and starving garrison lost hope for a successful defense, they destroyed the fort's stores and fortifications and fled to Crown Point (July 26, 1759). Rather than giving chase, Amherst rebuilt the fort and established secure supply routes. When he was informed by his rangers that Crown Point was evacuated in similar fashion (July 31), again Amherst refused to be drawn into pursuit. He consolidated his conquest by rebuilding Crown Point and constructing a road from Crown Point to Fort Number Four (in New Hampshire, on the Connecticut River). He also ordered the construction of a small flotilla to prevent the four French gunboats on Lake Champlain from attacking his forces.[108] These measures prevented Amherst from completing the conquest of Canada in 1759. But by consolidating British power in the northwest, Amherst simplified the 1760 campaign against Montreal, virtually guaranteeing success (and low casualty rates).[109]

The Montreal campaign testifies to the great achievements of Loudoun and Amherst as wilderness warriors, to their command of the territory and of enemy light troops. Although the capture of the city and of Canada was relatively serene and anticlimactic, it was one of the most difficult and impressive feats of the war. It was a logistical victory, however, rather than a tactical one. Amherst designed a three-pronged advance by three large British armies—from the west, south, and east—converging on Montreal. The operation was executed as planned, with all three armies (seventeen thousand troops in all) arriving at Montreal within forty-eight hours of one another, after crossing hundreds of miles of wilderness, dispersing enemy troops as they advanced. The British siege lasted two days, ending with the surrender of the city and of Canada on September 8, 1760.[110]

IT WAS THE GOOD FORTUNE of Jeffery Amherst and his generals to do battle in America at a time in which British command of the Atlantic was never seriously threatened. More than any other factor, the naval blockade was responsible for the success of British land forces against French and Indian troops during the Seven Years' War. William Pitt's navy maintained a steady pressure on French naval and military posts on the shores of France and the West Indies, preventing French authorities there from offering Canada the provisions and reinforcements it so desperately needed. Britain's blockade of the Gulf of Saint Lawrence provided a second, more effective line of defense for this purpose.

The blockade only exacerbated the acute economic advantage of Britain's American colonies over New France. The contemporary French historian Pierre Charlevoix's description from 1720 of this economic contrast alludes to the similarities between the Seven Years' War and the preceding wars of the colonists against their Indian neighbors. "There is . . . a wealth in New England . . . from which it appears those living there do not know how to draw profit; and in New France a poverty concealed under an air of ease in no way studied."[111] As in the earlier wars in America, attrition, rather than tactical victories, was the decisive factor in the eventual collapse of the Indians and the French.

The role of the British navy in the army's success in America cannot be overestimated. Nevertheless, significant developments in the administration of the army and its logistical support system played an equally important role. The chain of small forts and fortified trading posts along the northern frontier—created gradually during the 1730s and 1740s—led to the construction of more forts and, more important, of connecting roads to facilitate the secure movement of men and supplies. The defensive measures taken by Governors Andros and Dudley facilitated the gradual advance of English posts into Indian territory. Once an efficient supply and transport system was in place in London and America, this defensive system allowed the British Army to provide quick support for its forward positions against enemy attacks and the depredations of winter, helping to insure Loudoun's and Amherst's successes in the wilderness.

As spectacular as Braddock's defeat was, it was not characteristic of the true difficulties that hampered the army's performance in America. The Oswego debacle was more representative in this respect. Supply shortages and malnutrition made British troops vulnerable to attack and crippled their offensive operations during the first years of the war. Yet by 1758, the army had established an elaborate centralized logistical support system that enabled the British to capitalize on their natural advantages (numbers, resources, and control of the North Atlantic) and exploit French and Indian weaknesses.

In the west, success was harder to come by for the British. Since only a handful of advance posts had been created by colonial authorities prior to the outbreak of the Seven Years' War, British forces were forced to construct their own roads and build new forts as they advanced. Forbes's expedition against Fort Duquesne, for example, nearly failed because Forbes did not have an independent (that is, military) supply and transportation system like the one set up by Loudoun for forces on the northern frontier. The absence of secure roads and forts along the western frontier made it impossible at that time to form a sound and permanent logistical support system for operations in the west.[112]

British commanders at the start of the Seven Years' War encountered the same obstacles Dudley faced—logistical, strategic, and administrative incoherence on a regional level, and the amateurism of the officers and the men in colonial military establishments. Loudoun addressed the challenges of wilderness warfare with a timely and reliable supply of men and matériel to the front, enhanced British deployment on the frontiers, and the creation of a dependable corps of light troops. These forces provided intelligence, protected supply trains, and assisted infantry and artillery formations, allowing them the time to set up battles in which they could have a tactical—defensive—advantage. Mass deployment of men and matériel, made possible by centralized command and reliable logistical support, created a strong British presence on the frontiers, thus drawing enemy forces away from settlements in the interior and setting the stage for a European war in the American wilderness. It enabled British commanders to target strategically strong positions, forcing their opponents either to meet them on the battlefield at a disadvantage (as they did at the Plains of Abraham) or to forfeit the battle (as they did at Forts Duquesne and Ticonderoga). Thus, through conservative defensive deployment, British commanders gained decisive tactical advantages and avoided difficult battles.[113]

The French attempted to extricate themselves from this predicament by employing guerrilla tactics in an effort to draw the British into pursuits, away from their heavy formations and fortifications.[114] Whereas colonial forces in previous wars were vulnerable to such tactics, British commanders were more conservative and defensive-minded.

During all the colonial wars of the late seventeenth and eighteenth centuries, the French and Indians were driven by strategic and logistical *weakness* to employ the aggressive tactics of guerrilla warfare. Because they could not usually endure a long battle, their only chance of tactical success was to attack quickly, hoping to cause confusion and panic. Similarly, on a strategic level, they were too weak to survive a long, drawn-out war. Only the adoption of aggressive measures and offensive tactics offered them the prospect of a shortened war which they could possibly win. The British, in contrast, enjoyed a commanding numerical and economic superiority. Realizing that time was working against their enemies, they methodically consolidated their advantages rather than rushing into bold offensives that could have depleted their numbers. Leaving nothing to chance, British commanders made their positions invulnerable to enemy attack, conscientiously created a logistical support system for offensive expeditions, and then advanced carefully and in an orderly fashion on the weakened enemy.

Following Braddock's defeat, many Americans (including George Washington) felt that the French had prudently adjusted to war in America. They viewed the ever-popular actions of the rangers and the creation of British light-infantry units in the British Army as vital adjustments of Old World military practices to the unique conditions posed by America's battlefields. In fact, however, light troops had long been important participants on the battlefields of Europe, though only as auxiliaries since they did not and could not take the place of the large, heavy formations of the regular troops.[115]

In 1776, following the outbreak of the American War of Independence, Lewis Nicola wrote a military treatise "calculated for the Use of the Americans." Aware of the Americans' fascination with light troops, Nicola urged American authorities not to hang their hopes on the light infantry. He referred to Amherst's practice (inaugurated during his 1759 expeditions) of ordering his light infantry in a defensive line two-ranks deep ("the thin red line"), rather than in three ranks—the conventional formation for infantry battalions. In doing so, Amherst sacrificed volume of fire (for which the light infantry was not noted to begin with) for a longer frontage.[116] This deployment hampered the ability of enemy troops to flank the British formations. Although such formations had proved useful against light troops in the past (during the Seven Years' War), Nicola explained to his audience that sacrificing firepower for greater flexibility is a dangerous proposition when facing infantry formations drawn three-ranks deep.[117]

George Washington's conduct during the American War of Independence indicates that maturity and experience had altered his evaluation of European military conventions. Similarly, when dealing with the challenges of Indian warfare during the nineteenth century, the United States Army followed the example of Loudoun and Amherst, rather than Benjamin Church or Robert Rogers.[118]

LORD LOUDOUN's tenure in North America was difficult and strenuous. The negative press, personal ridicule, and political animosity directed at him by colonial authorities have created a lasting image of the general and his conduct in America: "he was haughty and blustering in peaceful communities, but very slow in facing the foe where actual danger and military duty called. . . . Loudoun was like the figure of St. George, painted on the sign boards—always on horseback but never riding on."[119] Charges of timidity and procrastination were leveled against General Amherst as well in 1759, when he chose to consolidate his control of Lake Champlain (through the construction of roads, fortifications, and a small fleet), rather than rush to Quebec to assist General Wolfe.[120]

Such disdain for and impatience with logistics and defensive preparation is characteristic of outsiders to the military profession; it explains the high opinion of Robert Rogers among civilians, in both Britain and the American colonies. Military professionals of high ranking, however, were compelled by the mantle of responsibility to take a more cautious approach. George Washington, for example, was transformed from a minor and relatively inexperienced officer to a commander in chief and sole protector of his nation's political existence. Consequently, his appreciation for "American tactics" was replaced by a cautious and defensive doctrine during the War of American Independence. Like General William Howe, Washington understood that his troops were his most valuable resource. Thus, like Howe, he was reluctant to squander them on bold but risky offensives that, at best, would have achieved nothing but a single tactical victory.

For British commanders, conducting military operations in America necessitated a higher degree of caution and conservatism than did combat in Europe. In European wars, the army's administrative and logistical center (London) was always close by. In America, however, commanders could not turn to London for additional funds, supplies, or reinforcements in times of sudden emergency. Thus, one tactical or logistical setback could scuttle an entire campaigning season, or even the entire war: "American conditions weighted the classic tension of warfare—boldness versus caution, surprise versus security—in favor of the cautious approach. Only bad luck could nullify the natural English superiority, and only rashness or faulty logistics could enhance the possibility of bad luck. . . . By 1758, the lessons of North American warfare were clear: leave nothing to chance, and take no chances."[121]

For this reason, Loudoun, Forbes, and Amherst "wasted" considerable time and money to protect against any twist of fate, secure their lines of communications, and consolidate their accomplishments. Although the army's progress in America was hampered by its dependence on supply trains, the high command did not abandon the idea of mass deployment. Rather, it invested in creating a flexible and far-reaching logistical support system, making the army an ever-present and irresistible force on all the frontiers and deep in enemy territory.

A QUICK GLANCE at the exact mathematical principles and geometrical schemes outlined in the military literature of the seventeenth and eighteenth centuries makes clear that contemporaries viewed the military profession as a *scientific* endeavor. Military men attempted to identify the factors that made one commander better than another, hoping to arrive at a formula that would eliminate chance and folly and insure consistent success. They believed that strict discipline and studious training could produce synchronized action and error-free execution, and that training-grounds performances could be replicated under fire, on the battlefield.

Some commanders and military theorists, however, convinced that this approach is unrealistic and doomed to failure (because of its disregard for the inconsistencies of human nature), have promoted the notion of the *art* of war. This view of warfare holds that the battlefield cannot be a place of rationality and order, and that dealing with chance and folly is one of the most important components of military command. Because this view of combat downplays the effectiveness of regimentation and emphasizes the role of irrational factors such as chance, genius, individual initiative and dedication, and patriotic enthusiasm, it has been linked with the ideological products of the Enlightenment—nationalism, democracy, and romanticism. In fact, the American Revolution and the Napoleonic wars did much to popularize this conception of warfare.

In America, the debate has been complicated by the notion of American exceptionalism and the enhanced military reputation of the American Indians.

The assumption that American conditions created a singular—even un-precedented—cultural reality in America has been continually debated since colonial times. On the military front of this debate, the favorable assessment of the Indians' soldiery has played a pivotal role in the exceptionalists' argument. American terrain and the Indians' irregular tactics, the argument goes, precluded the machinelike execution of European linear tactics. Thus, Indians were able to frustrate and overwhelm European forces, demonstrating to them that warfare in America dictated a reliance on Indian tactics.

Indian culture has been misrepresented for centuries as a means by which to critique European culture. When Indian societies are analyzed on their own terms, however, rather than as an ideological alternative to Western culture, a more realistic image emerges. By the late seventeenth and early eighteenth centuries, Indian tribes in the northeast had been severely weakened by epidemics. In their military engagements with Europeans, they were further handicapped by their relative poverty and by the absence of stable bureaucracies and political unity. On a logistical and strategic level, therefore, Indian tribes did not have the material, social, and political resources to compete with their European rivals. On a tactical level as well, however, they were forced to compete on unequal terms.

Although warfare figured prominently in Indian culture, Indian warriors did not enjoy the benefits offered by an organized and established state. Even if one assumes that Indians innately possessed greater physical strength and stamina than Europeans, it is unrealistic to expect these qualities to counteract the disciplined and coordinated action of large European formations. Unlike Europeans troops, Indians did not benefit from heavy investment in their martial education, extensive and disciplined training in large formations, standardized weaponry, and professional literature. Moreover, their offensive tactics prevented them from capitalizing on the defensive characteristics of the European weapons that they had adopted.

The first generation of colonial commanders—experienced European commanders, such as John Underhill and John Mason—were not impressed by the Indians' effectiveness in combat; nor were the British commanders who fought in North America during the Seven Years' War. Moreover, despite successful Indian attacks during the late seventeenth and early eighteenth centuries, English military establishments were not moved to adopt Indian tactics or to rely on Indian troops. Throughout the colonial era, English authorities did seek Indian alliances, but the evidence suggests that these alliances were a strategic, rather than tactical, asset.[1] The primary benefit these alliances offered was not Indian warriors to fight alongside the English. Rather, it was peaceful neighbors, helpful scouts, and intelligence.

The military education and conduct of English armed forces throughout the colonial era indicate that exposure to Indian tactics did not lead to a doctrinal transformation or reevaluation. From the battles of First Encounter and Mystic to the battle of the Plains of Abraham, English forces sought to take the strategic offensive but to rely on the strength and security of the tactical defense (forcing the enemy to attack at a disadvantage or withdraw). It is apparent, however, that during the wars of the late seventeenth and early eighteenth centuries, the amateurism of the colonies' military establishments led to a declining ability of colonial commanders to execute this conservative plan. Lacking practical experience in combat, formal training in command, and strict authority over their men, they repeatedly failed to keep up their guard and to maintain unit integrity and fire discipline. Thus, unlike the professional commanders of the first generation and those of the Seven Years' War, they were often surprised or tricked into assuming an offensive role.

The English owed their victories in these wars not to the tactical effectiveness of their fighting forces against Indian troops but to their commitment to a campaign of attrition against Indian agricultural fields, grain stores, and fisheries. In fact, the tactical *ineffectiveness* of colonial forces in these wars led colonial officials to seek a closer military cooperation with imperial administrators and professional British troops.

Throughout the colonial era, both colonial and British forces repeatedly demonstrated—whenever they maintained a defensive stance—that American terrain and the Indians' fighting methods did not make conventional European tactics obsolete. Because defensive tactics proved effective against Indian forces, colonial and British military authorities were never moved by the likes of Benjamin Church and Robert Rogers to doubt the value of European military conventions. Church and Rogers did, however, enjoy great popularity in the popular press.[2] Although newspaper stories and their own narratives overstated the importance and achievements of their combat missions, Church and Rogers captured the public's imagination. They promoted the concept of the art of war and fostered among outsiders to the military profession the romantic belief that in America, irregular terrain and the irregular tactics of the enemy rendered the scientific principles of European warfare invalid.

The consistent progress of British forces during the Seven Years' War belied this belief. During the war, British administrators demonstrated that even if combat is more an art than a science, wars are governed by universal and timeless scientific principles, "applicable to all cases, and differing only in point of numbers."[3] Aware that wars are administrative and organizational contests, rather than merely a series of tactical confrontations, British administrators slowly built a naval and military infrastructure in North America, setting the stage for an effective naval blockade and mass deployment of land forces on the frontiers. Commanders countered the enemy's speed and guerrilla tactics by establishing effective communications between units and by strong defensive deployment. They secured their positions by providing the means for effective supply and relief—constructing roads through the wilderness, securing them with strong garrisons, clearing forests along these routes, protecting supply trains, and establishing front-line depots.

Consistent improvement in the army's state of preparedness went hand in hand with the organization of supplies, men, and procedures, ensuring that British administrative and military posts were always well protected against enemy assaults. Similarly, forces in the field conducted themselves as a mobile fortresses. Mass deployment and defensive preparations, therefore, forced enemy forces into costly and fruitless attacks on strong or fortified positions. Whether enemy troops chose to launch such assaults or withdraw from these battles, this strategy ensured that the war would be a lengthy one. Thus, as the colonies had done in previous wars, Britain exploited the enemy's relative poverty and brought its logistical superiority to bear against the French and their Indian allies. In time, Canada and the west were conquered not through tactical brilliance but through a systematic campaign of attrition.

In America, as in Europe, there were commanders who lacked the patience for such methodical campaigning. Only a few of these offensive-minded commanders were successful, though all suffered high casualty rates. Most military men, however, preferred "to conquer the enemy with famine than with yron," realizing that logistical superiority, mass deployment, and defensive preparations enabled them to avoid difficult battles "in the victory of which, fortune may doe much more than valour."[4] Thus, they minimized the opportunities in which chance and other unpredictable factors could play an adverse role. Consequently, they seldom had to be bold and aggressive, choosing instead to deploy defensively in anticipation of enemy attacks.[5]

British achievements in the northeast during the Seven Years' War high-lighted the shortcomings of colonial armed forces in previous generations (including amateurism and poor discipline, defensive laxness, lack of atten-tion to mundane details, insufficient funding, logistical lack of preparedness, and administrative fragmentation).[6] These structural deficiencies made it difficult for provincial troops to commit themselves to the tactical defense, since maintaining formation in combat situations required patience, disci-pline, and faith (all of which were usually the product of repetitive drilling, strict discipline, and experience).[7] Nevertheless, when colonial troops were able or were forced to resist the impulse to break formation, even they could effectively repel Indian assaults. These episodes demonstrated that tight formations of musketeers made effective military machines, enabling small units to repel larger attacking forces.[8] Understanding that massed fire max-imized the effectiveness of projectile weapons—smoothbore firearms in particular—the colonies' military and political leadership did not encourage officers to rely on irregular tactics. Rather, it consistently adhered to the time-tested conventions of European warfare.

The first battles of the American War of Independence—Lexington and Concord and Bunker Hill—illustrate this point. Although few historians would argue that such tactical victories were responsible for the American victory in the war—most look to the naval war, imperial economics, and logistics to explain the failures of the British army and the loss of the Amer-ican colonies—these two battles remain the cornerstones of an American mythology of military prowess. The battle of Lexington and Concord, in particular, has been used to illustrate the superiority of American settlers over the redcoats in wilderness warfare. It has been presented as a contest be-tween the old and the new, the past and the future. A closer analysis reveals, however, that both British defeats resulted not from the shortcomings of European tactics but from a failure to execute the fundamentals of Euro-pean warfare.

Like Braddock's debacle at the Monongahela, the defeat along the Lexing-ton road should be viewed as a failure of command. Lieutenant Colonel Smith and Lord Percy, the British commanders on the march from Concord to Charlestown, could hardly have known that they were involved in a war. Even after the first shots were fired on the Lexington green, the general uprising was a surprise. Since Smith's assignment was not planned as a military cam-paign, his force was not outfitted for intense combat; indeed, the fact that the redcoats did not have a supply train or carry reserves of ammunition played a crucial role in the battle). Thus, being vastly outnumbered once the fighting began in earnest, the redcoats found themselves out of position and ill-equipped to effectively defend themselves. Even when British flanking parties were able to clear and hold the high ground commanding the road, their efforts were in vain, since the main force on the road was out of control—having already suffered significant casualties and being dangerously low on ammunition, the British column outran its flankers in panic. By ignoring officers' pleas for calm, the redcoats failed to take advantage of the protection offered by these flanking parties and exposed themselves to American fire. Moreover, the main force was not there to support the flankers when they were attacked.[9]

American forces again engaged the British from a position of strength in the battle of Bunker Hill. Whereas the battle of Lexington and Concord was an unscripted affair, the battle of Bunker Hill was executed by both sides according to a preconceived plan. When formulating a battle plan, the American high command chose to take the tactical *defense*. The British, in contrast, disregarded the maxims of European warfare and launched frontal assaults on the strong American positions. Just as the French had done at Ticonderoga in 1758, the Americans waited until the British were within effective musket range and then decimated them with devastating volleys of fire.

The success of American forces in the early battles of the American Revolution do not warrant a favorable assessment of "American tactics." Like earlier colonial wars, the American War of Independence consistently demonstrated the wisdom and tactical efficacy of European military conventions. Thus, despite the American victory in the war, the military leadership of the United States did not formulate a uniquely American military doctrine for the republic's armed forces. Rather, it looked to Europe for guidance in the science of warfare and the art of combat.

NOTES /

INTRODUCTION

1 Williams, *American Indian in Western Legal Thought*, 280 n. 8.

2 Drake, *King Philip's War*, 2, 133, 151, 153; Whisker, *American Colonial Militia*, 1:1; Keeley, *War before Civilization*, 74–75; Malone, *Skulking Way of War*, 59–60, 87–88, 90–98, 100; Bourne, *Red King's Rebellion*, 175, 181–84, 188–89; Selesky, *War and Society*, 10; Starkey, *European and Native American Warfare*, 2–4, 53, 71–82, 94–96; Ferling, "New England Soldier"; Axtell, *European and the Indian*, 139–41, 146–47, 299–302; Leach, *Arms for Empire*, 60–61; idem, *Flintlock*, 70–71; Simpson and Mary Simpson, "Introduction," in Church, *Diary*, 30; Smith, *Treatise*, 9–12.

3 The distinction between an army's tactical role and a society's political role in relation to its neighbors is crucial. Tactics relate strictly to battlefield conduct. Thus, in any military contest, the aggressor—the side that promoted antagonism, sought armed conflict, or even launched the first strike—can employ either offensive or defensive tactics. The other side, as well, is not compelled by its defensive role in the political arena to adopt a defensive role on the battlefield.

4 The term *strategy* refers to the planning of a diplomatic, political, and military course of action, the formulation of a tactical doctrine, and the deployment of forces in accordance with that doctrine. Logistics involve the mobilization and movement of men and materiel (military equipment). Whereas strategy and logistics involve preparations for battles, the term *tactics* refers to actual combat—the method by which a military force attempts to accomplish its mission on the field, during a battle.

5 Peter Paret argues that this historiographical position has been closely linked with American patriotism and European liberalism. "Colonial Experience," 366.

6 Segal and Stineback, *Puritans, Indians, and Manifest Destiny*, 185, 219.

7 Ferling, *Wilderness of Miseries*, 199. Like *Puritans, Indians, and Manifest Destiny*, both *Manitou and Providence* and *Wilderness of Miseries* are militant in their denunciation of the English settlers. Other analyses of the process of colonization suggest that the gradual conquest of North

America was a nuanced affair, governed more often by practical and pragmatic considerations than by religious or racial fanaticism. While Segal and Stineback, Salisbury, and Ferling emphasize the differences between twentieth-century Americans and the colonists, authors such as Karen Kupperman and Richard White offer a more recognizable image of the settlers. Through the narratives of Kupperman and White, seventeenth and eighteenth-century Americans seem not monstrous but *human*, even if not particularly humane.

8 Colonists' concerns about the "Indianization" of European warfare are also presented by Axtell (*European and the Indian*, 140–47, 275–84) and by Johnson ("Search for a Usable Indian").

9 Most proponents of the Americanization thesis focus on King Philip's War, the most devastating and traumatic military contest in the history of colonial New England. Douglas Edward Leach's *Flintlock Tomahawk* is still considered the most authoritative account of the war and its battles, although Eric Schultz and Michael Tougias (*King Philip's War*), Russel Bourne (*Red King's Rebellion*), and James Drake (*King Philip's War*) provide interesting narratives of the conflict.

10 The most exhaustive treatment of the Seven Years' War in North America is provided by Fred Anderson in *Crucible of War*.

CHAPTER ONE

1 Hilaire Belloc, quoted in Turney-High, *Practice of Primitive War*.

2 It is no surprise, therefore, that European powers so often met on the plains of the Netherlands for their military conflicts. Forcing an opposing army to fight on unfavorable terrain was practically impossible because the formations were so massive. Furthermore, setting an army in formation was such a lengthy and cumbersome undertaking that it was virtually impossible to organize quickly for an attack and surprise the enemy. More often than not, major battles occurred at a time and place convenient for both sides.

3 Peterson, *Encyclopedia of Firearms*, 68; Hamilton, *French and Indian Wars*, 82–86. For the purpose of this work, the terms *flintlock* and *snaphance* are interchangeable, as are the English lock, the dog lock, and the "true" flintlock. The distinctions between these fairly similar mechanisms are mostly modern. Peterson, *Arms and Armor*, 26.

4 Elton, *Compleat Body of the Art Military*, 2.

5 Malone, "English and Indian," 124.

6 Marlborough's offensive success ought to be attributed, to a large extent, to his understanding of the tactical effectiveness of light artillery against infantry. In addition to the regular cannon batteries, Marlborough supplied every battalion with two light guns (1.5 to 3 pounders). Being very mobile, these were advanced to the front as the offensive line progressed. Firing grapeshot and canister at close range transformed these guns into devastatingly effective offensive assets.

7 French, "Arms and Military."

8 Shelley, *John Underhill*, 131; Ellis, "Life of John Mason," 339; Adams, *History of Ancient Wethersfield*, 73–74; Trumbull, 1, 4, 15, 28, 74, 125; Shurtleff, *Records of the Governor* (1853–54), 1, 84, 85, 93, 198; Pulsifer, *Records of the Colony* (1855–61), 6, 11, 171.

9 Banks, *History of Martha's Vineyard* 295–96; Labaree, *Royal Instructions*, 392–93; Morton, "Origins of American Military Policy," 79; Eames, "Rustic Warriors," 375–476; Sharp, "New England Trainbands," 167–68, 189–95; Malone, *Skulking Way of War*, 54–55; Gildrie, "Defiance, Diversion, and the Exercise of Arms," 54.

10 Malone, "English and Indian," 91; idem, *Skulking Way of War*, 35.

11 Contemporary military manuals and treatises list between 33 and 51 separate stages and motions in this procedure. Ward, *Animadversions*, 215–21; French, "Arms and Military," 15.

12 For example, the matchlock musket was useless in damp, rainy, and windy weather since the serpentine had to remain lit at all times. This was not a major problem on the battlefields of Europe, where combat took place only during "the season" (that is, the spring and summer months). In America, however, the colonists' enemies threatened them year-round. Furthermore, because of the musket's size, weight, and delicacy, it was more suited to stationary or slow-moving troops. The Indians' reliance on stealth and surprise attacks made the flintlock a much more effective weapon. It ignited automatically (a musketeer could, therefore, fire a first shot at a moment's notice); it did not require a stand, enabling a musketeer to fire quickly in any direction; and because of its shorter and simpler loading procedure (twenty-six motions, compared with the matchlock's forty-four), the flintlock produced more than twice the firepower of the matchlock. The flintlock also had a more reliable firing mechanism (especially in the hands of unskilled troops)—the misfire rate fell from 50 to 33 percent with the transition from matchlocks to flintlocks. Nosworthy, *Anatomy of Victory*, 40. Furthermore, the matchlock's burning serpentine made it a relatively ineffective firearm in an ambush. The adoption of the flintlock was also encouraged by the needs of private citizens. Simpler, quicker, and more accurate, the flintlock was much more suitable for hunting, as well as home defense (especially since it was light enough to be operated by women and adolescents). Its only drawback was its price.

13 Peterson, *Arms and Armor*, 44–46; Malone, "English and Indian," 92–94. A similar policy was adopted in Virginia following the Jamestown massacre of 1622. Successful Indian attacks against the settlers in Virginia in 1622, as in New England in 1675–76, very clearly demonstrated the deficiencies of the matchlock musket.

14 Peterson, "Military Equipment," 200–201; Malone, "English and Indian," 98. The full-pike was fourteen to sixteen feet long; the half-pike was six to ten feet long.

15 A leather strap from which hung wooden cylinders containing one complete musket charge.

16 Shurtleff, *Records of the Governor* (1968), 1:125. When colonial armed forces could not furnish soldiers with a sufficient number of muskets, "unarmed" troops were formed into pike companies as late as King Philip's War. Another piece of European military equipment that proved to be disappointing in New England was the body armor. By the end of the Pequot War, the corselet (back and breast plates), tasses (thigh guards), thule (loin guard), and gorget (neck guard) were mostly discarded. Buff coats of leather or quilted cloth were lighter and less restrictive, while providing effective protection against Indian arrows. Gardiner, *Lion Gardiner*, 14, 55; Peterson, *Arms and Armor*, 44–46, 79–81; Malone, "English and Indian," 99–103.

CHAPTER TWO

1   Hodges, *Apprenticeship of Washington*, 121.

2   Shelley, *John Underhill*, 131; Ellis, "Life of John Mason," 339; Adams, *History of Ancient Wethersfield*, 73–74; Trumbull, *Public Records of the Colony of Connecticut*, 1, 4, 15, 28, 74, 125; Shurtleff, *Records of the Governor* (1853–54), 1, 84, 85, 93, 198; Pulsifer, *Records of the Colony*, 6, 11, 171.

3   Erwin, "Captain Myles Standish's Military Role," 2; Hodges, *Apprenticeship of Washington*, 100.

4   Parker, *Discoverers and Pioneers*, 278–79.

5   Physically, Miles Standish was quite unimpressive. Thomas Morton, of Merrimount, referred to him as "captaine shrimpe." Morton, *New English Canaan*, 285. An Indian admirer from Wessagusett commented that Standish was "a great captain, yet he was but a little man." Winslow, *Good Nevves*, 43.

6   Ellis, "Life of John Mason," 314–15; Sylvester, *Indian Wars of New England*, 1:245, n.1; Gardiner, *Lion Gardiner*, 46–47.

7   Mason also served Dorchester as a representative in the Massachusetts General Court in 1634–35. In Boston (at Castle Island) Mason served with captains Underhill, Patrick, Trask, and Turner and Lieutenants Feaks and Morris. Ellis, "Life of John Mason," 319–21.

8   Gardiner, *Lion Gardiner*, 46–47, 49.

9   The new colony, Connecticut, was meant to serve as a haven for John Winthrop Jr.'s gentlemen backers from England (including Lord Say and Seal, and Lord Brooke), in case Charles I implemented his "tyrannical designs" for England. Gardiner, *Lion Gardiner*, 50–51.

10   In his family Bible, Lion Gardiner noted that his son, David, held the distinction of being the first white child born in Connecticut (April 29, 1635). Ellis, "Life of John Mason," 22, n.1.

11   Bradford, *History of Plymouth Plantation*, 1:57.

12   Porter, *Inconstant Savage*, 424. There were a number of dangerous and action-packed encounters between pilgrims and wolves during the first year after settlement. Winslow, *Relation or Iournall*, 29.

13   Their first success at fishing occurred in January 1621: "one of the saylers found alive upon the shore an Hering." Winslow, *Relation or Iournall*, 26. The settlers' attempts at hunting and farming were as pathetic and discouraging.

14   Ibid., 29.

15   In all, the Indian population in New England in the mid-seventeenth century is estimated at more than eighteen thousand. As late as 1670, Connecticut's settler population numbered a mere ninety-five hundred (including slaves)—two colonists per square mile. Porter, *Inconstant Savage*, 429; Garvan, *Architecture and Town Planning*, 2–3. These figures, especially for the Indian population, are rough estimates. The estimates given by Porter and Garvan are reasonable but in no way uncontested.

16   Horowitz, *First Frontier*, 21.

17   Porter, *Inconstant Savage*, 429; Abbott, *Miles Standish*, 111. The hostility of the coastal Indians to the settlers was the result of their previous dealings with white slave traders. Especially

traumatic for them were the slaving expeditions of the notorious Captain Hunt (an associate of captain John Smith of Virginia). In one of these expeditions, Squanto—who would later become a friend and ally of the Plymouth settlers—was kidnapped and sold as a slave in Spain. Soon after, in 1614, a ship owned by Sir Ferdinando Gorges was attacked by bands of New England Indians. The ship's captain (Hobson) was able to escape. He and his crew returned to England "bringing nothing back with them but the News of their bad success, and that there was a War broke out between the English, and the Indians." The Indians' "traitorous and deceitful" treatment of Captain Hobson was well publicized in England long before the pilgrims set sail for America. Mather, *Early History*, 53–56, 57.

18 Bradford, *Bradford's History*, 102–3; see also ibid., 98, 100–102; Porter, *Inconstant Savage*, 424–26; Winslow, *Relation or Iournall*, 6–7, 11–12, 18–19; Hodges, *Apprenticeship of Washington*, 112.

19 Abbott, *Miles Standish*, 62; Hodges, *Apprenticeship of Washington*, 112.

20 Winslow, *Relation or Iournall*, 18–19; Bradford, *Bradford's History*, 103. My emphasis.

21 The men at the boat had no fire to light their matchlocks. A soldier from the other group carried a burning log from the campfire to them. Abbott, *Miles Standish*, 63.

22 Bradford, *Bradford's History*, 103. The arrows fired at the European company were mostly ineffective, thanks to the Europeans' wooden barricade and their coats of mail. There were no English casualties.

23 Winslow, *Relation or Iournall*, 19.

24 *Bradford's History*, 103.

25 In summer 1621, Squanto and Hobomac (Massasoit's war captain) were kidnapped by Corbitant, a sachem of a smaller Wampanoag band allied with the Narragansetts against Massasoit. To rescue Squanto and honor the alliance with Massasoit, Governor William Bradford ordered Captain Standish to launch an attack against Corbitant. Standish launched a minor attack on Nemasket, Corbitant's residence, in which three Indians were injured (they were taken to Plymouth where they were treated by the surgeon Samuel Fuller). Corbitant himself escaped but soon after arrived at Plymouth to sign a peace treaty with his brother and his European allies. Bradford, *Bradford's History*, 119–20; Heath, *Mourt's Relation*, 73–75; Vaughan, *New England Frontier*, 76; Abbott, *Miles Standish*, 153.

26 Hubbard, *Present State of New England*, 7; Heath, *Mourt's Relation*, 56–57. The treaty specified that no Indian shall injure the English; that no Indian shall visit Plymouth carrying a weapon; that no Englishman shall visit the Indians carrying weapons; that an offending Indian will be punished by the English authorities; that stolen English goods will be returned; that stolen Indian goods will be returned; that the English and Massasoit will help each other in war; and that Massasoit inform his allies of his alliance with the English.

27 Vaughan, *New England Frontier*, 77.

28 Porter, *Inconstant Savage*, 431.

29 Morton, *New Englands Memoriall*, 41.

30 The new settlers were not at all welcome by the original pilgrims. Porter, *Inconstant Savage*, 501.

31 Ibid.; Morton, *New Englands Memoriall*, 41.

32 Winslow, *Good Nevves*, 43.

33 Morton, *New Englands Memoriall*, 41–43; Porter, *Inconstant Savage*, 501–2; Winslow, *Good Nevves*, 43–44. When John Robinson, the legendary former pastor of the Plymouth settlers, received news of this massacre, he wrote Governor Bradford a sharp rebuke: "Concerning the killing of those poor Indians. . . . Oh how happy a thing it had been if you had converted some before killing any!" Robinson argued that the Indians were provoked to violence by the "heathenish Christians" of Weymouth. He saw no need of killing so many and observed that the excess of violence resulted not from professional and objective considerations but "merely from a human spirit." As for Miles Standish, Robinson suggested that he "may be wanting that tenderness of the life of man (made after God's image) which is meet." Salisbury, *Manitou and Providence*, 134; Porter, *Inconstant Savage*, 501.

34 Winslow, *Good Nevves*, 43–44; Hodges, *Apprenticeship of Washington*, 132–33; Salisbury, *Manitou and Providence*, 130.

35 The Narragansetts were the least affected by the European epidemics that decimated their enemies in New England earlier in the century.

36 Cannonicus sent the colonists five arrows bound with rattle-snake skin. After the meaning of this act was explained to the settlers, Governor Bradford sent back the snake skin filled with gun powder. Cannonicus feared that the snake skin contained a secret and fatal charm for his destruction. He refused to touch it, destroy it, or have it in his home. It was moved from place to place until, eventually, it found its way back to Plymouth. Abbott, *Miles Standish*, 181–82.

37 Winslow, *Good Nevves*, 36.

38 Bradford, *Bradford's History*, 97, 110–11; Abbott, *Miles Standish*, 182; James, *Three Visitors*, 24; Winslow, *Good Nevves*, 36.

39 One of the companies was designated as a fire brigade. In case a fire broke out during an attack, these specialists were to surround the burning building, with their backs to the fire, in order to defend the civilian fire fighters from an Indian attack. Winslow, *Good Nevves*, 36; Erwin, "Captain Miles Standish's Military Role," 5.

40 Winslow, *Good Nevves*, 37; see also Morton, *New Englands Memoriall*, 37. The settlers' fears of an Indian attack intensified in 1622 also because in November 1621 the settlement received a shipment of European supplies (aboard the *Fortune*). Winslow was concerned that these supplies might attract Indian raids.

41 The fact that this very modest fort took ten months to complete indicates just how weak and undermanned the settlers were. Winslow, *Good Nevves*, 42.

42 Parker, *Discoverers and Pioneers*, 295; see also James, *Three Visitors*, 11, 76–77; Steele, *Warpaths*, 87; Bradford, *Bradford's History*, 138–39; Morton, *New Englands Memoriall*, 37.

43 Malone, "English and Indian," 103.

44 Ibid.

45 Davis, *Records of the Town of Plymouth*, 1:18. This type of communication system often served the settlers very effectively. Winthrop, *Winthrop's Journal*, 80–81.

46 Vaughan, *New England Frontier*, 97. Plymouth's European population in 1637 was roughly 600. The number of Europeans in New England at the time is estimated at 15,000 to 20,000.

47 Ibid., 97, 103.

48 Shelley, John Underhill, 108–16. As early as 1629, for example, the Massachusetts Bay Company commissioned John Winthrop Jr. (Governor Winthrop's son, and the future governor of Connecticut) to survey the architectural and military plans of the impressive fortress at Harwich, England. In a letter to Governor Winthrop, Isaac Johnson, one of the members of the company's informal inner cabinet, explained: "I hope he will sufficiently inform himself of the dimensions of the Fort and all things about it, as, likewise, of what several materials, what kind earth or wood the several parts are framed of. It is likely he may enquire of some thereabouts, labourers, or artificers or artists, that helped make it. Let him take special notice of the thickness of the walks, where the ordnance is laid forth, and how long our ordnance had need to be in that regard, and send what speedy word may be with conveniency." Ibid., 116.

49 The General Court repeatedly issued legislation and exhortations regarding the importance of enforcing previous legislation regarding nightly watches. This suggests that vigilance tended to lag during periods of relative peace. Shurtleff, Records of the Governor (1968), 1:85, 190.

50 In summer 1631 the court designated one day a month as general training day. Captains were instructed to perform these large-scale maneuvers close to neighboring Indian villages in order to deter and impress. De Forest, Captain John Underhill, 9; Vaughan, New England Primer, 101–2. The towns were permitted to elect their own officers, to which captains Underhill and Patrick protested fiercely (Underhill and Patrick were commissioned as instructors to the colony's militias). De Forest, Captain John Underhill, 10–11.

51 Similar legislation was enacted by the Connecticut General Court soon after its establishment. Trumbull, Public Records of the Colony of Connecticut, 1:1, 4, 15, 28, 74, 79, 125; Adams, History of Ancient Wethersfield, 73–74; Ellis, "Life of John Mason," 339.

52 Shurtleff, Records of the Governor 1:85; Vaughan, New England Primer, 101–2.

53 Vaughan, New England Primer, 103.

54 The Massachusetts Bay Company had greater authority in New England than did the New England Company. Shurtleff, Records of the Governor, 1:386–94; Vaughan, New England Primer, 95–96.

55 Ellis, "Life of John Mason," 339. Like the ancient Philistines (with respect to the Judaeans), the English immigrants in New England were determined to deny the Indians access to iron and steel: "Forasmuch as the Indeans growe insolent and combyne theselues togather, being suspect to prpare for warr, It is Ordered, that no Smith wthin these libertys shall doe any worke for them, nor any prson wthin these libertys shall trade any Instrument or matter made of iron or steele wth them." Trumbull, Public Records of the Colony of Connecticut, 74. In 1628, the six plantations in the Boston Bay area, and other small plantations along the coast, initiated and participated in the military campaign of Plymouth against Thomas Morton's settlement of Merrymount. As frontier settlements, they were more vulnerable to Indian attack because of their size and location. These communities urged Governor William Bradford to lead their men into battle against Morton because he sold arms to their Indian neighbors and even instructed them in the repair of firearms (in violation of a royal proclamation by King James). Vaughan, New England Primer, 90–91.

56 Vaughan, New England Primer, 127–28.

57 Ibid.; Hubbard, *Present State of New England*, 118.

58 Underhill recounts the assault on the shore: "Myself received an arrow through my coat sleeve, a second against my helmet on the forehead; so as if God in his providence had not moved the heart of my wife to persuade me to carry it along with me, (which I was unwilling to do), I had been slain. Give me leave to observe two things from hence; first, when the hour of death is not yet come, you see God useth weak means to keep his purpose unviolated; secondly, let no man despise advice and counsel of his wife, though she be a woman." Underhill, "Nevves from America," 52.

59 Captain Turner approached the swamp. Locating a band of Indians, he charged. The assault was very quickly beaten back when Turner was shot. Ibid., 53–54. Turner was only slightly wounded, however. The English suffered no fatalities, compared with roughly forty Indian fatalities (according to Underhill's somewhat-unreliable account).

60 Ibid.; Sylvester, *Indian Wars*, 228–29, n. 2. The failure of the Block Island mission is attributed by some (e.g., De Forest, *Captain John Underhill*, 16) to the fact that Endicott was a political nomination and militarily inexperienced.

61 Gardiner, *Lion Gardiner*, 11. Being a European veteran and a "master of works of fortification," Gardiner knew that against a fortified force, starvation was usually more prudent a policy than violence.

62 The number of casualties on both sides was very small. Underhill, "Nevves from America," 60.

63 Gardiner, *Lion Gardiner*, 12–13; Mather, *Early History*, 164; Vincent, "A True Relation," 100.

64 Vincent, "A True Relation," 100.

65 Adams, *History of Ancient Wethersfield*, 63–64; Mason, "Brief History," 18; Vaughan, *New England Primer*, 133.

66 Mason was promoted to the rank of major.

67 Vaughan, *New England Primer*, 139; Hubbard, *Present State of New England*, 122. Ever since December 13, 1636, the Bay Colony's military establishment had consisted of three regiments—East (under Colonel John Winthrop Sr. and Lieutenant Colonel Thomas Dudley), North (Colonel John Hayes and Lieutenant Colonel Roger Harlakenden), and South (Colonel John Endicott and Lieutenant Colonel John Winthrop Jr.). Captains Traske, Patrick, and Underhill, respectively, were appointed as mustermasters of the three regiments. Shurtleff, *Records of the Governor* 1:186–87. It is clear that John Underhill was displeased with his position and rank, Drilling and training other people's forces, without a command of his own. In a 1637 letter to Governor Henry Vane he vented his frustrations and delivered a thinly veiled threat: "Vpon whatt juste grounde yow should be soe fearefull [to] aduance me, I knowe note, when as yow haue had so many pledges of my fidelity. . . . I hope [G]od will subdew me to his will: yett this I say, that such [treatment] of officers in forraine parts hath soe farre subuerted some of them, as to cause them turne publique rebbels againste theire state & kingdome." De Forest, *Captain John Underhill*, 18. Underhill's sound reasoning must have impressed the authorities; later that year he was appointed captain of the Boston militia company.

68 With Underhill and his twenty men already there, Mason sent away twenty of his men to reinforce their settlements. Mason, "Brief History," 20.

69   Gardiner, *Lion Gardiner*, 16; see also "Brief History," Mason, 20.

70   Gardiner demanded the same test of goodwill from a group of Long Island Indians who requested his permission to come to Connecticut to trade with the English. To prove that they were not in conspiracy with the Pequots, the Indians were required to kill a number of the Pequots and deliver their heads to fort Saybrook. On the receipt of twelve heads, lieutenant Gardiner gave the Indians his permission to visit and trade in Connecticut. Gardiner, *Lion Gardiner*, 17.

71   The captive, Kiswas, had lived in Fort Saybrook for years and acted as an interpreter for Lieutenant Gardiner. With the outbreak of hostilities, however, he joined the Pequot sachem Sassacus as a guide. Mason and Gardiner permitted Uncas to treat the captive in the Indian manner: Kiswas was tortured and then torn limb from limb. John Underhill ended his misery with his pistol. Ellis, "Life of John Mason," 372–73; Vaughan, *New England Primer*, 141; Vincent, "A True Relation," 101.

72   Mason, "Brief History," 21.

73   Ibid., 22.

74   The force that set out toward Mystic numbered seventy-seven Englishmen (a small party of Englishmen were left behind to sail back west and rejoin the company at Pequot Harbor), sixty Mohegans, and roughly two hundred Narragansetts.

75   Perhaps Mason feared that delaying the attack would compromise the element of surprise. Hubbard, *Present State of New England*, 123–24; Vaughan, *New England Primer*, 374, n. 45; Ellis, "Life of John Mason," 376.

76   Trumbull, *Compendium*, 51–52; Ellis, "Life of John Mason," 379.

77   Underhill, "Nevves from America," 79, 81; see also Benjamin Trumbull, *A Compendium*, 22–23, 52–53.

78   With twenty casualties, only forty fit Englishmen were left to give fire. Ellis, "Life of John Mason," 386.

79   Underhill, "Nevves from America," 81; see also Trumbull, *Compendium*, 53–54.

80   Mason, "Life of John Mason," 32; see also Morton, *New England Canaan*, 102; Lewis, *History of the Pequot War*, 13.

81   Underhill, "Nevves from America," 82; see also Ellis, "Life of John Mason," 387–88; Sylvester, *Indian Wars*, 1:277–80.

82   The fact that he was also an adulterer complicated his struggle to preserve his political and social status. De Forest, *Captain John Underhill*, 24–25.

83   Fred Anderson argues that the colonial military establishments were "in fact a confederation of tiny war bands, bound together less by the formal relationships of command than by organic networks of kinship and personal loyalties." Anderson, *People's Army*, 48. John Underhill and his subordinates may serve as an example of this: captain Underhill's second lieutenant (Richard Morris), third lieutenant (Edward Gibbons), three sergeants (Robert Harding, William Balstone, and Ralph Spragg), and his corporal (John Oliver), were all avid Hutchinsonians. Some of them shared Underhill's dishonor and dismissal. Richard Morris followed Underhill to New Hampshire after his own banishment from Massachusetts. Shelley, *John Underhill*, 136–37.

84   De Forest, *Captain John Underhill*, 31–43. John Underhill spoke Dutch and was married to a

Dutch woman; he had served in the Netherlands; and he was an experienced Indian fighter, a rare commodity in New Netherland.

85   Jameson, *Narratives*, 226–34; Mead, *Historie*, 10–13; Winthrop, *Winthrop's Journal*, 96, 138; Huntington, *History of Stamford*, 103–4; De Forest, *Captain John Underhill*, 49–50. Among the victims was Anne Hutchinson, who resided in Eastchester at the time.

86   Winthrop, *Winthrop's Journal*, 95–96, 161; De Forest, *Captain John Underhill*, 50.

87   Jameson, *Narratives*, 280.

88   De Forest, *Captain John Underhill*, 52–53. Underhill's new rank—sergeant major—is the equivalent of "major" in the modern rank hierarchy. Thus, by serving the Dutch, Underhill was able to secure a promotion for himself, as well as money and notoriety.

89   Mead, *Historie*, 14, 16. Trelease, *Indian Affairs*, 78.

90   A letter by major John Mason to John Winthrop about this affair indicates that Patrick indeed knowingly sent the Dutch on a wild goose chase, while he was privately negotiating or trading with the Indians at his house. Jameson, *Narratives*, 280–81; De Forest, *Captain John Underhill*, 53–54; Huntington, *History of Stamford*, 104–5.

91   The settlers of Hempstead were doubtless fearful of the consequences of trying and punishing the Indians themselves. Later, when it was too late, it was discovered that Englishmen, not Indians, were responsible for the terrible pig massacre.

92   "They then took the other four with them in the sailing boat, two of whom were towed along by a string round their necks till they were drowned" (De Forest, *Captain John Underhill*, 56).

93   "When they had been kept a long time in the *corps de garde*, the director became tired of giving them food any longer, and they were delivered to the soldiers to do as they pleased with." Naturally, the two did not survive the experience. Ibid.

94   O'Callaghan, *Documents*, 193–94; Mead, *Historie*, 18; De Forest, *Captain John Underhill*, 57; Hauptman, "John Underhill," 105.

95   Underhill decided to land at Greenwich, rather than Stamford, because from Greenwich he could approach the village unobserved and then attack the Indians by surprise.

96   Trelease, *Indian Affairs*, 79–80; see also Mead, *Historie*, 19; De Forest, *Captain John Underhill*, 57; Jameson, *Narratives*, 282–84; Hauptman, "John Underhill," 105.

97   This expedition was Underhill's last Indian campaign. He went on to live a contentious but interesting life in New Netherland, until the Dutch authorities banished him in 1654. He then moved to Rhode Island, where he served as an officer in the colonial militia and spent a short term in prison before returning to Long Island. Barred from Dutch territories, he lived in several English settlements there under the jurisdiction of New Haven. He did not stay long in any one of these settlements, sometimes because of personal choice and at other times because of public demand.

98   A peace treaty was signed with them on April 6, 1644, at Fort Amsterdam.

99   As John Underhill observed, Indians were not very effective as shock troops: "they might fight seven years, and not kill seven men."

100 Eid, "Neglected Side," 14–15, 17. The feigned retreat, which was so effective against Gardiner, was totally ineffective against John Mason during his retreat from Mystic. Unlike Gardiner, Mason refused to be drawn into unplanned offensive pursuits. He kept to his original goal (advancing toward the boats at Pequot Bay) while repelling—but not pursu-

ing—the Pequot skirmishers who harassed his flanks and rear. Mason knew that his army was depleted by injuries and running out of ammunition. By remaining on the defensive— by relying on his musketeers' firepower—Mason was able to conserve his resources.

101 As Colin Calloway argues in *Western Abenakis of Vermont*, Indian tribes successfully avoided extinction by migrating away from war zones.

102 Bradford, *Bradford's History*, 338.

103 Winthrop, *Winthrop's Journal*, 75–76.

104 Ibid., 96.

105 A system of communal defense was particularly essential for frontier communities. Thus, it is not surprising that the formation of the United Colonies of New England (a confederation between the colonies of Massachusetts, Plymouth, Connecticut, and New Haven) was initiated by Connecticut and New Haven, which were more vulnerable to Indian and Dutch violence from the west. Ibid., 99, n. 1.

106 In "Newes from America" (51), John Underhill expresses a need to explain and justify to his European readers the surprisingly small size of the companies sent by Massachusetts to Block Island: "God stirred up the heart of the honored Governor, Master Henry Vane . . . to send forth a hundred well appointed soldiers, under the conduct of Captain John Hendicot, . . . Captain John Underhill, Captain Nathan Turner, Captain William Jenningson, besides other inferior officers. I would not have the world wonder at the great number of commanders to so few men, but know that the Indians' fight far differs from the Christian practice; for they most commonly divide themselves into small bodies, so that we are forced to neglect our usual way, and to subdivide our divisions to answer theirs." In the Netherlands, Underhill attended the famous military academy founded by Maurice of Nassau. This academy stressed, among other things, the division of an army into smaller tactical units that could react faster in combat. Hauptman, "John Underhill," 102. It seems that Underhill felt a need to provide a utilitarian, tactical justification for a situation that was in fact forced on the colony by its demographics.

107 Gardiner, *Lion Gardiner*, 12–13; see also Mather, *Early History*, 164; Vincent, "A true Relation," 100.

108 Mason, "Brief History," 21.

109 Both Mason and Underhill took the strategic offensive but relied on the tactical defense (using the firepower of the musketeers). The settlers' threatening position forced the Indians to react in self-defense by charging their defensive formations.

110 Vulnerability to surprise attacks convinced both Indians and settlers to use dogs in order to help them detect approaching enemy troops or warn them of ambushes. Pulsifer, *Records* (1855–61), 10:168; James, *Three Visitors*, 15–16. Thus, Endicott and Underhill killed as many dogs as they could during their destructive spree on Block Island. Preventing the enemy the use of dogs undoubtedly weakened it militarily.

111 Marshall, *Expedition*, 6; Heath, *Mourt's Relation*, 77; Winslow, *Relation or Iournall*, 7, 17, 58.

112 Winslow, *Relation or Iournall*, 7.

113 Garvan, *Architecture and Town Planning*, 24–40. Later on, toward the late seventeenth century, the nuclear town was gradually transformed, often remaining a town in name alone. Newly established towns were in fact a collection of individual farms spread out over a

large territory. Reps, *Town Planning*, 147; Garvan, *Architecture and Town Planning*, 51–77; Wood, *New England Village*, 41–46). This new town structure necessitated a formulation of a different type of defensive strategy. Harold Selesky (*War and Society*) identifies this period as the stage in which the militia system was transformed. No longer an ad hoc military force based on the idea of communal defense, it became offensive-minded (conducting preemptive raids in the periphery), with a strong emphasis on scouting missions.

114 For example, a system of isolated farmhouses, separated by individual land holdings. Garvan, *Architecture and Town Planning*, 26–40.

115 Ibid., 39.

116 Ibid., 42–43, 93; Reps, *Town Planning*, 189–92.

117 Underhill, "Nevves from America," 66.

118 Hubbard, *Present State of New England*, 119; Eid, "Neglected Side," 19.

119 Underhill, "Nevves from America," 60–61.

120 Gardiner, *Lion Gardiner*, 9.

121 Ibid., 23.

122 John Underhill's amphibious assault at Block Island displayed his reliance on the offensive. Nevertheless, even Underhill used defensive tactics when threatened, as at Pound Ridge.

123 Ward, *Animadversions of Warre*, 2:63.

124 Ibid., 2:64. One incident that occurred during King George's War belied Machiavelli's twenty-sixth rule: in 1747, an apparently starving French and Indian raiding party set siege to Fort Number Four, New Hampshire. After attempting to burn the fort, the French commander demanded that the besieged English troops provide his men with food. When refused, he threatened to storm the fort and slaughter its inhabitants. After a while, however, the French commander called for another parley, suggesting that if the English sold his men some food, they would leave the territory peacefully. This offer was refused as well, and the French and Indians were forced to withdraw. Eames, "Rustic Warriors," 153–54.

125 Underhill utilized this superiority to his advantage during the assault on Block Island and in his confrontation with the Pequots during the retreat from Mystic.

126 Underhill, "Nevves from America," 82; Ellis, "Life of John Mason," 387–88; Sylvester, *Indian Wars*, 1:277–80.

127 Underhill, "Nevves from America," 84.

128 Mason, "Brief History," 39.

129 Mather, *Early history*, 165–66.

130 Although the use of small shot increased the likelihood of a hit, it decreased the musket's effective range. Hitting the target with less force, small shot was less likely than a single ball to produce a fatal or incapacitating wound.

131 Ellis, "Life of John Mason," 391.

132 Mason, "Brief History," 40–41. Connecticut set a bounty on Pequot scalps and bodies. Ellis, "Life of John Mason," 396.

133 Sylvester, *Indian Wars*, 291–92, 301; Ellis, "Life of John Mason," 393.

134 Perry, *Great Swamp Fight*, 7; Ellis, "Life of John Mason," 394. A similar assault, with similar results, was attempted by Captain Turner on Block Island.

135 Mason, "Brief History," 37–39; Bradford, *Bradford's History*, 340–42; Ellis, "Life of John Mason," 395.

136 It was with regard to this encounter that John Mason mentioned the use of small shot. Mason, "Brief History," 39; Perry, *Great Swamp Fight*, 9.

137 Ellis, "Life of John Mason," 396; Bradford, *Bradford's History*, 340–42.

138 Sylvester, *Indian Wars*, 330, n.1. On September 21, 1638, the Treaty of Hartford officially brought the war to an end. Pequot survivors were divided between the Mohegans and Narragansetts.

CHAPTER THREE

1 Mahon, "Anglo-American Methods," 255. The English were not the only ones responsible for the Indians' acquisition of firearms. French and Dutch traders were heavily involved in the arms trade in New England. The inability of the English governments in New England to prevent the Indians from purchasing firearms prompted them to turn a blind eye to, and profit from, this lucrative enterprise. These firearms, referred to as "trade muskets," were similar to those used by colonial militias, but they were usually cheaply made and were not fitted to mount bayonets.

2 Sylvester, *Indian Wars*, 330, n.1.

3 The English population of Massachusetts numbered approximately seventeen thousand. Plymouth, Rhode Island, and Connecticut had roughly five thousand, four thousand, and ten thousand English settlers, respectively. The number of Indians in New England in 1675 is estimated at twenty-five thousand (five thousand of them men of fighting age). Tebbel and Jennison, *American Indian Wars*, 31; Church, *Diary*, 2, 4; Phillips, *Salem in the Seventeenth Century*, 228. On the Indian side, roughly three thousand Indian warriors died during the war. Many more noncombatants perished from hunger and disease during and after the war. Phillips, *Salem in the Seventeenth Century*, 241; Leach, *Arms for Empire*, 65; Tebbel and Jennison, *American Indian Wars*, 51; Schultz and Tougias, *King Philip's War*, 5, n.6.

4 Drake, *King Philip's War*, 2, 133, 151, 153; Whisker, *American Colonial Militia*, 1:1; Keeley, *War before Civilization*, 74–75; Malone, *Skulking Way of War*, 59–60, 87–88, 90–98, 100; Bourne, *Red King's Rebellion*, 175, 181–84, 188–89; Selesky, *War and Society*, 10; Starkey, *European and Native American Warfare*, 2–4, 53, 71–82, 94–96; Ferling, "New England Soldier"; Axtell, *European and the Indian*, 139–41, 146–47, 299–302; Leach, *Arms for Empire*, 60–61; idem, *Flintlock*, 70–71; Alan Simpson and Mary Simpson, "Introduction," in Church, *Diary*, 30; Smith, *Treatise*, 9–12.

5 Tebbel and Keith, *American Indian Wars*, 34–37; Phillips, *Salem in the Seventeenth Century*, 229; Leach, *Flintlock*, 30–33; Melvoin, *New England Outpost*, 97–98.

6 Mather, *History of King Philip's War*, 53–54; Church, *The entertaining history*, 10–12; Leach, *Flintlock*, 36; *Present State*, 4–5; Tebbel and Jennison, *American Indian Wars*, 38; Wade, *Brief History*, 35.

7 Mather, *History of King Philip's War*, 54–55; Leach, *Flintlock*, 37–38.

8 Wade, *American Indian Wars*, 36; Leach, *Flintlock*, 38.

9 Church, *The entertaining history*, 10–12; Melvoin, *New England Outpost*, 97; Leach, *Flintlock*, 43.

Mather, *History of King Philip's War*, 55–56; Tebbel and Jennison, *American Indian Wars*, 38–39. Moseley was a tough and experienced soldier-adventurer. A few weeks before receiving his commission at the outbreak of King Philip's War, he had fought a company of pirates, bringing them to trial in Boston. (Increase Mather, *History of King Philip's War*, 55–56; Leach, *Flintlock*, 45–47.) The force sent from Massachusetts included a few dogs, for tracking and detecting Indians in the woods.

10 Leach, *Flintlock*, 40, 50–51.

11 The Wampanoags had been weakened in the mid-seventeenth century by the conversion of the Nausets of Cape Cod to Christianity. Phillips, *Salem in the Seventeenth Century*, 227; Leach, *Flintlock*, 51.

12 Church, *Entertaining History*, 12–13; Mather, *History of King Philip's War*, 57; Leach, *Flintlock*, 51–52.

13 Mather, *History of King Philip's War*, 57; Markham, *Narrative History*, 112–13; Leach, *Flintlock*, 52–54; Church, *Entertaining History*, 13.

14 Markham, *Narrative History*, 113.

15 On this assignment the English were relatively successful. Between Swansea and Rehoboth they came upon a group of enemy Indians. They pursued the Indians, killing many of them, including their sachem. Leach, *Flintlock*, 55.

16 In Northampton the Indians were able to penetrate the palisaded territory, where they encountered heavy fire. Trapped between the fortified English settlers and the palisade, the Indians suffered heavy casualties as they attempted to flee. Many more examples illustrate this pattern, such as the attacks against Lancaster, Brookfield, and Pocumtuck (Deerfield). *A New and Further Narrative*, 3; Melvoin, *New England Outpost*, 100–101, 113; Markham, *Narrative History*, 225; Hubbard, *Narrative*, 92–93.

17 Mather, *History of King Philip's War*, 66–68; Markham, *Narrative History*, 129–136; Tebbel and Jennison, *American Indian Wars*, 43–45; Leach, *Flintlock*, 81–83. Major Simon Willard was seventy years old at the time.

18 Four of these garrison houses were positioned strategically, within musket-shot of each other, and overlooking a meadow in the center of the village, where the cattle was placed at times of danger. The fifth garrison house was a mile away. May, *Plantation*, 32, 187–88, 192; Markham, *Narrative History*, 226–27.

19 The Indian forces that attacked Durham and the fort at Pemaquid during King William's War employed a similar strategy. Drake, *Border Wars*, 28–29, 38, n.2. These attacks indicate that the Indians understood that they were not successful against fortified houses. Thus, they attempted to draw defenders away from their fortifications (targeting enemy troops, and weakening their forts in the process), as the Pequots had attempted to do at the outbreak of the Pequot war when they tried to draw Gardiner and his men away from Fort Saybrook.

20 Hubbard, *Narrative*, 139–40; May, *Plantation*, 188; Markham, *Narrative History*, 228.

21 Hubbard, *Narrative*, 139–40; Markham, *Narrative History*, 228–29.

22 Sometimes, the governments placed troops as garrisons within towns to bolster their defense. A counterpart to this measure was the commissioning of scouting units ("flying dragoons") to patrol the region (to "seek and destroy"), alarm the towns and the govern-

ments of impending danger, and rush as relief forces to besieged towns. Pynchon, *Pynchon Papers*, 225.

23 Leach, *Flintlock*, 157–59.

24 *Present State*, 18–19; *Farther Brief and True Narration*, 5.

25 Church, *The entertaining history*, 17–18; Mather, *History of King Philip's War*, 60–61; Leach, *Flintlock*, 63–64.

26 Church, *The entertaining history*, 18–20; Leach, *Flintlock*, 64–65; Markham, *Narrative History*, 113–23; Tebbel and Jennison, *American Indian Wars*, 40; Mather, *History of King Philip's War*, 60–61.

27 Two of Pierce's men, one Indian and one Englishman, made their escape by feigning a chase. The Indian soldier, brandishing a tomahawk, chased the Englishman until both men were far enough away and out of danger. Forbes, *Other Indian Events*, 2–3.

28 *New and Further Narrative*, 5–6; Markham, *Narrative History*, 231–32; De Forest, *History of the Indians*, 282.

29 The survivors escaped to a nearby mill, where they defended themselves till nightfall, when they were rescued by a relief force led by Captain Prentice. Church, *History of King Philip's War*, 70, n.1; *New and Further Narrative*, 10; Ellis and Morris, *King Philip's War*, 211.

30 Mather, *History of King Philip's War*, 61–62; Tebbel and Jennison, *American Indian Wars*, 42; Leach, *Flintlock*, 68–69.

31 Church, *History of King Philip's War*, 53; Tebbel and Jennison, *American Indian Wars*, 42; Leach, *Flintlock*, 68–69.

32 Osgood, *American Colonies*, 1:111.

33 Church, *History of King Philip's War*, 53–55; Melvoin, *New England Outpost*, 98; Leach, *Flintlock*, 69–72; Tebbel and Jennison, *American Indian Wars*, 42.

34 Phillips, *Salem in the Seventeenth Century*, 227–28.

35 At that time Philip was traveling in the southwestern corner of Plymouth colony. Markham, *Narrative History*, 113; Leach, *Flintlock*, 40–42, 57.

36 Wade, *Brief History*, 35; Leach, *Flintlock*, 58–61. Massachusetts' peace mission to the Narragansetts was complicated by the intervention of Connecticut representatives. Massachusetts was more aggressive in the negotiations and more willing to back its demands with force of arms. Connecticut was more appeasing because, among other things, it was closer geographically to the Narragansetts than Massachusetts. The situation Connecticut faced in July 1675 was somewhat similar to its position at the outbreak of the Pequot War. In both cases Massachusetts took an aggressive, even belligerent, stance against Indian tribes that threatened Connecticut settlements more than Massachusetts settlements. For this reason, Lion Gardiner was displeased to see Captains Endicott and Underhill at Saybrook's gates at the start of the Pequot War: "You come hither to raise these wasps about my ears, and then you will take wing and flee away." Gardiner, *Lion Gardiner*, 11. Furthermore, Connecticut had to placate the enemy from the east (the Narragansetts) because of military commitments on its western frontier. Governor Edmund Andros of New York had challenged Connecticut's jurisdiction over the territory between the Hudson and Connecticut Rivers (a territory that included, among other towns, Hartford, Windsor, Wethersfield, and New Haven). This was a standing border dispute between the two colonies from the time

New York was still occupied by the Dutch. Connecticut's security concerns in summer 1675 enabled Governor Andros to press the matter with military force. On July 8, 1675, Andros and his troops arrived at Saybrook, intent on enforcing New York's claim to the disputed territory. By mid-July, however, Andros had left Connecticut peacefully.

37   Hubbard, *Narrative*, 86–87; Philips, *Salem in the Seventeenth Century*, 230–31; Melvoin, *New England Outpost*, 102–3.

38   Massachusetts was to supply 527 men, Connecticut was to mobilize 315 Englishmen and 150 Mohegans, and Plymouth was to supply 158 men to the force. *Farther Brief and True Narration*, 9; Wade, *Brief History*, 35–36.

39   Tebbel and Jamison, *American Indian Wars*, 48; Hubbard, *Narrative*, 99–101; Wade, *Brief History*, 36; Leach, *Flintlock*, 120–23.

40   Each company numbered roughly 75 men (527 men in total). The infantry companies were commanded by Major Appleton and Captains Samuel Moseley, James Oliver, Isaac Johnson, Nathaniel Davenport, and Joseph Gardiner. Captain Thomas Prentice commanded the cavalry unit. Plymouth supplied the intercolonial army with two infantry companies (under the command of Major William Bradford and Captain John Gorham). Connecticut provided five infantry companies (approximately sixty men each). *Farther Brief and True Narration*, 9; Philips, *Salem in the Seventeenth Century*, 233; Leach, *Flintlock*, 123–25, 128.

41   *Brief and True Narration*, 9; Philips, *Salem in the Seventeenth Century*, 234.

42   Most of these Indian captives were shipped to Aquidneck Island and interned there. *Farther Brief and True Narration*, 9; Leach, *Flintlock*, 125–26.

43   Wade, *Brief History*, 38.

44   Ibid.; Leach, *Flintlock*, 129; Tebbel and Jennison, *American Indian Wars*, 48.

45   *Farther Brief and True Narration*, 9.

46   The fortifications in this section were not completed but were protected by makeshift impediments and a block house. Trumbull, *Compendium of the Indian Wars*, 41; Leach, *Flintlock*, 129.

47   Church, *Entertaining Passages*, 14.

48   Some of the Indian defenders had run out of powder and were forced to resort to bows and arrows. Trumbull, *Compendium*, 40–43; Leach, *Flintlock*, 129–30; Wade, *Brief History*, 38–40; Tebbel and Jennison, *American Indian Wars*, 48; Philips, *Salem in the Seventeenth Century*, 234–35, 237.

49   Trumbull, *Compendium*, 41; Leach, *Flintlock*, 130.

50   Church, *Entertaining Passages*, 16; Wade, *Brief History*, 40; Leach, *Flintlock*, 133, 136.

51   Winslow's army did march back to Wickford that night, suffering from extreme hunger and exhaustion. Yet, they were not pursued. By resorting to the use of fire, Winslow ensured the completion of his assignment and reduced the chance of Indian attacks on his retreating forces. Even if the English could have conquered the fort by nightfall without resorting to the use of fire, camping in the fort overnight would have been very risky. By morning, the English could easily have been surrounded by enemy troops.

52   When conducted properly, the outcome of a siege is virtually predetermined. An efficient siege enables a commander to reduce the role of chance, bad judgment under fire, and misfortune.

53 Had Benjamin Church not been able to breach the wall and attack the Indians from the rear, the Great Swamp Fight would have ended as one of the greatest military disasters in the history of England's North American colonies.

54 Tebbel and Jennison, *American Indian Wars*, 49.

55 Wade, *Brief History*, 40–41; Leach, *Flintlock*, 131–32; Tebbel and Jennison, *American Indian Wars*, 49.

56 In this respect, "King Philip's War" is a misnomer—it was neither Philip's, nor a war. It was, in fact, a general uprising.

57 Mather, *History of King Philip's War*, 58–60, 68–69; Leach, *Flintlock*, 66; Church, *History of King Philip's War*, 70, n.1; *A New and Further Narrative*, 5–6, 10; Ellis and Morris, *King Philip's War*, 211; Markham, *Narrative History*, 231–32; De Forest, *History of the Indians*, 282.

58 Canonchet was captured by Dennison's men. He chose not to sign a peace treaty with the colonies, explaining that he "liked it well that he should die before his heart was soft or that he said anything unworthy of himself." He was delivered to, and executed by, the Mohegans and Pequots of Connecticut. De Forest, *History of the Indians*, 282–83; Lewis, *History of the Pequot War*, 16–17.

59 De Forest, *History of the Indians*, 282; Leach, *Flintlock*, 222–24, 229, 233.

60 Philip was beheaded and quartered. His head was placed on display in Plymouth and left there for the next twenty years as a threatening reminder to visiting Indian sachems and envoys. One of his hands was sent to Boston, where it was exhibited for years to come. His body was left on the battlefield to rot (the Plymouth government issued a strict prohibition against his burial). Tebbel and Jennison, *American Indian Wars*, 50–51; Leach, *Flintlock*, 209–10, 215–20, 230–36.

61 Indians did use small shot for hunting (Malone, *Skulking Way of War*, 65) and might have done so in combat as well. Even when loaded with small shot, however, smoothbore muskets were inaccurate when fired individually.

62 With only fifty men, Captain Wadsworth was able to hold off a force of over four hundred men for more than four hours. The Indians were finally able to dislodge the English company when they set fire to the woods. *New and Further Narrative*, 10–11.

63 Melvoin, *New England Outpost*, 116, 121. In the June attack the Wampanoag camp was inhabited by noncombatants as well as warriors. All suffered the same fate.

64 Ibid.

65 Eames, "Rustic Warriors," 455 n. 69.

66 Connecticut's Mohegan troops, for example, were not substantial contributors in the Great Swamp Fight. Wade, *Brief History*, 36.

67 Malone, "English and Indian," 280, 282–83.

68 Ibid., 280, 283, 286; Pynchon, *Pynchon Papers*, 225; Melvoin, *New England Outpost*, 110.

69 Pynchon to Leverett, September 30, 1675, Pynchon, *Pynchon Papers*, 154–55.

70 Drake, *King Philip's War*, 2, 133, 151, 153; Whisker, *American Colonial Militia*, 1:1; Keeley, *War before Civilization*, 74–75; Malone, *Skulking Way of War*, 59–60, 87–88, 90–98, 100; Bourne, *Red King's Rebellion*, 175, 181–84, 188–89; Selesky, *War and Society*, 10; Starkey, *European and Native American Warfare*, 2–4, 53, 71–82, 94–96; Ferling, "New England Soldier," 26–45; Axtell, *European and the Indian*, 139–41, 146–47, 299–302; Leach, *Arms for Empire*, 60–61; idem,

Flintlock and Tomahawk, 70–71; Simpson and Simpson, "Introduction," in Church, *Diary*, 30; Smith, *Treatise*, 9–12.

In *Flintlock and Tomahawk*, 70–71, Leach discusses the failure of Captain Cudworth to capture Philip at the Pocasset swamp. He argues that the English "continued to place too much faith in old European drill manuals, which had not been written with American conditions in mind. Fast moving, forest-wise Indian war parties repeatedly were able to baffle ponderous English units, retreating successfully when necessary." But Leach himself later asserts that Cudworth's failure did not result from an ill-advised plan. Rather, Leach criticizes Cudworth for poor execution of his conservative, European-minded plan, suggesting that a more "ponderous" deployment of troops would have sealed Philip's fate.

71 Malone, "English and Indian," 128–29, 141. Unlike Malone, most historians who refer to the settlers' increased reliance on individual marksmanship do not offer useful evidence to demonstrate a growing dedication to marksmanship training.

72 Some American manuals were simply reprints of European texts, whereas others were edited specifically edited for use in North America.

73 New Hampshire Militia, *For Promoting Military Discipline*, 18; Windham, *Plan of Exercise*, 15.

74 Accounts of colonial battles reveal no evidence of competent marksmen among colonial troops. One comes across few instances in which colonials displayed even adequate accuracy in their shots (that is, a satisfactory hit ratio).

75 Bland, *Abstract*, 7; Windham, *Plan of Discipline*, 16; Eames, "Rustic Warriors," 392.

76 Bland, *Treatise*, 21; Barriffe, *Militarie Discipline* (1661), 2. The American edition of Bland's *Abstract* does reflect other adjustments, in comparison with the original British edition. For example, the loading sequence was abridged and simplified, reflecting the widespread use of paper cartridges. Stanley, "Preliminary Investigation," 10–11; Eames, "Rustic Warriors," 392.

77 Bland, *Abstract*, 7; idem, *Treatise*, 21; Barriffe, *Militarie Discipline* (1661), 2.

78 New Hampshire Militia, *For Promoting Military Discipline*, 18; Windham, *Plan of Exercise*, 15–16 Johnson, *Manual Exercise*, 8; Bland, *Abstract*, 6–7, 37–38; Boone, *Military Discipline* (1701), 12; *Military discipline: The Compleat Soldier: To Which is Added, the Military Law of the Province of the Massachusetts-Bay in N.E.* (Boston: B. Green, 1706), 13.

79 American editions of European manuals and treatises tended to be more utilitarian and simplified than the European originals. The terminology in some of them was less professional (sometimes these manuals included definitions for conventional military terms) and some of the military maneuvers that they detailed were simplified. See, for example, in addition to Boone, Nicola, *Treatise of Military Exercise*. See also Eames, "Rustic Warriors," 392; Stanley, "Preliminary Investigation," 10–11.

80 Boone, *Military discipline*, 4.

81 Conversely, in European rifle corps (sniping units), soldiers were allowed a much greater freedom of action in targeting, aiming, and firing.

82 Stanley, "Preliminary Investigation," 2–11, 6, 46; Eames, "Rustic Warriors," 392; Whisker, *American Colonial Militia*, 1:79.

83 Windham, *Plan of Exercise*, 40, n.1, 40, n.2, 42–44, 46, 48, 51–72; Boone, *Military discipline* (1706), 11–68.

84 von Steuben, *Baron von Steuben's Revolutionary War Drill Manual*, 17, 63–67.

85 Mather, *Early History*, 165–66; Mason, "Brief History," 39, 138; Malone, "English and Indian," 89–90, 104, 138–139; Brown, *Firearms*, 85, 114, 126, 128. The majority of full-bore muskets were usually 12 gauge (that is, their bullets weighed one twelfth of a pound). Bastard muskets, or calivers (fusils), had a shorter and narrower barrel and, therefore, a higher gauge (a smaller bullet). Peterson, *Arms and Armor*, 14.

86 Peterson, *Encyclopedia of Firearms*, 52; Tonso, *Gun and Society*, 64.

87 Tonso, *Gun and Society*, 64–66.

88 Hubbard, *Narrative*, 92–93; Pynchon, *Pynchon Papers*, 139; Tebbel and Jennison, *American Indian Wars*, 43–45; *Present State*, 18–19; *Farther Brief and True Narration*, 5; Markham, *Narrative History*, 130–36, 226–27; Malone, "English and Indian," 278; Church, *Entertaining History*, 10–12; *New and Further Narrative*, 3; Boorstin, *Americans*, 349; Colden, *History of the Five Indian Nations*, 118.

89 Pynchon, *Pynchon Papers*, 142; Parkman, *Half Century of Conflict*, 1:39, 58; Chapman, "Block and Garrison Houses," 39, 45–49; Selesky, *War and Society*, 18–19; May, *Plantation*, 32; Eames, "Rustic Warriors," 78; Malone, "English and Indian," 223–25, 227; Mahon, "Anglo-American Methods," 261; Huntington, *History of Stamford*, 70, 113.

90 Settlers were ordered not to leave their towns alone and unarmed and were given a wider latitude to kill armed Indians. Selesky, *War and Society*, 18–19, 24; Melvoin, *New England Outpost*, 113; Mahon, "Anglo-American Methods," 258.

91 The involvement of the Narragansetts and their tributaries in the war threatened English settlements in the east, rather than in the western counties. Of the various Narragansett sachems, only Ninigret (sachem of the Niantics) allied himself with the English (along with the Mohegans and Pequots of Connecticut). During the war, therefore, life in the interior (Plymouth, eastern Massachusetts, Rhode Island, and eastern Connecticut) was more hazardous than along the western frontiers. Church, *Diary*, 10–11; Pynchon, *Pynchon Papers*, 142, 157, 221; Selesky, *War and Society*, 21, 28–29; Huntington, *History of Stamford*, 113.

92 Bland, *Treatise*, 134–35; Simes, *Military Medley*, 125–26; Parker, "Anglo-American Wilderness Campaigning," 277. It is clear that although Indian warfare differed from European warfare, it did not present unprecedented challenges to experienced European soldiers. The warnings of Bland and Simes indicate that ambushes and feigned retreats (or real ones, supported by a second line of troops to attack the pursuers) had been employed in Europe as they were in New England. Experienced commanders, as well as readers of classical and contemporary military history, would have been familiar with such tactics. Thus, surprise tactics were less likely to succeed against experienced European commanders.

93 Hubbard, *History*, 1:113–16.

94 Armed with a smoothbore musket, it took a skilled marksman to hit an individual target at forty to fifty yards. Malone, "English and Indian," 124. Because a ball fired from a smoothbore firearm is not forced by rifling to turn on its central axis, it leaves the barrel turning toward its heaviest or densest side. This irregular movement, combined with air friction, causes the ball to wobble and curve unpredictably. Tonso, *Gun and Society*, 64.

95 Hubbard, *Narrative*, 86–87.

96 Eames, "Rustic Warriors," 404.

97 Ibid., 375. Every settlement formed and maintained its own trained band (trainband), led by a captain. The members of the trainbands, who trained together a few days a year, maintained the town watch and performed defensive tasks at times of alarm. The trainbands' main purpose was to provide each New England settlement with defenders. Their secondary purpose was to prepare the men for service in the regional militia companies. Whisker, *American Colonial Militia*, 1:1, 3; Kenny, "Rhode Island Train Bands," 26–27.

98 Banks, *History of Martha's Vineyard*, 295–96; Labaree, ed., *Royal Instructions*, 392–93; Morton, "Origins of American Military Policy," 79; Eames, "Rustic Warriors," 375–476; Sharp, "New England Trainbands," 167–68, 189–95; Malone, *Skulking Way of War*, 54–55.

99 All able-bodied men (ages 16–60) were required to participate, including "all Scotsmen, Negers, & Indians inhabiting with or serving to the English." Shurtleff, *Records of the Governor* (1968), 2:24–25, 42–43, 120, 151, 223; 3:33–36, 40, 268; Eames, "Rustic Warriors," 377–78.

100 In European armies, the tactical counterpart of the company was the platoon, and the tactical counterpart of the regiment was the battalion. There was usually one battalion in a regiment, although some regiments—such as the 60th Royal Americans—were composed of up to four battalions.

101 Morton, "Origins of American Military Policy," 80; Anderson, *People's Army*, 50–51.

102 Windham, *Plan of Exercise*, 34; Sharp, "New England Trainbands," 112–13, 116–19, 124–26.

103 Hubbard, *Narrative*, 95–97.

104 Leach, *Arms for Empire*, 60–61, 64–66; Whisker, *American Colonial Militia*, 1:1; Malone, *Skulking Way of War*, 59–60, 87–88, 90–98, 100; Starkey, *European and Native American Warfare*, 2–4, 53, 71–82, 94–96; Bourne, *Red King's Rebellion*, 175, 181–84, 188–89; Drake, *King Philip's War*, 2, 133, 151, 153; Keeley, *War before Civilization*, 74–75; Simpson and Simpson, "Introduction" in Church, *Diary*, 30.

105 The term *rangers* did not come into use until King George's War. The flying dragoons, patrols, scouting units, and raiding parties of the colonial wars of the seventeenth and early eighteenth centuries, however, were ranger units in their composition and size, their offensive doctrine, and in their assignments. Their mission was to scout, gather intelligence, alert towns of the movements and intentions of enemy troops, relieve besieged towns, and seek out and engage enemy forces in the field. Since mobility and stealth were essential for the success of such missions, rangers were light troops, unencumbered by supply trains and heavy equipment. For this reason Benjamin Church made extensive use of whaleboats in his raids along the northern New England coastline during King William's War and Queen Anne's War. The mobility that whaleboats offered ranger units enabled them to surprise enemy troops: "Being farr nimbler then any pinnace, able to carry 15 men each being about 36 foot long, yet so light that two men can easily carry one of them." They were "of so great use for surprizing of places and vessels in the night, their padles making no noise as oars do." Eames, "Rustic Warriors," 163, 166, 135, n.1; Selesky, *War and Society*, 23.

106 Frontier settlements were perpetually at odds with colonial governments regarding the deployment of provincial troops in the towns in support of local garrisons. At times of distress on the frontiers, governments yielded to public pressure in this regard.

107 As their interaction with Europeans intensified throughout the seventeenth century, the sachems' political authority further deteriorated. When Ninigret, the great Narragansett sachem, for example, declared himself an ally of the English, he was forced to forfeit his political authority over his "subjects." He could no longer command the obedience of his warriors, who chose to join the uprising. Lincoln, *Narratives*, 60–61; White, *Middle Ground*; Calloway, *Western Abenakis*; Eames, "Rustic Warriors," 26; Ellis and Morris, *King Philip's War*, 236.

108 Lincoln, *Narratives*, 61.

109 *Farther Brief and True Narration*, 9; Lincoln, *Narratives*, 59.

110 Ellis and Morris, *King Philip's War*, 130, 156, 162, 248; Leach, *Flintlock*, 157, 207.

111 Melvoin, *New England Outpost*, 114–16; Ellis and Morris, *King Philip's War*, 236; Leach, *Flintlock*, 178–80, 199, 207, 209, 213–15.

112 James Smith, *A Treatise on the Mode and Manner of Indian War*, 9–12; Axtell, 140–41.

113 Melvoin, *New England Outpost*, 115. According to information obtained by the English, there were approximately sixty five warriors in the camp. The rest were noncombatants. Ibid.

114 Ibid., 115–16.

115 On the defense, English forces were hampered by the same obstacles, but their incompetence was compensated for by their fortifications and by the Indians' own inadequacies.

116 Gardiner, *Lion Gardiner*, 9.

117 Ward, *Animadversions of VVare*, 2:63.

118 Indian forces did not differ from English ones in this respect. Their lack of professionalism manifested itself, as it did with the settlers, in poor vigilance and a lack of attention to details. As Henry Turney-High observes in his study of primitive warfare, for all their reliance on surprise tactics, Indians rarely took steps to prevent a surprise attacks on themselves. Eames, "Rustic Warriors," 455, n.69.

119 Drake, *King Philip's War*, 2, 133, 151, 153; Whisker, *American Colonial Militia*, 1:1; Keeley, *War before Civilization*, 74–75; Bourne, *Red King's Rebellion*, 175, 181–84, 188–89; Malone, *Skulking Way of War*, 59–60, 87–88, 90–98, 100; Starkey, *European and Native American Warfare*, 2–4, 53, 71–82, 94–96; Axtell, *European and the Indian*, 139–41, 146–47, 299–302; Leach, *Arms for Empire*, 60–61; idem, *Flintlock*, 70–71; Simpson and Simpson, "Introduction," in Church, *Diary*, 30.

120 Church, *History of King Philip's war*, 108–9; Malone, "English and Indian," 287, 291; Leach, *Arms for Empire*, 64–65. Marching in loose formation, however, reduced the effective fire that Church's force could generate. A more cautious and conventional commander would have followed the recommendations of William Barriffe (Barriffe, *Militarie Discipline* [1661], 12) and kept the bulk of his troops closer together, while maintaining advance and rear guards marching at a distance from the main force. The advance and rear guards would have borne the brunt of a surprise attack, only to be rescued by the rest of the force. Conversely, in case of an attack on the main force, these detachments would have been able to relieve it. Before Benjamin Church's second expedition of King William's War in September, 1690, he was instructed by Governor Hinkley of Plymouth to observe these precautions. By this time, however, Church was already set in his Americanized ways. Church, *Entertaining History*, 112.

121 Leach, *Flintlock*, 217–18; Malone, "English and Indian," 290–91.

122 The Indians were slowed down not only by exhaustion. Because their villages were constantly raided by English forces, the few remaining bellicose war bands were forced to carry all their possessions with them. For the same reason, they traveled with their families, which slowed them down even more. Leach, *Flintlock*, 220, 222–24, 229, 233.

CHAPTER FOUR

1 In Europe, the peace of Rijswijk (September 30, 1697) brought an end to hostilities until the breakout of the War of Spanish Succession in 1701. In North America, however, violence persisted despite the European truce. In North America, Queen Anne's War was merely a continuation, if not a repetition, of King William's War. Parkman, *Half-Century of Conflict*, 1:50–51; Pynchon, *Pynchon Papers*, 305.

2 Hutchinson, *History of the Colony*, 2:151; Eames, "Rustic Warriors," 105–7.

3 Eames, "Rustic Warriors," 109–0.

4 For a fort to be tactically effective, all parts of the fortification must be viewed ("flanked") from some other part, within musket range, to enable the defenders, behind their fortifications, to defend every part of the outer wall. Thus, the enemy is unable to find a portion of the outer wall where they can situate themselves safely (in order to dismantle the fortifications) without attracting defensive fire. "For if there is any part that is not seen or defended, the enemy might approach that way under cover, and make themselves masters of it, without much trouble or loss." Muller, *On Fortification*, 69; Robinson, *American Forts*, 11.

5 Lincoln, *Narratives*, 240–41; Eames, "Rustic Warriors," 103, 108–9; Drake, *Border Wars*, 83–85; Osgood, *American Colonies*, 1:111.

6 Parkman, *Half-Century of Conflict*, 9.

7 Muller, *On Fortifications*, 152–55.

8 Frontenac replaced the Marquis de Denonville as the governor of Canada in 1689. Even though he was seventy years old at the time, historians and contemporaries have considered him to be without equal in North America as a military commander.

9 Hutchinson, *History of the Colony*, 2:51–52; Drake, *Border Wars*, 89–90.

10 Prior to the campaigning season of 1694, French magistrates and missionaries worked tirelessly to induce these eastern Abenaki tribes to rejoin the fight against the English. Hutchinson, *History of the Colony*, 2:55, 61; Drake, *Border Wars*, 93–94.

11 Settlers serving in the armed forces were compensated for their public service in order to ensure that they would not desert their units in order to tend to their fields, businesses, and families. Shurtleff, *Records of the Governor*, 3:42.

12 Marcus, "Connecticut Valley," 236–38.

13 The cost of the defense of Hampshire County (from August 1703 to August 1704) was estimated by Connecticut at eleven thousand pounds. Such estimates were a central issue in the constant bickering between the Councils of Connecticut and Massachusetts over the financing and command of Connecticut forces serving in Massachusetts. Ibid., 237–38.

14 As towns developed, they expanded geographically and required more garrison houses for effective defense. Just as fortresses were stronger when attention was paid to lines of fire

along the walls, so garrison houses were more effective when they were positioned "properly"—each house within view and within musket-range of others (these little forts, therefore, "viewed" or "flanked" one another).

15 Ibid., 230.

16 Between 1670 and 1715 Deerfield suffered thirty Indian attacks. In the 1704 attack on Deerfield three-fifths of the townspeople (290) were either killed or taken captive. For an interesting and innovative account of this raid and its impact, see Demos, Unredeemed Captive.

17 In 1703, after attacks on Saco and Winter Harbor, the authorities instructed the inhabitants there to evacuate all the women and children. The men were forbidden to leave; they were to remain there, under pay for their service. Osgood, American Colonies, 1:407; Melvoin, New England Outpost, 214; Leach, Northern Colonial Frontier, 112; Eames, "Rustic Warriors," 70–74; Philips, Salem in the Eighteenth Century, 9.

18 Drake, Border Wars, 173, n.3. The valley settlements were placed under the military charge of Colonel Samuel Partridge.

19 Pynchon, Pynchon Papers, 157.

20 Ibid., 221.

21 Parkman, Half-Century of Conflict, 1:13–14, 32–33; Selesky, War and Society, 33–34.

22 The Glorious Revolution in England (1688) sparked a series of coups against royal governors in North America, including Andros (The Glorious Revolution in America, 1688–89).

23 Hutchinson, History of the Colony, 2:10.

24 Osgood, American Colonies, 1:99–100, 102–5, 110; Marcus, "Connecticut Valley," 232–34.

25 Osgood, American Colonies, 1:102.

26 In England, Dudley became a Member of Parliament and, later, the lieutenant-governor of the Isle of Wight. While in London, he was very active in undermining Sir William Phips's position in Massachusetts. Church, History of Philip's War, 249–50, n.1; Parkman, Half-Century of Conflict, 1:105–8, 121; Hutchinson, History of the Colony, 2:60–64, 145, n.1.

27 Mather, Deplorable State, 4–6, 30–32; Philopolites [Mather], Memorial, 1–7, 16–37; Hutchinson, History of the Colony, 2:111–15, 117–20; Marcus, "Connecticut Valley," 236; Parkman, Half-Century of Conflict, 1:105–8, 121.

28 Springfield and Westfield are only twenty-five miles from Hartford. Hadley and Hatfield are forty miles away, and Deerfield ten miles farther.

29 Parkman, Half-Century of Conflict, 8; Marcus, "Connecticut Valley," 232–33, 235–38.

30 Ibid., 239. In Connecticut, tax rates did not increase dramatically throughout the war (ibid., 235).

31 With a population of 21,500, the Connecticut militia numbered roughly 3,000 (ibid., 233–34).

32 Ibid., 239.

33 Morrison, Embattled Northeast, 109–22; Church, History of Philip's War, 154, 164, n.1, 151–52, n.2; Osgood, American Colonies, 1:69; Drake, Border Wars, 10–11; Penhallow, History of the Wars, 5–6, 10.

34 Selesky, War and Society, 38; Osgood, American Colonies, 1:69.

35 Egeremet also informed his captives that St. Castin offered the eastern Indians all the powder and ball that they needed in order to fight the English. Drake, The Border Wars, 11.

36 Andros also built one fortress (Fort Anne) during this expedition. The fort, on the Kennebec River, was meant to impress and threaten the Kennebecs, thereby keeping them in check. Church, *History of Philip's War*, 164, n.1, 151–52, n.2, Osgood, *American Colonies*, 1:69–70; Drake, *Border Wars*, 12; Murrin, "Anglicizing an American Colony," 65.

37 Drake, *Border Wars*, 13; Osgood, *American Colonies*, 1:71; Murrin, "Anglicizing an American Colony," 65–66.

38 The author of this report was taken captive. His account of his capture seems uniquely gentle: "My brother ran one way, and I another, and looking over my shoulder I saw a stout fellow, all painted, pursuing me, with a gun in one hand and a cutlass glittering in the other, which I expected in my brains every moment. I soon fell down, and the Indian seized me by the left hand. He offered me no abuse, but tied my arms, then lifted me up and [led me away]. When we came to the place, I saw two men shot down on the flats, and one more or two more knocked on the head with hatchets, while crying out 'O, Lord! O, Lord!' etc. . . . After doing what mischief they could, the Indians sat down, and made us sit with them. After some time we arose [and] marched about a quarter of a mile then made a halt. Here they brought my father to us. They made proposals to him by old Moxus, who told him that those were strange Indians who shot him, and that he was sorry for it. My father replied that he was a dying man, and wanted no favor but to pray with his children. This being granted, he commended us to the protection . . . of God almighty . . . and took his leave of us for this life, hoping that we should meet in a better." Later, his Indian captors sold him to a Jesuit in Canada. "He gave me a biscuit, which I put in my pocket, and not daring to eat, I buried under a log, fearing he had put something in it to make me love him." Drake, *Border Wars*, 29–33.

39 In a subsequent attack on Durham, the Indians employed the same tactics—placing detachments between the fields and the houses in order to engage the men in the open field, where they could not use fortifications. After successfully dealing with the men in the field, the Indians turned on the garrison houses. There the defenders—women and children— held off the attackers. Unable to force their way in, the Indians opened negotiations. The defenders surrendered when they received assurances that no harm would come to them. Following the surrender, four of the boys were immediately killed. Ibid., 31–32; 38, n.2. The similarity between this attack and the 1689 attack on Pemaquid illustrates that English garrison houses and blockhouses were impregnable fortresses for Indian forces. Furthermore, it indicates that Indian leaders were very much aware of their impotence against fortified positions.

40 Frontenac was recalled into service because the French had been suffering terrible losses to the Iroquois in the Great Lakes region. Frontenac maintained a defensive presence in the west, against the Iroquois, while taking the offensive in the east.

41 In Salmon Falls, the French troops were unable to capture the town's three garrison houses. Despite the settlers' lax defensive preparations and despite the element of surprise, these houses were surrendered through negotiations, rather than combat. Osgood, *American Colonies*, 1:77–78; Drake, *Border Wars*, 50; Wade, *Brief History*, 43.

42 Osgood, *American Colonies*, 1:73; Drake, *Border Wars*, 36, 50.

43 Portneuf's men were not equipped for construction assignments but found digging tools

in the village. The mostly Indian troops were not used to digging trenches (rather than fighting), nor did they like the assignment. Nevertheless, Portneuf was convinced that the trench was essential and his men industriously complied with his demands. Drake, *Border Wars*, 52.

44 Osgood, *American Colonies*, 1:78; Drake, *Border Wars*, 53.

45 Originally, the campaign was to be a private expedition. The Massachusetts merchants were permitted to raise volunteers for the campaign. But the offer of shares in the prospective plunder did not attract the requisite number of volunteers. Thus, the expedition became a state enterprise. Phillips, *Salem in the Eighteenth Century*, 10–11; Osgood, *American Colonies*, 1:82–83.

46 Phips was an inexperienced commander and a novice at war. Originally a ship's carpenter in Maine and later a sea captain, Phips became one of Boston's wealthiest gentlemen. Phips allied himself to Increase Mather in his opposition to Sir Edmund Andros's administration, leading up to the colony's Glorious Revolution. Through initiative and marriage, and thanks to the recovery of a large treasure from a Spanish galleon that had sunk in the West Indies, Phips was awarded a baronetcy and eventually—in 1692, after his disastrous expedition against Quebec—the governorship of Massachusetts. His position in New England was undermined in London by Joseph Dudley's endeavors to replace him. Phips died in England (while answering charges leveled against him by Dudley) on February 18, 1695, and was succeeded by Richard Coote, the Earl of Bellomont. *Journal of the Proceedings*, 3; Church, *History of Philip's War*, 207, n.2; Hutchinson, *History of the Colony*, 2:59, 63–64; Drake, *Border Wars*, 57; Osgood, *American Colonies*, 1:84.

47 *Journal of the Proceedings*, 1:85; Drake, *Border Wars*, 57.

48 Selesky, *War and Society*, 40–41; Osgood, *American Colonies*, 1:86–87; Wade, *Brief History*, 44; Hamilton, *French and Indian Wars*, 37–39.

49 Wade, *Brief History*, 44; Osgood, *American Colonies*, 1:89; Selesky, *War and Society*, 40–41.

50 By the time the English arrived, the French defenders already outnumbered (and outgunned) the English attackers. Osgood, *American Colonies*, 1:90–91.

51 This plan, which failed in King William's War, worked perfectly during the Seven Years' War. The decisive difference between the two campaigns was in logistical preparation.

52 Because Montreal was no longer threatened by New York's army, Frontenac was able to dedicate all of his forces to the defense of Quebec.

53 Walley, "Major Walley's Journal," 460, 463–64, 467.

54 Wade, *Brief History*, 44; Osgood, *American Colonies*, 1:90–92; Drake, *Border Wars*, 58–65; Melvoin, *New England Outpost*, 188; Hamilton, *French and Indian Wars*, 37–39.

55 Some of the fort's ninety-five defenders were killed (contrary to the terms of surrender) but most were allowed to return to Boston unharmed. Captain Chubb was tried for high treason but was not convicted. He died soon after, during an Indian attack on Andover. Church, *History of Philip's War*, 219–20, n.1; Hutchinson, *History of the Colony*, 2:69–70; Hamilton, *French and Indian Wars*, 43; Drake, *Border Wars*, 72, 109–12, 114–15; Osgood, *American Colonies*, 1:113.

56 Dummer, *Letter to a Noble Lord*, 3–8; Penhallow, *History of the Wars*, 13, 26.

57 Mather, *Decennium luctuosum*, 31; Drake, *Border Wars*, 71–74, 76–80, 108–9, 117–33; Osgood,

American Colonies, 1:96–97, 112; Peckham, Colonial Wars, 42–43; Hamilton, French and Indian Wars, 43; Melvoin, New England Outpost, 198–99, 211; Banks, History of York, 1:228–29, 290–91, 294.

58 Church, History of Philip's War, 165–66; idem, Entertaining History, 98–101.

59 Church told the Indian women who remained in the village to tell Kankamagus and Worombo who he was, what he had accomplished during King Philip's War, and where to bring English captives in order to redeem their wives and children. Church, Entertaining History, 108, 115–17; Church, History of Philip's War, 182–84, 186–89.

60 Church, Entertaining History, 118.

61 In July 1691, four English companies, under the command of Captain John March, set out on an expedition against the Pejobscots. Like Church, March could not find any Indians to fight; like, Church, he encamped at Purpooduc Point on his way home; and like Church, March's force was attacked by the Indians he was hunting. Church, Entertaining History, 119–22; idem, History of Philip's War, 192–96; Drake, Border Wars, 71–72.

62 A third expedition, led by Church in August 1692, also ended in frustration. Church's last expedition took place during Queen Anne's War, in 1704. Church, Entertaining History, 129–35, 164–88; idem, History of Philip's War, 212–14; Peckham, Colonial Wars, 44; Drake, Border Wars, 68–69, 112–13; Osgood, American Colonies, 1:111–12.

63 To prevent the evacuation of the frontiers (thus exposing the more established settlements on the interior), permanent garrisons were established or strengthened in Amesbury, Haverhill, Billerica, Chelmsford, Dunstable, Groton, and Marlborough. Simultaneously, the colonial governments enforced legislation forbidding settlers on the frontier from abandoning their estates on pain of forfeiture. Osgood, American Colonies, 1:94, 111; Drake, Border Wars, 70–71, 95, 108–9, 117–33; Melvoin, New England Outpost, 198–99, 211.

64 Thomas Bickford's garrison was located near the river. When the attack began, Bickford's wife and children escaped in a boat. Bickford remained in the house alone, unmoved by his besiegers' threats and generous terms of surrender. He fired at them as quickly as possible from different locations along the stockade surrounding the house. To further impress the Indians with the number of men under his command, Bickford shouted orders to "his men" and wore different hats as he moved from one firing position to another. The bluff worked and the Indians left the house unmolested. Peckham, Colonial Wars, 47; Hutchinson, History of the Colony, 2:61–62; Drake, Border Wars, 96–101, 102, n.1.

65 Hutchinson, History of the Colony, 2:62; Drake, Border Wars, 102.

66 Mather, Deplorable State, 4–6, 30–32; Philopolites [Mather], Memorial, 1–7, 16–37; Hutchinson, History of the Colony, 2:111–15, 117–21.

67 The negotiations were concluded with an Indian ceremony in which they piled stones in two columns ("two brothers"), symbolizing mutual friendship and respect. Hutchinson, History of the Colony, 2:100–101; Parkman, Half-Century of Conflict, 1:36–37; Peckham, Colonial Wars, 62; Reid, "Unorthodox Warfare," 211.

68 Massachusetts, By His Excellency (1703); Reid, "Unorthodox Warfare," 212, 213–14; Hamilton, French and Indian Wars, 48.

69 Parkman, Half-Century of Conflict, 1:47.

70 The Five Nations of the Iroquois had been New York's allies against the French and their

Indian allies. New York's failure to come to their aid effectively during King William's War, however, chilled the Iroquois' enthusiasm for war. They had suffered Indian attacks during King William's War, as well as successive epidemics. Their numbers had decreased by half, and by 1703 they could field only twelve hundred warriors. Parkman, *Half-Century of Conflict*, 1:10, 48, 55–56; Hamilton, *French and Indian Wars*, 48.

71 Penhallow, *History of the Wars*, 14; Hutchinson, *History of the Colony*, 2:106–7; Osgood, *American Colonies*, 1:409–18; Drake, *Border Wars*, 187–88.

72 Parkman, *Half-Century of Conflict*, 1:42–46, 48; Osgood, *American Colonies*, 1:405–7; Peckham, *Colonial Wars*, 62; Drake, *Border Wars*, 154–55, 158–61; Phillips, *Salem in the Eighteenth Century*, 48–49.

73 Penhallow, *History of the Wars*, 6–8; Parkman, *Half-Century of Conflict*, 1:45–46; Osgood, *American Colonies*, 1:405–7; Peckham, *Colonial Wars*, 62; Drake, *Border Wars*, 158–60; Phillips, *Salem in the Eighteenth Century*, 48–49.

74 Penhallow, *History of the Wars*, 11–16, 19, 23–25, 31–33, 44–48, 58–59; Hutchinson, *History of the Colony*, 2:110, 121–22, 129–30, 134, 140–41, 149–50; Parkman, *Half-Century of Conflict*, 1:94–98; Drake, *Border Wars*, 162–65, 167–69, 189–90, 205–7, 216–19.

75 Penhallow, *History of the Wars*, 11–13; Church, *History of Philip's War*, 243–44; Hutchinson, *History of the Colony*, 2:103–4; Parkman, *Half-Century of Conflict*, 1:56–57, 61–67; Demos, "Deerfield Massacre," 84, 86–87; Peckham, *Colonial Wars*, 63; Melvoin, *New England Outpost*, 216–20; Hamilton, *French and Indian Wars*, 49; Osgood, *American Colonies*, 1:410–12; Leach, *Northern Colonial Frontier*, 119–20; Demos, *Unredeemed Captive*, 20.

76 Parkman, *Half-Century of Conflict*, 1:50, 122–23; Osgood, *American Colonies*, 1:413–14, 417; Peckham, *Colonial Wars*, 64; Eames, "Rustic Warriors," 167; Drake, *Border Wars*, 194–203, 207–8; Philips, *Salem in the Eighteenth Century*, 49.

77 As mentioned above, the coercive powers of governments and of military commanders were limited in the colonies.

78 Eames, "Rustic Warriors," 167–68.

79 Ibid.

80 Provincial troops received ten pounds a scalp during Queen Anne's War, whereas volunteers without pay were awarded fifty pounds a scalp. Provincial troops that came to the relief of towns or garrisons received thirty pounds a scalp. (*Present State*, 9; Trask, *Letters*, 112, 117; Penhallow, *History of the Wars*, 39; Hutchinson, *History of the Colony*, 2:106; Axtell, *European and the Indian*, 223–24; Eames, "Rustic Warriors," 170–72; Osgood, *American Colonies*, 1:408; Melvoin, *New England Outpost*, 183, 201; Philips, *Salem in the Eighteenth Century*, 15–17; Drake, *Border Wars*, 166–67, 191–92).

81 Provincial soldiers usually volunteered for service, counting on lucrative personal contracts. Only rarely were men pressed for service in colonial armies. In many sources, bounty hunters are referred to as "volunteers." They were not, however, provincial troops.

82 Selesky, *War and Society*, 61–66, 70–71. The coercive powers of colonial governments were limited. Because public approval and consent were imperative, governments were unable to impress men into service for assignments that took them far from their own borders.

83 As soon as news of the attack on Wells reached Boston, Dudley's government ordered the improvement of fortifications in Wells, Berwick, and other settlements in Maine. Dudley

also recruited 150 men from the Massachusetts southern regiments for service in Maine. Meanwhile, Dudley dispatched a force of 100 dragoons to Wells and also sent the *Province Galley* north to patrol the coast as far as the Saint Croix River (this galleon saved Fort Casco in late August). Osgood, *American Colonies*, 1:406–7.

84 Throughout the winter of 1703–4, six hundred men ranged the woods along the northern frontier in an effort to seek and destroy enemy war bands and prevent their penetration into English territory (the attack on Deerfield demonstrated that the borders were porous despite these defensive measures). During summer 1704, over nineteen hundred men were posted along the borders of Maine and New Hampshire. Parkman, *Half-Century of Conflict*, 1:100.

85 Massachusetts, *By His Excellency* (1703).

86 Selesky, *War and Society*, 49; Osgood, *American Colonies*, 1:407; Murrin, "Anglicizing an American Colony," 80.

87 Hutchinson, *History of the Colony*, 2:123; Osgood, *American Colonies*, 1:423–25.

88 Commenting on this attack, Francis Parkman explained that "Canadian feudalism developed good partisan leaders, which was rarely the case with new England democracy." The force attacking Port Royal was "a crowd of ploughboys, fishermen, and mechanics, officered by tradesmen, farmers, blacksmiths [and so on]." Parkman, *Half-Century of Conflict*, 1:125–29; see also Penhallow, *History of the Wars*, 41–42; Hutchinson, *History of the Colony*, 2:124; Philips, *Salem in the Eighteenth Century*, 51.

89 Hutchinson, *History of the Colony*, 2:124–25; Parkman, *Half-Century of Conflict*, 1:128–31; Osgood, *American Colonies*, 1:425–26; Drake, *Border Wars*, 224–36.

90 Mather, *Deplorable State*, 4–6, 30–32; Philopolites [Mather], *Memorial*, 1–7, 16–37; Hutchinson, *History of the Colony*, 2:125, 127.

91 When John March returned to Boston, he was severely ridiculed. As he walked through the city, children would run after him, crying "wooden sword, wooden sword." An attempt was made to court martial March, but eventually the charges were dropped. Penhallow, *History of the Wars*, 43; Hutchinson, *History of the Colony*, 2:125–27; Parkman, *Half-Century of Conflict*, 1:128, 131; Philips, *Salem in the Eighteenth Century*, 50–51; Osgood, *American Colonies*, 1:427.

92 New York was to contribute 800 men, Connecticut 350 men, New Jersey 200 men, and Pennsylvania 150 men. Hutchinson, *History of the Colony*, 2:131; Penhallow, *History of the Wars*, 49–50; Osgood, *American Colonies*, 1:429–30.

93 Great Britain, *By the Honourable* (May 9, 1709); Great Britain, *By the Honourable* (May 26, 1709); Osgood, *American Colonies*, 1:429–30; Penhallow, *History of the Wars*, 49–50.

94 Early in 1709, the English suffered another setback on the eastern front. At dawn on January 1, 1709, a force of 164 men from Placentia (the chief French station in Newfoundland) attacked Fort William, the stronger of the two English forts in Saint John, Newfoundland. The outer gates of the fort were left wide open overnight. Undetected and unimpeded, the French advanced with ladders to the inner walls. The garrison awoke as the French climbed over the walls. Panic ensued, and the fort was captured. On January 2, the smaller fort ("the castle") surrendered, as did the village of Saint John itself. Despite his achievements, the governor of Placentia refused to commit the necessary funds and manpower to defend these new possessions against British attacks from the sea. The territory was therefore

abandoned the following summer. Parkman, *Half-Century of Conflict*, 1:131–33, 139–45; Selesky, *War and Society*, 55–56; Hutchinson, *History of the Colony*, 2:132; Osgood, *American Colonies* 1:430–35

95 Dummer, *Letter to a Noble Lord*, 3–8; Penhallow, *History of the Wars*, 13, 26; Massachusetts, *By His Excellency* (July 15, 1710); idem, *By His Excellency* (July 29, 1710); Penhallow, *History of the Wars*, 51–52; Hutchinson, *History of the Colony*, 2:134–35. Francis Nicholson served as Andros's lieutenant governor in New York. In 1689, with the arrival of the Glorious Revolution to America, Nicholson fled to England. He later served as governor of Maryland (1694–98) and of Virginia (1698–1705). Samuel Vetch was a Scottish immigrant who settled in Albany. While making a fortune trading with the Indians, Vetch involved himself in the government and administration of New York. After the capture of Port Royal, Samuel Vetch remained in Annapolis as Nova Scotia's military governor, with a garrison of 250 colonial soldiers and 200 British marines. In June 1711, Micmacs and Penobscots ambushed the English troops garrisoning Annapolis (70 soldiers were killed or captured). This attack, combined with desertion and disease, reduced the strength of the Annapolis garrison to 200 men fit for service. The success of the Indian attack, the weakness of the garrison, and the poor condition of the Annapolis fortifications encouraged the French Acadians. They joined the Indian revolt and lay siege to Annapolis (the besiegers numbered roughly 500). The French settlers begged Vaudreuil for military support. However, by that time Vaudreuil had already learned of Walker's expedition and decided to maintain as many defenders as possible in Montreal and Quebec. Without artillery and provisions, the siege of Annapolis soon dissolved. Parkman, *Half-Century of Conflict*, 1:151–54, 191–92; Penhallow, *History of the Wars*, 53–55; Hutchinson, *History of the Colony*, 2:135–37; Selesky, *War and Society*, 56; Osgood, *American Colonies*, 1:438–39; Drake, *Border Wars*, 260–61; Wade, *Brief History*, 48.

96 Dummer, *Letter to a Noble Lord*, 10–11; 13–17, 18–19; Penhallow, *History of the Wars*, 62–64; Hutchinson, *History of the Colony*, 2:142–43. Parkman, *Half-Century of Conflict*, 1:164–75; Selesky, *War and Society*, 57; Drake, *Border Wars*, 268–81; Osgood, *American Colonies*, 1:440–44.

97 Penhallow, *History of the Wars*, 65; Parkman, *Half-Century of Conflict*, 1:175–77; Wade, *Brief History*, 43; Hutchinson, *History of the Colony*, 2:144–46; Drake, *Border Wars*, 280–81; Osgood, *American Colonies*, 1:449–50.

98 Sandwiched between Nova Scotia and Newfoundland, Cape Breton Island controlled the entrance to the Gulf of Saint Lawrence. By controlling the Atlantic routes to New France, however, Britain turned the Mississippi into Canada's only lifeline. Parkman, *Half-Century of Conflict*, 1:185–86.

99 Drake, *Border Wars*, 289–93.

100 Parkman, *Half-Century of Conflict*, 1:232–39, 243–47, 253–64; Peckham, *Colonial Wars*, 84–85.

101 Parkman, *Half-Century of Conflict*, 1:185, 250–52.

102 To repeat, since early detection virtually insured defensive success, the presence of dogs was of critical importance to English defenders. Underhill, "Nevves from America," 79; James, *Three Visitors*, 15–16; Demos, 312–13; Drake, *Border Wars*, 20–21.

103 In a devastating surprise attack on Dover, New Hampshire (June 27, 1689), four of the town's five garrison houses were captured by the Indian attackers (52 inhabitants were

killed or captured). These houses were captured because Indian women, who had spent the night as guests in the houses, unlocked their gates in advance of the Indian assault. The one house that remained locked at the time of the attack remained unharmed. Drake, *Border Wars*, 14–21; Osgood, *American Colonies*, 1:71.

104 Banks, *History of York*, 1:317.

105 Relief forces rarely arrived in time to interrupt an Indian attack. On May 13, 1704, for example, messengers notified Hartford officials of an attack on Northampton. Men and horses were immediately impressed into service. They reached Northampton three hours later but were too late to relieve the inhabitants. Selesky, *War and Society*, 51.

106 Colonel Thomas Westbrook articulated these concerns over the inefficacy of ranger units ("scouts") and relief forces in comparison to permanent garrisons. He recommended that "it wou'd be best that all the Officers return to their Post as soon as their Affairs will admit of it, so that we may be in the best posture we can in all our Frontiers to receive the Enemy, in case they shou'd make their Attempts on us." Trask, *Letters*, 118.

107 Settlers threatened to leave their estates on the frontier (thus exposing the more populous counties to Indian raids) if they did not receive adequate protection. The governments responded by penalizing settlers who had abandoned their freeholds with fines and forfeiture of estates. The destruction of York, for example, in winter 1692, turned Wells into a more isolated and vulnerable outpost. Because the inhabitants made preparations to evacuate their homes, the garrison there was reinforced and the town's store rooms were stocked full, in case of a siege. To further assuage the inhabitants' fears, the surrounding countryside was diligently patrolled by ranger units. When the long-awaited attack on Wells finally materialized, however, Captain Converse had under his command only fifteen soldiers of the garrison, a handful of the town's inhabitants, and fourteen men who had arrived with provisions for the small fort. Behind effective fortifications, with the women firing alongside the men, these defenders repelled a succession of assaults by a force of over three hundred Indians (under Madockwando, Moxus, and Egeremet) and a small band of Canadian troops commanded by Captain Portneuf. Mather, *Decennium luctuosum*, 90–94; Drake, *Border Wars*, 76, 77–80; Peckham, *Colonial Wars*, 43.

108 Marcus, "Connecticut Valley," 231.

109 Trask, *Letters*, 111–12; Eames, "Rustic Warriors," 145; Penhallow, *History of the Wars*, 28–29.

110 Mather, *Decennium luctuosum*, 26; my emphasis. During Queen Anne's War, Governor Dudley wrote to the Board of Trade: "We may . . . destroy their corn and houses [but there is] no likelihood of seeing them, who will have their scouts out, and march off as we approach them . . . however the experience of the best men that have at any time been here can advise to no better method then by constant marches, especially in the winter to dislodge and starve them." Eames, "Rustic Warriors," 182–83.

111 Mather, *Duodecennium luctuosum*, 11; Eames, "Rustic Warriors," 146.

112 On a few rare occasions (such as the Great Swamp Fight, during King Philip's War), Indian forces were surprised in their villages. Saddled with the responsibility of defending their wives and children, they adopted a defensive doctrine (positional defense, relying on firepower). On August 12, 1724, for example, Captains Harmon and Moulton were led by their Indian guides to the Norridgwocks' principal village. Forced to defend the battlefield, the

Indians stood their ground, where they were decimated by massed fire (whereas the Norridgewocks fired wildly, the English never broke formation and fired by ranks). Parkman,
Half-Century of Conflict, 1:245–46; Peckham, *Colonial Wars*, 85.

113 During Sir William Phips's ill-conceived expedition against Quebec, Major John Walley
landed his troops and advanced toward the city (inexplicably expecting effective artillery
support). On their landing, they were harassed by French skirmishers who were sniping at
them, "galling them considerably." The English troops fired one massive volley in the direction of the French snipers and then advanced toward them, still in formation. Rather
than face another devastating volley, the French skirmishers fled to the cover of a nearby
swamp. Major Walley displayed his predisposition for the tactical defense in his approach
toward the city as well. He advanced toward the town, threatening it with an assault. But,
despite taking the strategic offensive, Walley adopted the tactical defense, choosing a site
"where wee had better shelter for the men, and a better place for our defence, where we
placed out guards, and put ourselves in the best posture we could to defend ourselves and
offend our enemies, if they had come upon us." Walley, "Major Walley's Journal," 461, 463.

114 An examination of military encounters during Dummer's or Lovewell's War (1721–25)
yields numerous examples of such misconduct. Penhallow, *History of the Wars*, 112–14;
Trask, *Letters*, 112, 114, 116–17; Symmes, *Brief History*, 12–13, 15–16; Parkman, *Half-Century of
Conflict*, 1:257–68; Baxter, "Campaign Against the Pequakets"; Chamberlain, "John Chamberlain," 3–4; Kidder, *Expeditions*, 11–13; Eames, "Rustic Warriors," 162–63, 177–78.

115 Mather, *Decennium luctuosum*, 26.

116 Hutchinson, *History of the Colony*, 2:111–14; Bradley and Camp, *Forts of Pemaquid*, 12; Osgood, *American Colonies*, 1:404.

117 The diligence with which Andros, Phips, and Dudley fortified the frontier demonstrates
that responsible military leaders in the colonies appreciated the wisdom and efficacy of European conventions. Conversely, throughout his career, Benjamin Church berated his superiors for their infatuation with fortifications and positional defense. When Captain Cudworth decided to consolidate his strategic advantage against Philip by building a fort in the
Mount Hope peninsula (and later on, in the Pocasset country), Church was outraged. He
believed that rather than being positions of military might that commanded their surroundings, forts were "nests for destruction" for the besieged defenders. Osgood, *American Colonies*, 1:111.

118 Artillery was employed in all successful attacks on American forts. Without artillery, the
defenders could be forced into surrender only by starvation (that is, a lengthy siege) or by
collapsing or burning the fort's outer walls.

119 Eames, "Rustic Warriors," 132–33.

120 Penhallow, *History of the Wars*, 11, 32; Banks, *History of York*, 1:325; Osgood, *American Colonies*,
1:408; Philips, *Salem in the Eighteenth Century*, 52.

121 Since the colonies had demonstrated their poor administrative skills in past conflicts, it
was no coincidence that a considerable portion of the logistical planning for these operations was conducted in London.

CHAPTER FIVE

1   Kopperman, *Braddock*, 131; McCardell, *Ill-Starred General*, 251.

2   Baker, *First Siege*, 4, 5, 7. The thick stone walls of Louisburg, built thirty feet high and surrounded by a wide ditch, were defended by three batteries (150 guns in all) within the town walls. The town was further defended by a heavy battery of thirty guns on an island at the entrance to the port, and another one (the Grand Battery, boasting forty-two-pounders) directly opposite the port's entrance. The French fishing industry in the region (564 vessels, employing 27,500 men) was estimated by Governor William Shirley at £1 million annually. French success cut into the profits of many New Englanders and destabilized the economies of the New England colonies. Phillips, *Salem in the Eighteenth Century*, 139–40, 143, 147.

3   The garrison numbered eighty-seven soldiers, one-third of whom were unfit for service. The French force consisted of over six hundred troops, supported by two small armed vessels. Parkman, *Half-Century of Conflict*, 2:60–62; Whitton, *Wolfe*, 110–11.

4   Drake, *Particular History*, 54–57; Phillips, *Salem in the Eighteenth Century*, 140–41; Whitton, *Wolfe*, 110–12; Baker, *First Siege*, 6.

5   At the time, the naval base at Halifax did not yet exist. The garrisons in Canseau and Annapolis were neglected and inexplicably small (especially considering the fact that nearly all of Nova Scotia's sixteen thousand inhabitants were French). In Annapolis, the ramparts "were crumbling into the ditches, and the cows of the garrison walked over them at their pleasure" on their way to pasture. The garrisons at Canseau and Annapolis were also poorly supplied, resulting in a few deaths in Canseau, due to malnutrition. Parkman, *Half-Century of Conflict*, 2:61; Whitton, *Wolfe*, 111.

6   Massachusetts, Connecticut, and New Hampshire contributed 3,250, 526, and 304 troops, respectively. Baker, *First Siege*, 7–9; Wade, *Brief History*, 52.

7   Bradstreet, *Diary*, 9; Parkman, *Half-Century of Conflict*, 2:68–69; Whitton, *Wolfe*, 114–16; Baker, *First Siege*, 7–9; Phillips, *Salem in the Eighteenth Century*, 142–43.

8   DeForest, *Louisbourg Journals*, 6, 67; Whitton, *Wolfe*, 116; Baker, *First Siege*, 9; Phillips, *Salem in the Eighteenth Century*, 149.

9   Stearns, "Louisburg," 320–21; Bradstreet, *Diary*, 11–19; Phillips, *Salem in the Eighteenth Century*, 150–51; Whitton, *Wolfe*, 116–17; Baker, *First Siege*, 9–13; Pomeroy, *Journals*, 16–34; Gibson, *Boston Merchant*, 42–71; DeForest, *Louisburg Journals*, 69–78; Parkman, *Half-Century of Conflict*, 2:97–101.

10 Stearns, "Louisburg," 323; Bradstreet, *Diary*, 21; Giddings, "Journal," 302; Phillips, *Salem in the Eighteenth Century*, 151; Whitton, *Wolfe*, 118. The capture of the *Vigilant*—a sixty-four-gun ship laden with provisions and munitions for Louisburg, as well as reinforcements of 560 men—was most devastating for the French. General Pepperrell was quick to inform the besieged troops of the abortive French attempt to resupply Louisburg and of the growing strength of the English forces. Stearns, "Louisburg," 322–23; Drake, *Particular History*, 209–11; Bradstreet, *Diary*, 10–13, 15; Giddings, "Journal," 298–99; Gibson, *Boston Merchant*, 51–52; Parkman, *Half-Century of Conflict*, 2:123–24; Baker, *First Siege*, 14; Whitton, *Wolfe*, 117.

11 H. T. Wade, *Brief History*, 54, 56. Ian Kenneth Steele refers to the siege as "a caricature of European warfare conducted with levity, recklessness, and indiscipline." Steele, *Guerrillas and Grenadiers*, 49.

12 Pepperrell's experience in military life consisted of an uneventful service in the colonial militia. Wade, *Brief History*, 54, 56.

13 Supplies sent from France to Louisburg in autumn 1744 did not reach Canada in time (before Louisburg's port was blocked by ice). The French supply ships continued to the West Indies and the fort's garrison was forced to persevere through the harsh winter without their usual annual consignment of commissary and military supplies. Because supply levels were so low in Louisburg, the English captives from Canseau were released and sent to Boston. They corroborated Vaughan's assertions about conditions in Louisburg. Parkman, *A Half-Century of Conflict*, 2:68; Baker, *First Siege*, 7, 11; Phillips, *Salem in the Eighteenth Century*, 142–43; Whitton, *Wolfe*, 110.

14 Baker, *First Siege*, 14.

15 The troops did exhibit amateurism and lack of discipline—nearly half of English casualties were caused by mismanagement of cannon. The garrison's weakness, however, coupled with the heavy bombardment and the tight naval blockade, prevented the French from exploiting the besiegers' weaknesses. Steele, *Guerrillas and Grenadiers*, 49.

16 Drake, *Particular History*, 103–6, 109–12, 114–18, 141–48, 153–73, 254–60; Phillips, *Salem in the Eighteenth Century*, 154–55; Steele, *Guerrillas and Grenadiers*, 51; Eames, "Rustic Warriors," 128–29.

17 Eames, "Rustic Warriors," 172.

18 Drake, *Particular History*, 175.

19 Parkman, *Half-Century of Conflict*, 1:185.

20 Gipson, *British Empire*, 4:7; C. Fuller, *British Light Infantry*, 78.

21 Parkman, *Half-Century of Conflict*, 2:56–58; Gipson, *British Empire*, 4:8, 106–7, 5:20, 6:100; Jackson, *Rogers' Rangers*, 14, 17; Whitton, *Wolfe*, 104–5; Hamilton, "Colonial Warfare," *Proceedings*, 6. During this period, Louisburg, Fort Niagara, and Crown Point were strengthened with added fortifications and weaponry. The new forts included Forts Rouille (Toronto), Presqu'Isle, and Le Boeuf, in the Great Lakes region, and Fort Chartres, along the upper Mississippi, in the Illinois country. Other, smaller forts and fortified depots (manned by French garrisons) were constructed throughout Indian territory in Canada and the west.

22 Robinson, *American Forts*, 39–42.

23 Ibid., 34–35; Melvoin, *New England Outpost*, 279; Eames, "Rustic Warriors," 107–9.

24 Robinson, *American Forts*, 34–35.

25 Jackson, *Rogers' Rangers*, 15.

26 Hargreaves, *Bloodybacks*, 130; Steele, *Guerrillas and Grenadiers*, 88; idem, *Warpaths*, 192–93; Jackson, *Rogers' Rangers*, 15; Anderson, *People's Army*, 114–15, 118–22. According to Captain Peter Wraxall, Johnson's secretary, the American army suffered such heavy casusalties "by neglecting to have advanced & flank, Guards." Gipson, *British Empire*, 6:170–71.

27 Hargreaves, *Bloodybacks*, 130. Despite the fact that Johnson failed to complete his mission, he was awarded with a baronetcy for his tactical victory at Lake George. Braddock's defeat and death had shocked the English public. By celebrating William Johnson's achievements, the Crown attempted to downplay Braddock's debacle.

28 Steele, *Guerrillas and Grenadiers*, 88; Hargreaves, *Bloodybacks*, 130–31; Jackson, *Rogers' Rangers*, 16; Parker, "Wilderness Campaigning," 142.

29 Darlington, History, 77; Parkman, Montcalm and Wolfe, 232, 238–39; Pargellis, Military Affairs, 188, 190–94; idem, Lord Loudoun, 148–49, 151.

30 Pargellis, Military Affairs, 211; idem, Lord Loudoun, 151–52.

31 Parkman, Montcalm and Wolfe, 231; Pargellis, Lord Loudoun, 152–53.

32 Pargellis, Military Affairs, 188–89; idem, Lord Loudoun, 156–59.

33 Cross, "Journal," 15–16; Pargellis, Military Affairs, 211–13; idem, Lord Loudoun, 158–59; Parkman, Montcalm and Wolfe, 236, 239–41; Whitton, Wolfe, 185–187; Hargreaves, Bloodybacks, 137–38.

34 Whitton, Wolfe, 192–93; Steele, Betrayals, 75–77.

35 Knox, Historical Journal, 1:67–70; Whitton, Wolfe, 193–95; Pargellis, Lord Loudoun, 243–50; Steele, Betrayals, 92–93, 98–110.

36 Jackson, Rogers' Rangers, 16; Hargreaves, Bloodybacks, 131.

37 Parkman, Montcalm and Wolfe, 272–73; Pargellis, Lord Loudoun, 211, 231–235. Long, Lord Jeffrey Amherst, 48. The battalion, rather than the regiment, was the army's basic tactical unit. The regiment was an administrative unit. Usually, there was one battalion in every regiment, although some regiments were comprised of up to four battalions (such as the 60th regiment, also known as the Royal Americans).

38 Pargellis, Military Affairs, 391–94, 396–97; idem, Pargellis, Lord Loudoun, 238–39, 243; Steele, Guerrillas and Grenadiers, 116.

39 Amherst, Journal of Jeffery Amherst, 48–72; idem, Journal of the Landing, 6–18; Knox, Historical Journal, 1:184, 243–50, 3:97–101, 104–6, 112–14; Long, Lord Jeffrey Amherst, 55–70; Mahon, Life of General James, 63–66; Hargreaves, Bloodybacks, 145–46; Darlington, History, 92; Leach, Arms for Empire, 422.

40 Steele, Guerrillas and Grenadiers, 124. Authorities in Britain shared this view and, therefore, stressed the importance of a strong blockade on the Gulf of Saint Lawrence. Great Britain, Proceedings and Debates, 100.

41 Knox, Historical Journal, 1:393–456; Parkman, Montcalm and Wolfe, 470–78; Anderson, Crucible of War, 352–63.

42 Pitt, Correspondence, 1:297–301; Knox, Historical Journal, 1:185–86; Pargellis, Military Affairs, 418–22; Leach, Arms for Empire, 426; Darlington, History, 92; Anderson, People's Army, 16–17; Hargreaves, Bloodybacks, 151, 153–54; Parkman, Montcalm and Wolfe, 365–67.

43 Steele, Guerrillas and Grenadiers, 119.

44 Parkman, Montcalm and Wolfe, 377–79; Anderson, People's Army, 17.

45 Amherst, Journal of Jeffery Amherst, 63–64, 67; Long, Lord Jeffrey Amherst, 67.

46 Parkman, Half-Century of Conflict, 1:232–39, 243–47, 253–64; Peckham, Colonial Wars, 84–85.

47 Eames, "Rustic Warriors," 110–11.

48 Kopperman, Braddock, 126.

49 McCardell, Ill-Starred General, 212, 216.

50 Pargellis, "Braddock's Defeat," 254, 256, 260–61.

51 Ibid., 257, 264–65; Young, "Essay," 5–6; Simes, Military Medley, 125–26; McCardell, Ill-Starred General, 242–47.

52 McCardell, Ill-Starred General, 241; Livingston, "Military Operations in North-America," 91–94; Pargellis, Military Operations, 113–18; idem, "Braddock's Defeat," 259–63; McCardell,

Ill-Starred General, 248–53; Mahon, "Anglo-American Methods," 269; Anderson, *Crucible of War*, 100–106; Russell, "Redcoats," 643–44.

53   Pargellis, *Military Operations*, 119; McCardell, *Ill-Starred General*, 254–57, 261, 265.

54   Pargellis, "Braddock's Defeat," 263–64; Shy, *Toward Lexington*, 89.

55   Forbes, *Writings*, 13–25, 31; Pitt, *Correspondence*, 1:xlii–xliii; Hargreaves, *Bloodybacks*, 155–56; Parker, "Wilderness Campaigning," 275–76; Parkman, *Montcalm and Wolfe*, 384.

56   Quoted in Parker, "Wilderness Campaigning," 265.

57   Ibid., 266; Forbes, *Writings*, 131–32, 216, 220, 242–43, 245, 267–68, 274, 276.

58   Forbes, *Letters*, 8; idem, *Writings*, xi, 106, 131–32, 144–47, 157, 159, 173, 180, 207–8, 214, 216, 219–20, 242–43, 245, 254, 260, 267–68, 274, 276, 283; Cort, *Col. Henry Bouquet*, 10–14; Steele, *Guerrillas and Grenadiers*, 122; Hargreaves, *Bloodybacks*, 156–57.

59   Parker, "Wilderness Campaigning," 275–76, 280–81, 284, 285–86.

60   By that time, the French lost the support of most of their Indian allies in the west. On October 7, 1758, Governors Bernard and Denny, of New Jersey and Pennsylvania, began a series of negotiations at Easton, Pennsylvania, with over five hundred Indian representatives of all the Six Nations and nine other Indian tribes. According to the terms of the Treaty of Easton, Pennsylvania released territories beyond the Appalachians back into Indian hands, with a mutual understanding that English settlement beyond the mountains would not be permitted. Having achieved their war aims, most of these tribes discontinued their military cooperation with the French. *British Empire*, 7:278–79.

61   Forbes, *Letters*, 6; Cort, *Col. Henry Bouquet*, 14–15; K. Parker, "Wilderness Campaigning," 288; Hargreaves, *Bloodybacks*, 157; Darlington, *History*, 93–95.

62   Only once during Forbes's expedition, at the battle of Loyal Hannah (September 14, 1758), did enemy troops manage to threaten British troops. A scouting force—eight hundred light troops under the command of Captain James Grant—carelessly revealed its position to the enemy by setting fire to a French warehouse. In advance of the Indian attack, Grant divided his already small force into four groups. Thus, unable to produce massed fire against their assailants, these groups were overrun by an overwhelming number of French and Indians. Three hundred were captured or killed. Grant himself was captured. Forbes, *Writing*, 232–33; Parkman, *Montcalm and Wolfe*, 392–94; Parker, "Wilderness Campaigning," 277–78; Gipson, *British Empire*, 7:268–70.

63   Frazier, *Mohicans of Stockbridge*, 117; Loescher, *History of Rogers' Rangers*, 23–24, 27–30, 33–35; Jackson, *Rogers' Rangers*, 2, 17–24; McCulloch, "Buckskin Soldier," 17–18.

64   McCulloch, "Buckskin Soldier," 18. See also Parker, "Wilderness Campaigning," 218–19.

65   Rogers, *Journals*, 104, 106–7; Pitt, *Correspondence*, 2:221–22; Amherst, *Journal*, 168; Frazier, *Mohicans*, 134–36; Jackson, *Rogers' Rangers*, 104–5; McCulloch, "Buckskin Soldier," 20–21; Calloway, *Western Abenakis*, 175–79.

66   Rogers, *Journals*, 107–14; Beattie, "Adaptation," 81; McCulloch, "Buckskin Soldier," 21–22; Frazier, *Mohicans*, 135–36. During this unimpressive retreat, some of the rangers were driven by hunger to eat their own excrements, as well as their fallen comrades. McCulloch, "Buckskin Soldier," 21–22.

67   Rogers, *Journals*, 30–32; Parker, "Wilderness Campaigning," 232–36; Parkman, *Montcalm and Wolfe*, 310.

68 Rogers estimated the number of French casualties at 116, whereas French accounts reported only 36. Rogers reported 13 English fatalities and 7 captured. Rogers, *Journals*, 32; See also Parker "Wilderness Campaigning," 236.

69 Quoted in Frazier, *Mohicans*, 133.

70 Forbes, *Writings*, 116, 118, 159, 192, 228; idem, *Letters*, 32; Amherst, *Journal of Jeffery Amherst*, 129–31, 133; Amherst, *Journal of William Amherst*, 42–43, 46; Frazier, *Mohicans*, 119, 125–26; Beattie, "Adaptation," 75; Russell, "Redcoats," 646–47; Rogers, *British Army*, 150; McCulloch, "Buckskin Soldier," 21; Jackson, *Rogers' Rangers*, 29–31, 33, 38–39, 41–42, 70–71.

71 Unaffiliated with the regiments, they could not be disciplined or held accountable by British officers.

72 Beattie, "Adaptation," 70, 74–75, Frazier, *Mohicans*, 127–29, 130–31, 137. In July 1757, for example, a company of rangers took two weeks off, vacationing on an island in Lake George, when they were supposed to be surveying enemy positions. Pargellis, *Lord Loudoun*, 303–4.

73 Mahon, "Anglo-American Methods," 265–66; Beattie, "Adaptation," 70.

74 Hamilton, "Colonial Warfare," 7; Pargellis, *Lord Loudoun*, 299–300; Russell, "Redcoats," 645; Parker, "Wilderness Campaigning," 238–40; Robson, "British Light Infantry," 209–10.

75 Quoted in Pargellis, *Military Affairs*, 224; see also idem, *Lord Loudoun*, 97–98, 300–301, 304–5; Long, *Lord Jeffrey Amherst*, 52; Anderson, *People's Army*, 18.

76 Long, *Lord Jeffrey Amherst*, 52; Beattie, "Adaptation," 68; Pargellis, *Lord Loudoun*, 97–98. General Forbes expressed a similarly low opinion of his provincial troops during his expedition against Fort Duquesne. Forbes, *Writings*, 198. As late as 1759, provincial troops distinguished themselves as careless and unprepared soldiers. They certainly fell short of their legendary reputation as a nation of rugged frontiersmen and expert riflemen. Upon inspecting his troops prior to his expedition against Ticonderoga, General Amherst was shocked to find that many provincials had only the most rudimentary understanding of the mechanics of their firearms. Few of them knew how to take care of their muskets and maintain them in working order. Amherst directed his officers to provide provincial units with Humphrey Bland's *Treatise of Military Discipline* and to give top priority to the training of provincial troops in the operation of their firearms. Whisker, *American Colonial Militia*, 1:78. He attempted to cure his provincials of their carelessness, lawlessness, and proclivity for desertion through a liberal application of the lash and the hangman's noose. Amherst, *Journal of Jeffery Amherst*, 113; Green, *Three Military Diaries*, 56–58, 63, 66–68.

77 Rogers, *British Army*, 72–73 Robson, "British Light Infantry," 211–14; Shy, *Toward Lexington*, 129–30; Russell, "Redcoats in the Wilderness," 645; Pargellis, *Lord Loudoun*, 304–5; Hargreaves, *Bloodybacks*, 148; Rogers, *British Army*, 71–72; Mahon, "Anglo-American Methods," 257, 260; Myatt, *British Infantry*, 55.

78 Paret, "Colonial Experience," 53–56; Russell, "Redcoats," 630, 634–35, 637, 638. Rifled firearms existed in Europe as early as 1477. Eighteenth-century rifles were capable of hitting a man-size target at a distance of over two hundred yards (maximal effective range). However, they were much slower to load (three to four times slower) and tended to jam more than the loose-fitting barrels of the muskets. Furthermore, rifle barrels were of smaller caliber than the muskets and were not uniform. Thus, each rifleman had to cast his

own bullets to fit his individual rifle. Similarly, each rifleman had to weigh and measure the powder charge to fit his rifle's specific requirements. Prepacked cartridges were, therefore, not available for riflemen, which slowed the loading process. Moreover, because they were not fitted for bayonets, rifles were a defensive liability in battles that could involve close-quarters combat. These characteristics made rifle units relatively ineffective against enemy formations of even average strength, which could generate more rapid and effective fire. Thus, detachments of riflemen (acting as snipers) were tiny and acted only as auxiliaries to larger light-infantry units furnished with muskets. Hamilton, "Colonial Warfare," 10; Mahon, "Anglo-American Methods," 256; Tonso, *Gun and Society*, 65; Beattie, "Adaptation," 73; Whisker, *American Colonial Militia*, 1:85.

79 Especially important in this respect was the enhanced role of artillery in European warfare. Larger artillery trains required added protection.

80 Light troops were required for this purpose especially when the army was on the march, because large forces required considerable time to transform themselves from a marching force (in columns) to a fighting force (in ranks).

81 Simes, *Military Medley*, 150–51.

82 Russell, "Redcoats," 637, 638.

83 Ibid., 632–35; Beattie, "Adaptation," 68; Fuller, *British Light Infantry*, 49–59.

84 Training in light-infantry tactics was discontinued in the British Army after the close of the Seven Years' War. Mahon, "Anglo-American Methods," 267. The British did not expect to fight another war in North America. Elsewhere throughout the empire, the army could rely on local irregulars to serve as light troops.

85 Russell, "Redcoats," 642.

86 General Forbes followed Braddock's lead in this respect, when he lost his five hundred Indian troops (driven off by boredom during the tedious construction of Forbes's road). Steele, *Warpaths*, 214.

87 Young, "Essay," 5–6; Simes, *Military Medley*, 125–26; Webb, *A military treatise*, 66–71; Beattie, "Adaptation," 58–59. See also Russell, "Redcoats," 642.

88 Quoted in Pargellis, *Military Affairs*, 129–32; see also Russell, "Redcoats," 643; Beattie, "Adaptation," 59.

89 Stevenson, *Military Instructions*, 8–12, 16–31, 99–148; Young, "Essay," 5–6, 9, 12–13; Simes, *Military Medley*, 125–26; Webb, *A military treatise*, 66–71.

90 Webb, *A military treatise*, 58–59.

91 Parker, "Wilderness Campaigning," 247–51. Redoubts are small square defensive works without any bastions.

92 Stevenson, *Military Instructions*, 52–53; see also 37–45.

93 Russell, "Redcoats," 649–50.

94 Hargreaves, *Bloodybacks*, 151–52. A similar course of action was taken by Colonel Bouquet in the Battle of Bushy Run, during Pontiac's Rebellion in 1763. Indian attackers were drawn and directed by light-infantry units toward the heavy infantry formations. There, the British decimated the Indians with a strong volley of fire. Amherst, *Journal of Jeffery Amherst*, 316–17; Parker, "Wilderness Campaigning," 302–8; Parkman, *Conspiracy of Pontiac*, 2:67–78, 369–74.

95　In the Battle of Bushy Run, Bouquet used the bayonet charge to direct a large body of Indians toward his strong formations of heavy infantry, where they were devastated by heavy fire and then chased off with yet another bayonet charge (inducing a quick withdrawal of the remainder of the Indian army). Amherst, *Journal of Jeffery Amherst*, 316–17; Parker, "Wilderness Campaigning," 302–8; Parkman, *Conspiracy of Pontiac*, 2:67–78, 369–74.

96　Hamilton, "Colonial Warfare," 7.

97　Beattie, "Adaptation," 62–63; Parker, "Wilderness Campaigning," 185–86; Pargellis, *Lord Loudoun*, 291–93. The stores supplied to Britain's troops were procured in the British Isles and in North America. Provisions of unsuitable quality were to be replaced immediately at the expense of Baker, Kilby, and Baker. In 1760, a different trading firm was contracted to supply the British Army in America.

98　The western frontiers were untracked. Almost all intercolonial commerce was conducted along the eastern seaboard and the waterways. To move large armies safely, in defensive formation, paths had to be cleared through the forests. One method of safeguarding roads was "to leave a small border of trees on each side of the road, and clear away beyond it. This makes a defence for any parties marching along the road and they command everything that passes the cleared part. By this means they are not so liable to be surprised by the skulking parties of Indians." Amherst, *Journal of William Amherst*, 40; Hamilton, "Colonial Warfare," 7.

99　Parker, "Wilderness Campaigning," xv–xvii, 145–47.

100　Beattie, "Adaptation," 64; Pargellis, *Military Affairs*, 263–85, 330–35; idem, *Lord Loudoun*, 296–98; Beattie, "Adaptation," 64–65; Anderson, *Crucible of War*, 180. In 1756, it cost nearly sixpence per mile to transport a barrel of beef from Albany to Lake George. By the end of 1757, it cost less than twopence.

101　On July 3, 1756, an ambush on a British supply convoy offered Loudoun's transport troops an opportunity to demonstrate their ability to defend themselves and their cargo. A convoy of supply boats on the return trip from Oswego to Albany was attacked by a force of nine hundred French and Indian troops. The boatmen settled into a lengthy and indecisive fire fight with their attackers. After several hours, the British troops launched a successful bayonet charge that dispersed the enemy and brought the battle to a close. Livingston, "Military Operations in North-America," 155–56; Bougainville, *Adventure in the Wilderness*, 6; Parkman, *Montcalm and Wolfe*, 229–30.

102　Beattie, "Adaptation," 65–67; Pargellis, *Military Affairs*, 263–85, 330–35.

103　Shirley was relieved of all official duties because of suspicious regarding financial malfeasance. He was replaced by Loudoun as commander in chief and by Thomas Pownall as governor of Massachusetts.

104　Pargellis, *Lord Loudoun*, 167–86, 212, 218–27, 263–78; Boorstin, *Americans*, 364–65; Steele, *Guerrillas and Grenadiers*, 95, 113; Anderson, *People's Army*, 12–14; idem, *Crucible of War*, 167, 180–83.

105　Pargellis, *Lord Loudoun*, 293, 306.

106　Brewer, *Sinews of Power*, 30; Pitt, *Correspondence*, 2:75–76, 86–87, 139; Steele, *Guerrillas and Grenadiers*, 94, 115–16. The high cost of executing the war in America led Britain to attempt to recuperate its losses by extracting greater revenues from the colonies in the 1760s and

1770s. These attempts led to the acrimony that preceded the outbreak of the American Revolution. By the end of the American War of Independence, Britain's national debt ballooned to £242,000,000, forcing Britain to cut its losses and discontinue hostilities against its many enemies.

107 Amherst, Journal, 113–32, 144–50, 198–226.

108 Ibid., 14, 143–51, 154; Pitt, Correspondence, 2:143–44, 201, 241, 244; Rogers, Journals, 103–4; Rogers, British Army, 136, 143; Shy, Toward Lexington, 90–91, 94–95; Hargreaves, Bloodybacks, 160; Anderson, People's Army, 18.

109 Ticonderoga and Crown Point served as valuable supply depots in later years.

110 Amherst, Journal of Jeffery Amherst, 227–47.

111 Quoted in Whitton, Wolfe, 96.

112 Loudoun's system in the north required a series of permanent fortified establishments of troops, rangers, artisans, and beasts of burden (complete with provisions, tackle, machinery, and ammunition).

113 As Daniel Defoe remarked, contemporary "maxims of war [were]—Never fight without an advantage, and always encamp so as not to be forced to it." Steele, Guerrillas and Grenadiers, 6.

114 In the early stages of the war, the French could still mobilize proper campaigns, complete with regular infantry battalions, supply trains, and artillery (in the expeditions against Oswego and Fort William Henry, for example). By 1758, however, New France was too weak to employ European tactics.

115 This is the reason why the battalions of Colonel Bouquet's 60th Royal Americans never fought as a unit during the war. Rather, the regiment's companies were attached to various other regiments to serve as light-infantry auxiliaries. Parker, "Wilderness Campaigning," 254, n.3.

116 Amherst argued that "if the men are silent, attentive, and obedient to their officers," the firepower produced by two ranks of musketeers was sufficiently powerful to repel light formations such as those of the Indians and Canadians. Beattie, "Adaptation," 78.

117 Nicola, Treatise of Military Exercise, vi–vii. By the middle of the eighteenth century, British regulars could produce between three and four shots per minute. Eames, "Rustic Warriors," 432; Hamilton, "Colonial Warfare," 10. Ordered in three ranks, the defensive line produced a massive volley of fire roughly every six seconds. Light formations in the field could not survive such devastating fire, nor could they match the firepower of larger infantry formations.

118 Utley, Frontier Regulars, 46–47. Utley comments that the army's strategy was a wise one but that the army was too small to make it as effective as it could have been: "The flaws in this system arose mainly from the small size of the army. To be truly effective, the network of forts needed to be comprehensive enough to cover all potential trouble spots and strongly enough held to permit the prompt application of force sufficient to meet probable contingencies." Utley's assessment of Custer's defeat at the Little Bighorn underscores the superiority of European tactics over Indian tactics. He states that Sitting Bull's troops were victorious partly because they outnumbered Custer's three to one and because they were motivated and self-assured. Nevertheless, Utley holds Custer responsible for his defeat because of his failure to conduct his men in proper formation. He asserts that a cardinal

factor in Custer's defeat was that his men "allowed themselves to be beaten in fragments. In each fragment, command and control collapsed, discipline evaporated, and men panicked." Utley, "Sitting Bull," 51.

119 Cort, *Col. Bouquet*, 9; see also Parker, "Wilderness Campaigning," xviii.

120 Amherst, *Journal of Jeffery Amherst*, 14; Shy, *Toward Lexington*, 94–95.

121 Shy, *Toward Lexington*, 88–89.

CONCLUSION

1 Steele, *Warpaths*, 222.

2 Leach, *Arms for Empire*, 407–8, n.44; McCulloch, "Buckskin Soldier," 18, 20.

3 Nicola, *Treatise of Military Exercise*, 84.

4 Ward, *Animadversions of Warre*, 2:63.

5 It is usually strategic or logistical weakness that impels a commander to adopt offensive tactics. Whenever possible, a military force is best served by preserving the protective gap between itself and the enemy. Only desperation or recklessness could move a commander to jeopardize his mission and his troops by eliminating this gap.

6 In a letter to Secretary of State Henry Fox, Peter Wraxall (William Johnson's secretary) complained about the quality of the army led by Johnson to Fort Saint Frederic: "The Officers of this Army with very few Exceptions are utter Strangers to military Life and most of them in no Respect superior to the Men they are put over, They are like the heads and indeed are the heads of a Mob. The Men are raw Country Men. They are flattered with an easy & a speedy Conquest; All Arts are used to hide future Difficulties and Dangers from them, and the whole Undertaking in all its Circumstances smoothed over to their Imaginations." Steele, *Guerrillas and Grenadiers*, 95. During the Seven Years' War, British military authorities were disappointed by the cost and performance of colonial soldiers. Like Governor Joseph Dudley, they considered provincial troops a broken reed and prevailed upon the British government in 1758 to allow twenty-four thousand regulars for service in America.

7 British soldiers were trained to "lock" their formations during battle—soldiers tightened and stabilized the ranks and the files by establishing physical contact between and within the ranks. Bland, *Abstract of Military Discipline*, 37–38; Eames, "Rustic Warriors," 391. This practice not only increased the effectiveness of a platoon's fire but also reassured each soldier that his comrades were maintaining their position. Thus, soldiers could feel secure in the knowledge that their flanks were not exposed. (Furthermore, even if a soldier felt the urge to break formation, he was "locked" into position by the men surrounding him.)

8 To paraphrase Rudyard Kipling ("The Law of the Jungle," *The Second Jungle Book*), the strength of the pack was the musketeer and the strength of the musketeer was the pack.

9 Fischer, *Paul Revere's Ride*, 227, 229, 230, 231, 242, 245–46, 253, 259.

BIBLIOGRAPHY /

PRIMARY SOURCES

Amherst, Jeffery. *Commissary Wilson's Orderly Book: Expedition of the British and Provincial Army, Under Major General Jeffrey Amherst, Against Ticonderoga and Crown Point, 1759.* Albany: J. Munsell, 1857.

——. *The Journal of Jeffrey Amherst, Recording the Military Career of General Amherst in America From 1758 to 1763.* Edited by J. C. Webster. Toronto: Ryerson Press, 1931.

——. *A Journal of the Landing of His Majesty's Forces on the Island of Cape-Breton, and of the Siege and Surrender of Louisbourg.* Boston: Green & Russell, 1758.

Amherst, William. *Journal of William Amherst in America, 1758–1760.* Edited by John C. Webster. Shediac, New Brunswick, 1927.

Arber, Edward. *The Story of The Pilgrim Fathers, 1606–1623 A.D. as Told by Themselves, their Friends and their Enemies.* London, 1897.

Banks, Charles E., ed. *The History of Martha's Vineyard.* Vol. 1. Boston: George H. Dean, 1911.

Barriffe, William. *Military Discipline: The Compleat Souldier . . . : To Which is Added, the Military Law of the Province of the Massachusetts-Bay in N.E.* Boston: B. Green, 1706.

——. *Military Discipline: The Compleat Souldier or Expert Artillery-Man . . . : To Which is Added, the Duties of All the Officers, in a Private Company: As Also the Military Law of the Province of the Massachusetts-Bay.* Boston: Nicholas Boone, 1701.

——. *Militarie Discipline: Or the Young Artillery-Man.* London: Gertrude Dawson, 1661.

——. *Militarie Discipline: The Yovng Artillery-Man: VVherein is Discoursed and Shown the Postures Both of Musket and Pike the Exactest Way, &c.: Together With the Exercise of the Foot in Their Motions, With Much Variety: As Also Diverse and Severall Formes For the Inbattelling Small or Greater Bodies, Demonstrated by the Number of a Single Company, With Their Reducements.* London: John Dawson, 1643.

Bland, Humphrey. *An Abstract of Military Discipline: More Particularly With Regard to the Manual Exercise, Evolutions and Firings of the Foot.* New York: Boston and New York: De Forest, 1754.

——. *A Treatise of Military Discipline.* London: S. Buckley, 1727.

Boone, Nicholas. *Military Discipline: The Compleat Souldier, or Expert Artillery-Man . . . : To Which is Added, the Duties of All the Officers, in a Private Company: As Also the Military Law of the Province of the Massachusetts-Bay: Being a Collection From Col. Elton, Bariff, and Others.* Boston: Nicholas Boone, 1701.

——. *Military discipline: The Compleat Soldier: To Which is Added, the Military Law of the Province of the Massachusetts-Bay in N.E.* Boston: B. Green, 1706.

Bougainville, Louis Antoine. *Adventure in the Wilderness: The American Journals of Louis Antoine de Bougainville, 1756–1760.* Edited and translated by E. P. Hamilton. Norman: University of Oklahoma Press, 1964.

Bradford, William. *Bradford's History of Plymouth Plantation.* Edited by William T. Davis. New York: Charles Scribner's Sons, 1908.

——. *History of Plymouth Plantation.* Edited by W. C. Ford. Boston: Massachusetts Historical Society, 1912.

Bradstreet, Dudley. *Diary Kept by Lieut. Dudley Bradstreet of Groton, Mass. During the Siege of Louisburg, April, 1745–January, 1746.* Cambridge: John Wilson and Son, 1897.

Breton, William. *Militia Discipline: The Words of Command, and Directions for Exercising the Musket, Bayonet, & Cartridge . . . For the Instruction of Young Soldiers [By William Breton; Printed at London, 1717]; To Which is Added, Some Further Directions for the Exercise of a Company or Battalion Drawn Up Three, or Six Deep; As Also, an Abstract of the Militia Law in This Province.* Boston: Printed for D. Henchman, 1733.

Church, Benjamin. *Diary of King Philip's War, 1675–76.* Chester, Conn.: Pequot Press, 1975.

Church, Thomas. *The entertaining history of King Philip's war, which began in the month of June, 1675. As also of expeditions more lately made against the common enemy, and Indian rebels, in the eastern parts of New England: with some account of the divine providence towards Col. Benjamin Church.* Newport, R.I.: Solomon Southwick, 1772.

——. *Entertaining Passages Relating to Philip's War Which Began in the Month of June 1675.* Boston, 1716.

——. *The History of King Philip's War, Commonly Called The Great Indian War of 1675 and 1676: Also of the French and Indian Wars at the Eastward in 1689, 1690, 1692, 1696, and 1704.* Boston: Thomas B. Wait and Son, 1827.

——. *The History of Philip's War, Commonly Called The Great Indian War of 1675 and 1676: Also of the French and Indian Wars at the Eastward in 1689, 1690, 1692, 1696, and 1704.* Boston: J. H. A. Frost, 1827.

Colden, Cadwallader. *The History of the Five Indian Nations of Canada Depending on the Province of New York in America.* New York: Bradford, 1727.o

Connecticut. *Public Records of the Colony of Connecticut.* Hartford: F. A. Brown, 1852.

Cross, Stephen. "Journal of Stephen Cross of Newburyport." *Essex Institute Historical Collection* 76 (1940): 14–42.

Davis, W. T., ed. *Records of the Town of Plymouth.* Plymouth, Mass.: Avery and Doten, 1889–1903.

DeForest, Louis E., ed. *Louisbourg Journals, 1745.* New York: Society of Colonial Wars in the State of New York, 1932.

Drake, Samuel G. *A Particular History of the Five Years French and Indian War in New England and Parts Adjacent: From its Declaration by the King of France, March 15, 1744, to the Treaty With the Eastern Indians, Oct. 16, 1749, Sometimes Called Gov. Shirley's War; With a Memoir of Major-General Shirley, Accompanied by his Portrait and Other Engravings.* Albany: Munsell, 1870.

Dummer, Jeremiah. *A Letter to a Noble Lord, Concerning the Late Expedition to Canada*. Boston: Eleazer Phillips, 1712.

Elton, Richard. *The Compleat Body of the Art Military: Divided into Three Books, the First Conteining the Postures of the Pike and Musket . . . The Second Comprehending Twelve Exercises . . . The Third Setting Forth the Drawing Up & Exercising of Regiments*. London: Robert Leybourn, 1650.

A Farther Brief and True Narration of the Great Swamp Fight in the Narragansett Country December 19, 1675. Written a Few Days Later and First Printed at London in February, 1676. Providence: Society of Colonial Wars in the State of Rhode Island and Providence Plantations, 1912.

Forbes, John. *Letters of General John Forbes relating to the Expedition against Fort Duquesne in 1758*. Edited by Irene Stewart. Pittsburgh: Allegheny County Committee, 1927.

——. *Writings of General John Forbes relating to His Service in North America*. Edited by Alfred Procter James. Menasha, Wis.: Collegiate Press, 1938.

Gardiner, Curtis A., ed. *Lion Gardiner and his Descendants*. St. Louis: A. Whipple, 1890.

Gardiner, Lion. "Relation of the Pequot Wars." In *Lion Gardiner and his Descendants*, edited by Curtis Gardiner, 7–24. St. Louis: A. Whipple, 1890.

Gibson, James. *A Boston Merchant of 1745; or, Incidents in the Life of James Gibson, a Gentleman Volunteer at the Expedition of Louisbourg*. Boston: Redding and Company, 1847.

Giddings, Daniel. "Journal Kept by Lieut. Daniel Giddings of Ipswich During the Expedition Against Cape Breton in 17445." *Essex Institute Historical Collections* 48 (1912): 293–304.

Great Britain. Parliament. *Proceedings and Debates of the British Parliaments Respecting North America*. Edited by Leo F. Stock.. Millwood: Kraus International Publications, 1982.

Great Britain. Sovereign. *By the Honourable Col. Francis Nicholson and Col. Samuel Vetch . . . A Proclamation, Whereas her Majesty hath been pleased to Instruct us with her Royal Commands*. May 9, 1709. Boston: 1709.

——. *By the Honourable Col. Francis Nicholson and Col. Samuel Vetch . . . A Proclamation, Whereas by a former Proclamation we had, in her Majestys Name, by virtue of her Royal Instruction . . . assured all of Her Majestys Subjects as should enlist themselves to go as Volunteers in the present Expedition, of a good Firelock . . .*, May 26, 1709. New York: Bradford, 1709.

Green, Samuel Abbott. *Three Military Diaries Kept by Groton Soldiers in Different Wars*. Groton: John Wilson and Son, 1901.

Hazard, Ebenezer. *Historical Collections; Consisting of State Papers, and Other Authentic Documents*. Philadelphia: T. Dobson, 1792–94.

Heath, Dwight B., ed. *Mourt's Relation: A Journal of the Pilgrims at Plymouth—A Relation or Journal of the English Plantation Settled at Plymouth in New England, by Certain English Adventurers Both Merchants and Others*. New York: Corinth Books, 1963.

Higginson, Francis. *New Englands Plantation; or, A Short and Trve Description of the Commodities and Discommodities of that Countrey*. Salem, Mass.: The Essex Book & Print Club, 1908.

Hubbard, William. *The History of the Indian Wars in New England: From the First Settlement to the Termination of the War with King Philip, in 1677*. Roxbury, Mass.: W. Elliot Woodward, 1865.

——. *Narrative of the Indian Wars in New England: From the First Planting thereof in the Year 1607 to the Year 1677*. Boston: Boyle, 1775.

——. *The Present State of New England. Being a Narrative of the Troubles with the Indians in New England, from the First Planting Thereof in the Year 1607, to this Present Year 1677: but Chiefly of the Late Troubles* in the Two Last Years 1675, and 1676. To which is Added a Discourse About the War with the Pequods in the Year 1637. London: Printed for Thomas Parkhurst, 1677.

Hutchinson, Thomas. The History of the Colony and Province of Massachusetts-Bay. Edited by Lawrence Shaw Mayo. Cambridge: Harvard University Press, 1936.

——, ed. The Hutchinson Papers. Albany: J. Munsell, 1865.

James, Sidney V., ed. Three Visitors to Early Plymouth: Letters about the Pilgrim Settlement in New England during Its First Seven Years. By John Pory, Emmanuel Altham, and Isaack de Rasieres. Plymouth, Mass.: Plimouth Plantation, 1963.

Jameson, Franklin, ed. Narratives of New Netherland, 1609–1664. New York: Charles Scribner's Sons, 1909.

Johnson, Guy. Manual Exercise, Evolutions, Manoeuvres, &c.: To Be Observed and Followed by the Militia of the Province of New-York: With Some Rules and Regulations for Their Improvement; &c. and an Explanatory Plate. Albany: Alexander and James Robertson, 1772.

A Journal of the Proceedings in the Late Expedition to Port-Royal, on Board Their Majesties Ship, the Six-Friends, the Honourable William Phipps Knight, Commander in chief, &c. Boston: Benjamin Harris, 1690.

Knox, John. An Historical Journal of the Campaigns in North-America, for the Years 1757, 1758, 1759, and 1760. Toronto: Champlain Society, 1914.

Labaree, Leonard Woods, ed. Royal Instructions to British Colonial Governors, 1670–1776. New York: Appleton-Century, 1935.

Lincoln, Charles Henry, ed. Narratives of the Indian Wars, 1675–1699. New York: Charles Scribner's Sons, 1913.

Livingston, William. "A Review of the Military Operations in North-America: From the Commencement of the French Hostilities on the Frontiers of Virginia, in 1753, to the Surrender of Oswego, on the 14th of August, 1756; in a Letter to a Nobleman: Interspersed With Various Observations, Characters, and Anecdotes, Necessary to Give Light into the Conduct of American Transactions in General; and More Especially in the Political Management of Affairs in New-York." In Collections of the Massachusetts Historical Society for the Year of M,DCCC, 67–136. Boston: Samuel Hall, 1801.

Mason, John. "A Brief History of the Pequot War, Especially the memorable Taking of their Fort at Mistick In Connecticut in 1637." In History of the Pequot War: The Contemporary accounts of Mason, Underhill, Vincent and Gardener, edited by Charles Orr, 1–46. Cleveland: Helman-Taylor Company, 1897.

Massachusetts, Militia. A Plan of Exercise, for the Militia of the Colony of the Massachusetts-Bay: Extracted From the Plan of Discipline, for the Norfolk Militia. Boston: Richard Draper, 1768.

Massachusetts, Province. By His Excellency, Joseph Dudley Esq. Captain General and Governour in Chief . . . A Declaration Against the Pennicooke and Eastern Indians, August 18, 1703. Boston, 1703.

——. By His Excellency, Joseph Dudley . . . A Proclamation. Whereas . . . Port Royal, July 29, 1710. Boston: B. Green, 1710.

——. By His Excellency, Joseph Dudley . . . A Proclamation for an Embargo, July 15, 1710. Boston: B. Green, 1710.

——. "Charter of the Province of the Massachusetts Bay." [1691]. Publications of the Colonial Society of Massachusetts, vol. 2. Boston: Colonial Society of Massachusetts, 1913.

Mather, Cotton. Decennium luctuosum: An history of remarkable occurrences, in the long war, which New England hath had with the Indian savages, from the year, 1688. To the year 1698. Boston: B. Green and J. Allen; 1699.

———. The Deplorable State of New England, By Reason of a Covetous and Treacherous Governour and Pusillanimous Counsellors. Boston, 1721.

———. Duodecennium Luctuosum. The History of a Long War With IndianSalvages, And their Directors and Abettors; From the Year, 1702. To the Year, 1714. Boston: B. Green, 1714.

Mather, Increase. Early history of New England: being a relation of hostile passages between the Indians and European voyagers and first settlers: and a full narrative of hostilities, to the close of the war with the Pequots, in the year 1637 ; also a detailed account of the origin of the war with King Philip. Boston: Samuel G. Drake, 1864.

———. A. History of King Philip's War: Also a History of the Same War by the Rev. Cotton Mather. Edited by Samuel Drake. Boston: Samuel Drake, 1862.

———. A relation of the troubles which have hapned in New England, by reason of the Indians there: From the year 1614 to the year 1675: Wherein the frequent conspiracyes of the Indians to cutt off the English, and the wonderfull providence of God, in disappointing their devices, is declared: Together with an historical discourse concerning the prevalency of prayer; shewing that New Englands late deliverance from the rage of the heathen is an eminent answer of prayer. Boston: John Foster, 1677.

Morton, Nathaniel. New Englands Memoriall; or, A brief Relation of the Most Memorable and Remarkable Passages of the Providence of God Manifested to the Planters of New England in America; With Special Reference to the First Colony Thereof, Called New Plimouth. Boston: The Club of Odd Volumes, 1903.

Morton, Thomas. New English Canaan. New York: Burt Franklin, 1967.

Muller, John. On Fortifications. London: J. Nourse, 1756.

A New and Further Narrative of the State of New England: Being a Continued Account of the Bloudy Indian-War, From March Till August 1676: Giving a Perfect Relation of the Several Devastations, Engagements, and Transactions There. London: J.B., 1676.

New Hampshire. Militia. For Promoting Military Discipline, This Plan of Exercise, Extracted From the Plan Practiced by the Norfolk Militia is presented . . . by the Province of New Hampshire. Portsmouth, N.H.: D. and R. Fowle, 1771.

Nicola, Lewis. A Treatise of Military Exercise Calculated for the Use of Americans: In Which Every Thing That is Supposed Can Be of Use to Them, Is Retained, and Such Manoeuvres, as Are Only for Shew and Parade, Are Omitted. Philadelphia, 1776.

O'Callaghan, E. B., ed., Documents Relative to the Colonial History of the State of New York. New York: AMS Press, 1969.

Pargellis, Stanley, ed. Military Affairs in North America, 1748–1765: Selected Documents from the Cumberland Papers in Windsor Castle. Hamden, Conn.: Archon Books, 1969.

Penhallow, Samuel. The History of the Wars of New England, With the Eastern Indians, or a Narrative of their continued Perfidy and Cruelty. Boston: T. Fleet, 1726.

Philopolites [Cotton Mather]. A Memorial of the Present Deplorable State of New England, with many Disadvantages it lyes under, by the Male-Administration of their Present Governour, Joseph Dudley, Esq. And his Son Paul, & c. Together With The several Affidavits of People of Worth, Relating to several of the said Governour's Mercenary and Illegal Proceedings. . . . Boston: S. Phillips, N. Buttolph, and B. Elliot, 1707.

Pitt, William, Earl of Chatham. *Correspondence of William Pitt, When Secretary of State, With Colonial Governors and Military and Naval Commissioners in America.* Edited by Gertrude Selwyn Kimball. New York: Macmillan, 1906.

Pomeroy, Seth. *The Journals and Papers of Seth Pomeroy, Sometime General in the Colonial Service.* Edited by Louis E. DeForest. New York: Society of Colonial Wars, 1926.

The Present State of new England, With Respect to the Indian War. London: Dorman Newman, 1675.

Pulsifer, David, ed. *Records of the Colony of New Plymouth in New England: Printed by Order of the Legislature of the Commonwealth of Massachusetts.* New York: AMS Press, 1968.

——. *Records of the Colony of New Plymouth in New England Printed by Order of the Legislature of the Commonwealth of Massachusetts.* Boston: 1855–61.

Pynchon, John. *The Pynchon Papers.* Edited by Carl Bridenbaugh. Boston: Colonial Society of Massachusetts, 1982.

Rogers, Robert. *Journals of Major Robert Rogers.* New York: Corinth Books, 1961.

Shirley, William. *Correspondence of William Shirley, Governor of Massachusetts and Military Commander in America, 1731–1760.* Edited under the Auspices of the Colonial Dames of America by Charles Henry Lincoln. New York: Macmillan, 1912.

Shurtleff, Nathaniel B., ed. *Records of the Governor and Company of the Massachusetts Bay in New England.* Boston: 1853–54.

——. *Records of the Governor and Company of the Massachusetts Bay in New England.* New York: AMS Press, 1968.

Simes, Thomas. *The Military Medley: Containing the Most Necessary Rules and Directions for Attaining a Competent Knowledge of the Art.* London: Thomas Simes, 1768.

Smith, James. *A Treatise on the Mode and Manner of Indian War . . . : Ways and Means Proposed to Prevent the Indians From Obtaining the Advantage: A Chart, or Plan of Marching and Encamping, Laid Down, Whereby We May Undoubtedly Surround Them if We Have Men Sufficient:: Also, a Brief Account of Twenty-Three Campaigns Carried on Against the Indians, With the Events Since the Year 1755, Gov. Harrison's Included.* Paris, Ky.: Joel R. Lyle, 1812.

Stearns, Benjamin. "Louisburg: Benjamin Stearns's Diary, 11 March–2 August, 1745." Edited by J. C. L. Clark. *Acadiensis* 8 (October 1908): 317–29.

Steuben, Frederick William, Baron von. *Baron von Steuben's Revolutionary War Drill Manual: A Facsimile Reprint of the 1794 Edition.* New York: Dover Publications, 1985.

Stevenson, Roger. *Military Instructions for Officers Detached in the Field: Containing, a Scheme for Forming a Corps of a Partisan: Illustrated With Plans of the Manoeuvres Necessary in Carrying on the Petite Guerre.* London: D. Wilson and T. Cadell, 1770.

Symmes, Thomas. *Brief History of the Battle Which Was Fought on the 8th of May, 1725, Between Capt. John Lovell and his Associates, and a Body of Indians Under the Command of Paugus, Sachem of the Pigwacket Tribe.* Portland: A. & J. Shirley, 1818.

Trask, William Blake, ed. *Letters of Colonel Thomas Westbrook and Others Relative to Indian Affairs in Maine, 1722–1726.* Boston: Littlefield, 1901.

Trumbull, Benjamin. *A Compendium of the Indian Wars in New England: More Particularly Such as the Colony of Connecticut Have Been Concerned and Active in New Haven, August 25th Anno 1767.* Hartford: Edwin Valentine Mitchell, 1926.

Trumbull, J. Hammond, ed. *The Public Records of the Colony of Connecticut, Prior to the Union with the New Haven Colony.* Hartford: Brown and Parsons, 1850.

Underhill, John. "Nevves from America; or, A new and Experimentall Discoverie of New England: Containing a Trve Relation of Their War-like Proceedings These Two Yeares Last Past, With a Figure of the Indian Fort, or Palizado." In *History of the Pequot War: The Contemporary accounts of Mason, Underhill, Vincent and Gardener*, edited by Charles Orr, 47–86. Cleveland: Helman-Taylor Company, 1897.

Vincent, Phillip. "A True Relation of the Late Battell Fought in New England, Between the English and the Pequet Salvages." In *History of the Pequot War: The Contemporary Accounts of Mason, Underhill, Vincent and Gardener*, edited by Charles Orr, 93–111. Cleveland: Helman-Taylor Company, 1897.

Walley, John. "Major Walley's Journal in the Expedition against Canada in 1692 [sic]." In Thomas Hutchinson, *The History of the Colony and Province of Massachusetts-Bay*, edited by Lawrence Shaw Mayo, 1:458–66. Cambridge: Harvard University Press, 1936.

Ward, Robert. *Animadversions of Warre; or, A Militarie Magazine of the Trvest Rvles, and Ablest Instrvctions, for the Managing of Warre. Composed, of the Most Refined Discipline, and Choice Experiments That These Late Netherlandish, and Swedish Warres Have Produced. With Divers New Inventions, Both of Fortifications and Stratagems. As Also Sundry Collections Taken Out of the Most Approved Authors, Ancient and Moderne, Either in Greeke, Latine, Italian, French, Spanish, Dutch, or English. In two bookes.* London: I. Dawson, 1639.

Webb, Thomas. *A military treatise on the appointments of the army: Containing many useful hints, not touched upon before by any author: and proposing some new regulations in the army, which will be particularly useful in carrying on the war in North-America: Together with a short treatise on military honors.* Philadelphia: W. Dunlap, 1759.

Windham, William. *A Plan of Discipline Composed for the Use of the Militia of the County of Norfolk.* London: Shuckburgh, 1759.

———. *A Plan of Exercise, for the Militia of the Colony of Connecticut: Extracted From the Plan of Discipline, for the Norfolk Militia.* Boston: 1774.

Winslow, Edward. *Chronicles of the Pilgrim Fathers.* New York, E. P. Dutton, 1910.

———. *Good Nevves From New England; or, A True Relation of Things Very Remarkable at the Plantation of Plimoth in Nevv-England . . . Wherevnto is Added by him a Briefe Relation of a Credible Intelligence of the Presente State of Virginia.* London, Printed by I. D. for William Bladen and Iohn Bellamie, 1624.

———. *A Relation or Iournall of the Beginning and Proceedings of the English Plantation Setled at Plimoth in New England, by Certaine English Aduenturers Both Merchants and Others. With Their Difficult Passage, Their Safe Ariuall, Their Ioyfull Building of, and Comfortable Planting Themseves in the Now Well Defended Towne of New Plimoth.* Edited by George Morton. London: Iohn Bellamie, 1622.

Winthrop, John. *Winthrop's Journal vol. II, "History of New England," 1630–1649.* Edited by James Kendall Hosmer. New York: Charles Scribner's Sons, 1908.

Wolfe, James. *General Wolfe's Instructions to Young Officers.* London: J. Milan, 1768.

Young, Alexander, ed. *Chronicles of the First Planters of the Colony of Massachusetts Bay, From 1623 to 1636: Now First Collected From Original Records and Contemporaneous Manuscripts.* Boston: C. C. Little and J. Brown, 1846.

———. *Chronicles of the Pilgrim Fathers of the Colony of Plymouth, From 1602 to 1625.* Boston: C. C. Little and J. Brown, 1844.

Young, William. "An Essay on the Command of Small Detachments." In *Military Manoeuvres.* London: J. Millan, 1766.

SECONDARY SOURCES

Abbott, John S. C. *Miles Standish, Captain of the Pilgrims*. New York: Dodd & Mead, 1872.

Adams, Sherman W. *The History of Ancient Wethersfield, Connecticut*. Vol. 1. Edited by Henry R. Stiles. New York: The Grafton Press, 1904.

Anderson, Fred W. *A People's Army: Massachusetts Soldiers and Society in the Seven Years' War*. Chapel Hill: University of North Carolina Press, 1984.

———. *Crucible of War: The Seven Years' War and the Fate of Empire in British North America, 1754–1766*. New York: Knopf, 2000.

Andrews, K. R., N. Canny, and P. E. H. Hair, eds. *The Westward Enterprise: English Activities in Ireland, the Atlantic, and America, 1480–1650*. Liverpool: Liverpool University Press, 1978.

Axtell, James. *The European and the Indian: Essays in the Ethnohistory of Colonial North America*. Oxford: Oxford University Press, 1981.

Baker, Henry M. *The First Siege of Louisburg, 1745*. Concord, N.H.: Rumford Press, 1909.

Banks, Charles. *The History of York, Maine, Succesively Known as Bristol (1632), Agamenticus (1641), Gorgeana (1642), and York (1652)*. Boston: Calkins Press, 1931–35.

Bartocci, Clara. "Puritans versus Pequots: Four Eye-Witness Reports of the First War in Colonial New England." *Storia Nordamericana* 4 (1987): 71–91.

Baxter, James Phinney. "The Campaign against the Pequakets: Its Causes and Its Results." In *Collections and Proceedings of the Maine Historical Society*, 353–71. Portland: Maine Historical Society, 1890.

Beattie, Daniel J. "The Adaptation of the British Army to Wilderness Warfare, 1755–1763." In *Adapting to Conditions: War and Society in the Eighteenth Century*, edited by Maarten Ultee, 56–83. Tuscaloosa: University of Alabama Press, 1986.

Bitterli, Urs. *Cultures in Conflict: Encounters between European and Non-European Cultures, 1492–1800*. Cambridge: Polity, 1989.

Boorstin, Daniel. *The Americans: The Colonial Experience*. New York: Random House, 1958.

Bourne, Russell. *The Red King's Rebellion: Racial Politics in New England, 1675–1678*. New York: Atheneum, 1990.

Bradley, Robert L., and Helen Camp. *The Forts of Pemaquid, Maine: An Archeological and Historical Study*. Augusta: Maine Historic Preservation Commission, Maine Archeological Society, and Maine Bureau of Parks and Recreation, 1994.

Brewer, John. *Sinews of Power: War, Money, and the English State, 1688–1783*. New York: Knopf, 1989.

Brown, M. L. *Firearms in Colonial America: The Impact on History and Technology, 1492–1792*. Washington: Smithsonian Institution Press, 1980.

Calloway, Colin G. *The Western Abenakis of Vermont, 1600–1800: War, Migration, and the Survival of an Indian People*. Norman: University of Oklahoma Press, 1990.

Canny, Nicholas P. *The Elizabethan Conquest of Ireland: A Pattern Established, 1565–76*. Sussex: Harvester Press, 1976.

———. *Kingdom and Colony: Ireland in the Atlantic World, 1560–1800*. Baltimore: Johns Hopkins University Press, 1988.

Canny, Nicholas, and Anthony Pagden, eds. *Colonial Identity in the Atlantic World, 1500–1800*. Princeton: Princeton University Press, 1987.

Chamberlain, George Walter. "John Chamberlain, the Indian Fighter at Pigwacket." In *Collections and Proceedings of the Maine Historical Society*, 2d ser., 9:1–15. Portland: Maine Historical Society, 1898.

Chapman, Leonard B. "Block and Garrison Houses of Ancient Falmouth." In *Collections and Proceedings of the Maine Historical Society*, 2d ser., 6:37–53. Portland: The Society, 1895.

Coleman, Roy V. *First Frontier*. New York: C. Scribner's Sons, 1948.

Colonial Society of Massachusetts. *Architecture in Colonial Massachusetts: A Conference Held by the Colonial Society of Massachusetts, September 19 and 20, 1974*. Boston: Colonial Society of Massachusetts, 1979.

Cort, Cyrus. *Col. Henry Bouquet and his Campaigns of 1763 and 1764*. Lancaster, Pa.: Steinman and Hensel, 1883.

Darlington, Mary Carson, ed. *History of Colonel Henry Bouquet and the Western Frontiers of Pennsylvania, 1747–1764*. Pittsburgh: privately printed, 1920.

Dederer, John M. *War in America to 1775: Before Yankee Doodle*. New York: New York University Press, 1990.

De Forest, John William. *History of the Indians of Connecticut from the Earliest Known Period to 1850*. Brighton, Mich.: Native American Book Publishers, 1991.

De Forest, Louis E. *Captain John Underhill: Gentleman, Soldier of Fortune*. New York: De Forest, 1934.

Demos, John, ed. "The Deerfield Massacre." *American Heritage* 44, no.1 (1993): 82–89.

———. *Remarkable Providence: Readings on Early American History*. New York: G. Braziller, 1972.

———. *The Unredeemed Captive: A Family Story from Early America*. New York: Vintage, 1995.

Drake, James D. *King Philip's War: Civil War in New England, 1675–1676*. Amherst: University of Massachusetts Press, 1999.

Drake, Samuel A. *The Border Wars of New England*. New York: Scribner, 1897.

Eames, Steven Charles. "Rustic Warriors: Warfare and the Provincial Soldier on the Northern Frontier, 1689-1748." Ph.D. diss., University of New Hampshire, 1989.

Eid, Leroy V. "The Neglected Side of American Indian War in the Northeast." *Military Review* 61 (1981): 9–21.

Ellis, George E. "Life of John Mason." In *The Library of American Biography*, edited by Jared Sparks, 2d ser. 3:207–428 (1855).

Ellis, George William, and John E. Morris. *King Philip's War: Based on the Archives and Records of Massachusetts, Plymouth, Rhode Island, and Connecticut, and Contemporary Letters and Accounts*. New York: Grafton Press, 1906.

Erwin, John S. "Captain Myles Standish's Military Role at Plymouth." *Historical Journal of Massachusetts* 13 (1985): 1–13.

Ferling, John E. "The New England Soldier: A Study in Changing Perceptions." *American Quarterly* 33 (1981): 26–45.

———. *A Wilderness of Miseries: War and Warriors in Early America*. Westport, Conn.: Greenwood Press, 1980.

Fischer, David H. *Paul Revere's Ride*. New York: Oxford University Press, 1994.

Forbes, Allan. *Other Indian Events of New England: A Collection of Interesting Incidents in the Lives of the Early Settlers and the Indians of This Country*. Boston, 1941.

———. *Some Indian Events of New England: A Collection of Interesting Incidents in the Lives of the Early Settlers of This Country and the Indians.* Boston: State Street Trust, 1934.

Frazier, Patrick. *The Mohicans of Stockbridge.* Lincoln: University of Nebraska Press, 1992.

French, Allen. "The Arms and Military of Our Colonizing Ancestors." *Proceedings of the Massachusetts Historical Society* 68 (1941-44): 3–21.

Fuller, J. F. C. *Armament and History.* London: 1946.

———. *British Light Infantry in the Eighteenth Century.* London: 1926.

Garvan, Anthony N. B. *Architecture and Town Planning in Colonial Connecticut.* New Haven: Yale University Press, 1951.

Gildrie, Richard P. "Defiance, Diversion, and the Exercise of Arms: The Several Meanings of Colonial Training Days in Colonial Massachusetts." *Military Affairs* 52 (April 1988): 53–55.

Gipson, Lawrence Henry. *The British Empire before the American Revolution.* New York: Alfred A. Knopf, 1961–68.

Hamilton, Edward P. "Colonial Warfare in North America." *Proceedings of the Massachusetts Historical Society* 80 (1968): 3–15.

———. *The French and Indian Wars: The Story of Battles and Forts in the Wilderness.* Garden City, N.Y.: Doubleday, 1962.

Hargreaves, Reginald. *The Bloodybacks: The British Servicemen in North America and the Carribbean, 1655–1783.* New York: Walker, 1968.

Hauptman, Laurence M. "John Underhill: A Psychological Portrait of an Indian Fighter, 1597–1672." *Hudson Valley Regional Review* 9 (1992): 101–11.

Hays, Samuel Hubbard, ed. *Taking Command: The Art and Science of Military Leadership.* Harrisburg, Pa.: Stackpole Books, 1967.

Historical Sketch of the Town of Weymouth. Weymouth, Mass.: Weymouth Historical Society, 1885.

Hodges, George. *The Apprenticeship of Washington and Other Sketches of Colonial Personages.* New York: Moffat, Yard and Company, 1909.

Horowitz, David. *The First Frontier: The Indian Wars and America's Origins, 1607–1776.* New York: Simon and Schuster, 1978.

Huntington, Elijah Baldwin. *History of Stamford, Connecticut, from Its Settlement in 1641, to the Present Time, including Darien, Which Was One of Its Parishes until 1820.* A corrected reprint of the 1868 edition. Harrison, N.Y.: Harbor Hill Books, 1979.

Isham, Edward Swift. *Frontenac and Miles Standish in the Northwest.* New York: Printed for the New York Historical Society, 1889.

Jackson, H. M. *Rogers' Rangers: A History.* Published by the author, 1953.

Jennings, Francis. *The Invasion of America: Indians, Colonialism, and the Cant of Conquest.* New York: Norton, 1976.

Johnson, Richard R. "The Search for a Usable Indian: An Aspect of the Defense of Colonial New England." *Journal of American History* 64 (1977): 623–51.

Keegan, John. *Warpaths: Travels of a Military Historian in North America.* London: Hodder & Stoughton, 1995.

Keegan, John, and Richard Holmes. *Soldiers: A History of Men in Battle.* New York: Viking, 1986.

Keeley, Lawrence. *War before Civilization.* New York: Oxford University Press, 1996.

Kenny, Robert W. "The Beginnings of the Rhode Island Train Bands." *Collections of the Rhode Island Historical Society* 33 (1940): 25–38.

Kidder, Frederic. *The Expeditions of Captain John Lovewell, and His Encounters with the Indians including a Particular Account of Pequauket Battle, with a History of That Tribe.* Boston: Bartlett and Halliday, 1865.

Kopperman, Paul E. *Braddock at the Monongahela.* Pittsburgh: University of Pittsburgh Press, 1977.

Kupperman, Karen O., ed. *America in European Consciousness, 1493–1750.* Chapel Hill: University of North Carolina Press, 1995.

Leach, Douglas Edward. *Arms for Empire: A Military History of the British Colonies in North America, 1607–1763.* New York: Macmillan, 1973.

———. *Flintlock and Tomahawk: New England in King Philip's War.* New York: Macmillan, 1958.

———. *The Northern Colonial Frontier, 1607–176.3* Albuquerque: University of New Mexico Press, 1974.

Lewis, George. *The History of the Pequot War and Battle of Stonington.* Bridgeport: Press of City Steam Printing, 1893.

Loescher, Burt Garfield. *The History of Rogers' Rangers.* Volume 1, *The Beginnings, January 1755–April 6, 1758.* San Francisco, 1946.

Long, John Cuthbert. *Lord Jeffrey Amherst: A Soldier of the King.* New York: Macmillan, 1933.

Mahon, John K. "Anglo-American Methods of Indian Warfare, 1676–1794." *Mississippi Valley Historical Review* 45 (1958): 254–75.

Mahon, R. H. *Life of General James the Hon. Murray: A Builder of Canada.* London: John Murray, 1921.

Malone, Patrick M. "English and Indian/Indian and English Military Systems." Ph.D. diss., Brown University, 1971.

———. *The Skulking Way of War: Technology and Tactics among the New England Indians.* New York: Madison Books, 1991.

Marcus, Richard H. "The Connecticut Valley: A Problem in Inter-Colonial Defense." *Military Affairs* 33 (1969): 230–42.

Markham, Richard. *A Narrative History of King Philip's War and the Indian Troubles in New England.* New York: Dodd, Meade & Company, 1883.

Marshall, Orsamus Holmes. *Expedition of the Sieur de Champlain Against the Onondagas in 1615, Comprising an Inquiry into the Route of the Expedition, and the Location of the Iroquois Fort Which it Besieged.* New York: New York Historical Society, 1876.

Mason, Louis B. *The Life and Times of Major John Mason of Connecticut, 1600–1672.* New York: G. P. Putnam, 1935.

Mathews, Lois Kimball. *The Expansion of New England: The Spread of New England Settlement and Institutions to the Mississippi River, 1620–1865.* Boston: Houghton Mifflin, 1909.

May, Virginia A. *A Plantation Called Petapawag: Some Notes on the History of Groton, Massachusetts.* Groton: Groton Historical Society, 1976.

McCardell, Lee. *Ill-Starred General: Braddock of the Coldstream Guards.* Pittsburgh: University of Pittsburgh Press, 1958.

McCulloch, Ian. "Buckskin Soldier: The Rise and Fall of Major Robert Rogers." *Beaver* 73 (1993): 17–26.

McKnight, Edward. *Myles Standish, Captain of Plymouth.* Chorley, Eng.: Sandiford, 1901.

Mead, Spencer Percival. *Ye Historie of ye Town of Greenwich, County of Fairfield and State of Connecticut.* Harrison, N.Y.: Harbor Hill Books, 1979.

Melvoin, Richard Irwin. *New England Outpost: War and Society in Colonial Deerfield.* New York: Norton, 1989.

Miles, H. H. *The History of Canada under French Regime, 1535–1763.* Montreal: Dawson Brothers, 1872.

Morrison, Kenneth M. *The Embattled Northeast: The Elusive Ideal of Alliance in Abenaki-Euroamerican Relations.* Berkeley: University of California Press, 1984.

Morton, Louis. "The End of Formalized Warfare." *American Heritage* 6 (1955): 12–19.

——. "The Origins of American Military Policy." *Military Affairs* 22 (1948): 75–82.

Murrin, John M. "Anglicizing an American Colony: The Transformation of Provincial Massachusetts." Ph.D. diss., Yale University, 1966.

Myatt, Frederick. *The British Infantry, 1660–1945: The Evolution of a Fighting Force.* Volume 1. Poole, Eng.: Blandford Press, 1983.

Nosworthy, Brent. *The Anatomy of Victory: Battle Tactics, 1689–1763.* New York: Hippocrene Books, 1990.

Osgood, Herbert L. *The American Colonies in the Eighteenth Century.* New York: Columbia University Press, 1924.

——. *American Colonies in the Seventeenth Century.* New York: Macmillan, 1907.

Pagden, Anthony. *The Fall of Natural Man: The American Indian and the Origins of Comparative Ethnology.* New York: Cambridge University Press, 1982.

Paret, Peter. "Colonial Experience and European Military Reform at the End of the Eighteenth Century." In *Warfare and Empire: Contact and Conflict between European and Non-European Military and Maritime Forces and Cultures,* edited by Douglas M. Peers, 357–70. Brookfield, Vt.: Ashgate, 1997.

Pargellis, Stanley McCrory. "Braddock's Defeat." *American Historical Review* 41 (1936): 253–69.

——. *Lord Loudoun in North America.* New Haven: Yale University Press, 1933.

Parker, H. F. *Discoverers and Pioneers of America.* New York: Derby and Jackson, 1860.

Parker, King Lawrence. "Anglo-American Wilderness Campaigning: Logistical and Tactical Developments." Ph.D. diss., Columbia University, 1970.

Parkman, Francis. *A Half-Century of Conflict.* Boston: Little, Brown, 1927.

——. *Montcalm and Wolfe.* New York: Atheneum, 1984.

——. *The Conspiracy of Pontiac and the Indian War after the Conquest of Canada.* Boston: Little, Brown, 1924.

Pearce, Roy Harvey. *Savagism and Civilization.* Baltimore: Johns Hopkins Press, 1953.

Peckham, Howard H. *The Colonial Wars, 1689–1762.* Chicago: University of Chicago Press, 1964.

Perry, John Hoyt. *The Great Swamp Fight in Fairfield.* New York, 1905.

Peterson, Harold. *Arms and Armor in Colonial America, 1526–1783.* Harrisburg: Stackpole, 1956.

——. "The Military Equipment of the Plymouth and Bay Colonies, 1620–1690." *New England Quarterly* 20 (June 1947): 197–208.

——, ed. *Encyclopedia of Firearms.* New York: E. P. Dutton, 1964.

Phillips, James Duncan. *Salem in the Eighteenth Century.* Boston: Houghton Mifflin, 1937.

——. *Salem in the Seventeenth Century.* Boston: Houghton Mifflin, 1933.

Porter, Harry Culverwell. *The Inconstant Savage: England and the North American Indian, 1500–1660.* London: Duckworth, 1979.

Radabaugh, Jack Sheldon. "The Militia of Colonial Massachusetts." *Military Affairs* 18 (spring 1954): 1–18.

Reid, John G. "Unorthodox Warfare in the Northeast, 1703." *Canadian Historical Review* 73 (1992): 211–20.

Reps, John William. *Town Planning in Frontier America.* Princeton: Princeton University Press, 1969.

Robinson, Willard B. *American Forts: Architectural Form and Function.* Chicago: University of Illinois Press, 1977.

Robson, Eric. "British Light Infantry in the Eighteenth Century: The Effect of American Conditions." *Army and Defense Quarterly* 61 (1952): 209–22.

Rogers, Hugh C. B. *The British Army of the Eighteenth Century.* London: George Allen & Unwin, 1977.

Russell, Peter E. "Redcoats in the Wilderness: British Officers and Irregular Warfare in Europe and America, 1740 to 1760." *William and Mary Quarterly* 35 (October 1978): 629–52.

Salisbury, Neal. *Manitou and Providence: Indians, Europeans, and the Making of New England, 1500–1643.* New York: Oxford University Press, 1982.

Schultz, Eric, and Michael Tougias. *King Philip's War: The History and Legacy of America's Forgotten Conflict.* Woodstock, Vt.: Countryman Press, 1999.

Segal, Charles, and David Stineback. *Puritans, Indians, and Manifest Destiny.* New York: G.. Putnam's Sons, 1977.

Selesky, Harold E. "Military Leadership in an American Colonial Society: Connecticut, 1635–1785." Ph.D. diss., Yale University, 1984.

——. *War and Society in Colonial Connecticut.* New Haven: Yale University Press, 1990.

Sharp, Morrison. "The New England Trainbands in the Seventeenth Century." Ph.D. diss., Harvard University, 1938.

Sheldon, George. *A History of Deerfield, Massachusetts.* Somersworth: New Hampshire Publishing Company, 1972.

Shelley, Henry C. *John Underhill: Captain of Connecticut and New Netherland.* New York: 1932.

Shepard, James. *Connecticut Soldiers in the Pequot War of 1637.* Meriden, Conn.: Journal Publication Company, 1913.

Shy, John. *Toward Lexington: The Role of the British Army in the Coming of the American Revolution.* Princeton: Princeton University Press, 1965.

Slotkin, Richard. *Regeneration through Violence: The Mythology of the American Frontier, 1600–1860.* Middletown, Conn.: Wesleyan University Press, 1973.

Stanley, John Henry. "A Preliminary Investigation of Military Manuals of American Imprint Prior to 1800." Master's thesis, Brown University, 1964.

Starkey, Armstrong. *European and Native American Warfare, 1675–1815.* Norman: University of Oklahoma Press, 1998.

Steele, Ian Kenneth. *Betrayals: Fort William Henry and the "Massacre."* New York: Oxford University Press, 1990.

——. *Guerrillas and Grenadiers: The Struggle for Canada, 1689–1760.* Toronto: Ryerson Press, 1969.

——. *Warpaths: Invasions of North America.* Oxford: Oxford University Press, 1994.

Sylvester, Herbert Milton. *Indian Wars of New England.* Boston: W. B. Clarke, 1910.

Tebbel, John, and Keith Jennison. *The American Indian Wars*. New York: Harper and Brothers, 1960.

Tonso, William R. *Gun and Society: The Social and Existential Roots of the American Attachment to Firearms*. Lanham, Md.: University Press of America, 1982.

Trelease, Allen W. *Indian Affairs in Colonial New York: The Seventeenth Century*. Ithaca: Cornell University Press, 1960.

Turney-High, Henry H. *The Practice of Primitive War*. Missoula: Montana State University Press, 1942.

Ultee, Maarten, ed. *Adapting to Conditions: War and Society in the Eighteenth Century*. Tuscaloosa: University of Alabama Press, 1986.

Utley, Robert M. *Frontier Regulars: The United States Army and the Indian, 1861–1891*. New York: Macmillan, 1973.

——. "Sitting Bull: The Lance and the Shield." In *Books at Brown*, 1998, 44–52. Providence: Friends of the Library of Brown University, 1998.

Vaughan, Alden T. *New England Frontier: Puritans and Indians, 1620–1675*. Norman: University of Oklahoma Press, 1995.

Wade, Herbert T. *A Brief History of the Colonial Wars in America from 1607 to 1775*. New York: Society of Colonial Wars, 1948.

Weigley, Russell F. *The Age of Battles: The Quest for Decisive Warfare from Breitenfeld to Waterloo*. Bloomington: Indiana University Press, 1991.

Weymouth [Mass.] Historical Society. *Proceedings on the Two Hundred and Fiftieth Anniversary of the Permanent Settlement of Weymouth*. Boston: Wright & Potter, 1874.

Whisker, James Biser. *The American Colonial Militia*. Lewiston, N.Y.: Edwin Mellen Press, 1997.

Whitton, F. E. *Wolfe and North America*. Boston: Little, Brown, 1929.

Williams, Robert A. *The American Indian in Western Legal Thought: The Discourse of Conquest*. New York: Oxford University Press, 1990.

Wood, Joseph. *The New England Village*. Baltimore: Johns Hopkins University Press, 1997.

Wooster, Robert. *The Military and United States Indian Policy, 1865–1903*. New Haven: Yale University Press, 1988.